At H

At Home in Holland

A Practical Guide for Living in the Netherlands

11th Edition

Eburon Delft
2009

Acknowledgements

The 11th Edition of "At Home in Holland" is the result of a common effort of the following volunteer expatriates and their Dutch friends. I would like to thank each of them. With their dedication of time, effort and knowledge, they created this book.

Editor	Susanne Bomhard
Co-Editor	Teresa Mahoney
Co-Editor	Melissa White
Proof Reading	Judith Treanor
IT	Kay van der Made

Chapter Editors

Kathy Anderson
Celeste Brown
Pat Fennell
Laurie Keckley
Theresa Milcik
Barb Stoebe
Melissa White
Betsy Blauvelt
Stacie Coates
Deb Filkins
Pam Legvold
Beth Mothershead
Judith Treanor
Susanne Bomhard
Phoebe Fagan
Darlene Fleming
Kay van der Made
Georgina Regnault
Lisa Wildeman

On behalf of our team above I would like to thank:
Jozias van Aartsen – Mayor of Den Haag and the patron of our book who generously hosted the Book Launch
John Protor for donating the painting on the book cover for the Charity Auction
Hannelore de Boer – Hospitality Centre Den Haag
Patricia Hollamby – PR and Book Launch
Others: Merel Ohr, Huib Versluys, Maarten Fraanje of Eburon Publishing

Sincerely

Susanne Bomhard
Editor
11th Edition "At Home in Holland"
February 2009
www.athomeinholland.com

American Women's Club of The Hague
Nieuwe Duinweg 25
2587 AB Den Haag
☎ (070) 350-6007
www.awcthehague.org

Table of Contents

At Home in Holland

The Netherlands, tucked into the northwest corner of Europe between Belgium, Germany and the North Sea, is a country with a population of about 16.4 million people of which 3.2 million inhabitants are from a foreign background. You are now one of them!

This remarkable country is known for its liberal ideas and social politics. The tolerance shown towards foreigners goes back to the "Golden Age" in the 17th century when the Netherlands was one of the world's leading powers. As the leading maritime power of that time, the Dutch lived with a variety of cultures in their midst and that has created a multi-ethnic society that continues today.

Today's statistics show the Netherlands is the country with the tallest population, the happiest children and the easiest investment climate in the Euro zone.

As a low country bordering the North Sea, the Dutch have to deal with the water—the water from the sea, the water from the sky and the water from the rivers. Over the centuries they have continued to reclaim land. About one fifth of the country is reclaimed from the sea. One famous example is the Zuiderzee, an arm of the North Sea which was drained and that created a freshwater lake, IJselmeer. When stormy sea waters inundated the Zeeland islands in 1953, the great Delta Works were built in order to shut the door on future floods in that region. As a result, 50% of the Netherlands today is situated below sea level.

The Dutch will make it easy to welcome you as long as you remember to adjust and not expect them to change. Remember that there is more than one way to do things. Enjoy the local holidays, attend the jazz festivals, eat the herring, drink the beer, drink the beer, sample the cheese, marvel at the tulips, witness the arrival of Sinterklaas at the harbor, and celebrate the Queen's birthday with the rest of her nation on *Koniginnedag*.

With this book you possess a valuable resource for making your stay a successful and enjoyable one. This is the Eleventh Edition of *At Home in Holland*. First printed in 1963, it is the result of the combined resources and knowledge of hundreds of volunteer expatriates and their Dutch friends over the years. We hope that this guide will help you to feel "At Home in Holland."

We dedicate this book to our wonderful hosts – the people of the Netherlands.

Susanne Bomhard
Editor

Notes

Throughout this book, Dutch translations of many English words are shown in *italics*.

Websites are also shown in *italics*, and should be consulted for the latest information. It is common to list the homepage, which in many cases will be in Dutch. To find if English pages are available, look for a British or American flag, the word "English" or the abbreviation "En" near either the top or the bottom of the homepage.

We most commonly refer to the country we live in as "the Netherlands," which is the correct terminology. "Holland" is actually the name of two provinces, North and South Holland (Noord Holland and Zuid Holland). You will see the region of Den Haag often called "The Hague," which is the English translation. In your travels around The Hague, you might also come across its official name which is 's-Gravenhage. Throughout this book, you will see references to the area of The Hague, but address information shown with Den Haag.

Prices quoted are subject to change.

Chapter 1

Culture Shock

One's destination is never a place, but a new way of seeing things. Henry Miller

The experience of living in the Netherlands can be a special and rewarding one; it may bring opportunities for personal growth, career development and educational advancement. All of these, along with the fun of seeing Europe, can become personal high points if you keep a few things in mind. Before leaving home, take the time to say good-bye to family, friends, co-workers and the life you leave behind. This is a parting. Be gentle with yourself and allow yourself time alone to process your feelings about moving. Plan ways to keep in touch with people you leave behind, but remember that you—and they—will surely change before you meet again. It is sometimes easier to keep in touch with short emails and notes, rather than with longer letters.

If you plan to work here, be prepared to take some time to find employment. An employer will need to be able to prove that a similarly skilled Dutch person could not do the job as well as you, an expatriate, and that can slow the process of finding work. If you are more concerned with keeping up your skills for your career upon returning to your home country, take a volunteer position when you arrive. It's one of the best ways to meet friends and garner a support network, as well as develop valuable career skills. Remember, volunteer employment is no different on a resumé than work you are paid for–it takes the same dedication and skills. Choose something that will allow you to achieve your goals. Be sure to keep a detailed record of what you do and letters of recommendation from your supervisor, club president or fellow co-workers.

Once you have arrived, bear in mind that you and your family have begun an adventure that will hold new and exciting experiences and opportunities. What may surprise you is that this adventure will bring challenges, difficulties and, in some cases, tears. With preparation, perseverance and patience, your stay can be happy and successful.

People function well in their home country because they can pick up and respond to thousands of subtle cues. They know the "rules" for shopping, driving, banking, using the phone book and hundreds of other activities of everyday life. Nonverbal signals tell them when it is time to end a conversation, change the subject or take their turn.

Phases of Adjustment

When you and your family arrive in the Netherlands, suddenly you will not know the rules anymore. What is worse, when you ask what the rules are, the instructions may only be available in Dutch! Being exposed to many new sights, sounds, foods and ways of doing things can be fun, but it also means that you will experience a period of adjustment known as culture shock. Culture shock is a normal part of any move, and experiencing it does not mean you are weak or incapable. What it does mean is just what the name implies. Your system has experienced a shock. Be prepared to slow down and expect things to take a little longer than they do at home. Doing routine chores in a foreign country with a foreign language takes more time and a lot more energy. Expect to be able to do about half of the duties that you would normally do at home in one day during the first six months of your move here. Culture shock has predictable stages, although the amount of time it takes each individual to go through these stages varies from person to person. Each person has her own way of reacting in the various stages of culture shock.

It begins with what could be called "The Tourist Phase" or "Honeymoon Phase." Your new life is exciting and everything seems charming and quaint. (You might find yourself saying, "Oh, I love this place, let's not move home!")

This fun ends in what might be called the "Disenchantment Phase" or the "I-Hate-This-Country Phase." Suddenly, those delightful differences become irritating. Life is frustrating. You may feel depressed, anxious and even hostile. (You might find yourself thinking, "What have we done?")

The next step is the "Adjustment and Acceptance Phase" when you begin to adjust to your new environment and even enjoy it. It becomes home. (You'll know that you made it when you say "I want to get home," and by home you mean the Netherlands!)

Another phase is "Reverse Culture Shock." You might be surprised that returning to your home culture after growing accustomed to a new one can produce the same effects as described above. Learn more about this in our **Repatriation** chapter.

Options for Settling In

Although culture shock can be emotionally painful, it will, more often than not, pass. You will manage the stress, cope with the frustrations and learn to appreciate life in the Netherlands. What works for one person may not work for another, but here are a few suggestions for coping.

▸ Attend a Newcomer's Group

Several of the clubs listed in the **Church and Community** chapter are excellent for newcomers. They often help you to make new friends who are also experiencing the same feelings. They are also sources of information on how to:

- Navigate in your new home
- Use public transportation
- Find food stores with familiar products
- Find volunteer organizations
- Contact a doctor (*huisarts*)
- Find a hairdresser

If you are a single person making the move to the Netherlands, it becomes even more important to network with the local agencies that have newcomer's groups. The group leaders and members who know other singles will act as sponsors and may network introductions for you. Through informal introductions such as these, many singles—and couples with one Dutch partner and one expat partner—have come together to make fast friendships.

▸ Learn as Much as You Can

The more familiar you become with the Netherlands and the Dutch people, the more comfortable you will feel. Take the time to learn some of the language, history and culture. The books *The Low Sky* and *Dealing with the Dutch* both take an informative tack in helping you understand differences from a cultural perspective. If you are frustrated, you may want to read the humorous *The Undutchables*, a book on the foibles of the Dutch. Knowing that you are not alone may make you feel better! All of these books are available at The American Book Center (*www.abc.nl*).

The experience of working in the Netherlands can turn into the opportunity of a lifetime, if you take the time to try to understand the Dutch system of workplace relationships. Many expatriates who come here to work are initially frustrated by the seemingly slow pace of business and decision making. Again, it is vital to try to learn as much as you can by reading books such as *Dealing with the Dutch* in order to be able to go with the flow and participate in the Dutch business culture. Keep in mind that true success comes with learning to swim in the sea you are in and that may take some experimenting and changing of old habits.

Learn the Language

Learning a new language is difficult, particularly for adults. This task alone is quite enough to cause frustration and anxiety. However, once you begin to be able to carry on a friendly conversation with your neighbors or on trips to the shops, you not only gain confidence and a feeling of power, but a whole world of cultural meanings open up for you.

Keep an Open Mind

It is only natural to make comparisons with home, but bear in mind that your way is not the only way—it just happens to be the more familiar one. Relax, try new things and above all, keep your sense of humor.

Develop a Routine

Create a daily framework for your life here, and build upon it as your circle of friends grows and you settle in. In the beginning this helps your positive frame of mind. You have things to do and a reason to do them.

Get Involved

Helping an organization with its newsletter, library or a fund raiser can really boost your self-confidence and esteem. Look into your community for places to use your skills. You can find a place where you belong and that needs you. This simple act of charity may be the kindest thing you do for yourself. Try to have contact with the new culture. Learn the language and volunteer in community activities that allow you to practice. See the **Church and Community** chapter for organizations that might need your help.

▸ Get Enough Daylight

Keep in mind that the winter months may seem longer and darker, because the Netherlands may be a lot farther from the equator than your home. This means that you may be susceptible to a mild form of depression caused by lack of full-spectrum light. Taking an hour walk outdoors in the morning should be all you need to keep feeling at the top of your form. Some people invest in a sunlamp to provide light and warmth that is lacking during the winter months. Another option is to plan a vacation to a warm, sunny location during January or February.

▸ Get Enough Exercise

Exercise relieves stress and increases endorphins in the body, the "feel good" chemicals that help combat depression. There are many fitness clubs, swimming pools and sports clubs. Cycling is very popular and is truly the best way to see the country. Make sure to invest in some good waterproof rain gear. You will quickly learn that there is no such thing as bad weather—just bad clothing.

▸ Keep a Journal

Keeping a journal can be a very effective coping mechanism, as well as a wholly original souvenir of your Dutch experience. Perhaps you can try your hand at writing a blog, an online journal where you can post photos and stories to share with your family and friends. With *www.blogger.com* you don't have to be very computer savvy to set up your own blog. It is a great way to document how you spend your time and the many things you have accomplished...in a foreign country!

▸ Share Your Experiences

Talk them over with your family and friends. You will certainly find that others have had similar experiences and the feedback you get will help you feel supported and give support to others. If you are lucky, you will also gain an appreciation for the inevitable absurdities of your own culture.

▸ Ask for Help if You Need It

Seek out advice and friendship from other expatriates—they have been through the same experiences and understand your feelings. It is especially helpful to seek out another newcomer to share your feelings. Try also to connect with a Dutch person, someone who can help you by acting as a cultural interpreter of sorts. You will be less likely to fall into an unconstructive "us" versus "them" mentality with their aid. It also might be helpful to talk with one of the professional counselors referred by ACCESS (Administrative Committee to Coordinate English-Speaking Services), which is a non-profit organization staffed fully by volunteers. ACCESS helps anyone from anywhere to settle with ease in the Netherlands. They provide free information in English for the international community, free counseling referrals, educational seminars, workshops and other services.

▸ ACCESS

Outside of office hours you may leave a message and someone will call you back.
Stadhuis, Spui 70 Den Haag
☎ (070) 346 25 25
Prinses Irenestraat 59, 1077 WV Amsterdam
☎ (020) 423 32 17
www.access-nl.org

▸ Experience is the Best Teacher

Keep in mind that no one is ever thrilled at the prospect of being the new kid on the block—no matter what age kid you may be. Trying to become part of an already established society can bring its share of stress and frustration to every member of the family. It is only a matter of time until we realize that this transient group we are a part of is like no other. Making friends is a quick process, if you are open to it, because so many of us are here for just a short period of time.

Nevertheless, first-timers may have some uncomfortable moments and moves can bring apprehension about everything that is new and so unlike home. No matter how much we are advised and forewarned, newcomers are bound to have a few trying experiences before they learn the system. Eventually we laugh about it, but it can be rough at first. Many people confessed that in the first six months of their move to the Netherlands their normal quota of confidence and assertiveness seemed to dry up. They were less likely to want to make phone calls where they might not be understood, speak to people in stores and even felt intimidated at the grocery store until friends helped them.

Maintain a Positive Attitude

Only you can control your experience of living in the Netherlands. You have a choice every day regarding the attitude that you embrace for that day. As Charles Swindoll has inspired others in his motivational speeches, "We cannot change our past...we cannot change the fact that people will act in a certain way. We cannot change the inevitable. The only thing we can do is play on the one string we have and that is our attitude. Life is 10% what happens to me and 90% how I react to it. And so it is with you...we are in charge of our attitudes." Armed with a positive attitude and inner strength, your new challenge will be a wonderful new experience.

May all your trails be crooked, winding, lonesome, dangerous, leading to the most amazing view ... where something strange and more beautiful and more full of wonder than your deepest dreams waits for you. Edward Abbey

Reichman & Rommelaar

Two names, one business, one philosophy. With a thorough approach that brings supply and demand together. Solidly traditional when it comes to professionalism, trust and commitment. Contemporary when it comes to knowing the market, taking swift action, using information technology, and networking.

the Hague

Voorschoten

Repeat orders from 9 out of every 10 clients
Since the establishment of the business in 1961, we have always been fully licensed by the NVM, the Netherlands Association of Real Estate Brokers and Immovable Property Experts. We see this as an obvious choice and entirely in line with our focus on providing our clients with fine quality and service. And the success of such a strategy can be seen in the fact that nine out of ten of our new clients come back to us again for all future transactions. What better proof of customer satisfaction!

Saving time and effort
Buying, selling or renting a house: it takes a lot of time and effort. But the assistance provided by Reichman & Rommelaar will spare you much of this. After all, the searching and negotiating will be done for you - by professionals who know everything about the market, who will be there to help you throughout the process and who will involve you at the crucial stages of the process. One less thing to worry about. We make extensive use of the on-line NVM market system, our own networks, and, of course, our relationships with satisfied clients we have built up over the years. This strategy plus personal involvement has been the key to our success.

Voorburg showcase

Relocation Service Reichman & Rommelaar - Totally at home in the region
Temporarily working abroad has its attractive as well as its less attractive aspects. For several years now, our Expat Establishment Service has been successfully assisting employees of large international businesses settle into the Netherlands. Not only are they assured of suitable housing, but also of a professional approach that goes far beyond just finding a home.

Wassenaar

We give you more than just a home
Our Establishment service comprises, among others: the handling of visa applications, working permits, parking permits, local procedures, contacts with international schools, renovation and redecoration management. Reichman & Rommelaar has what it takes to make every ex-pat feel completely at home in The Hague within the shortest possible time. The members of our team have years of experience in the special skills required in international relocation services.

Cornelis de Wittlaan 39
2582 AB Den Haag
Tel. 070 - 354 66 00
Fax 070 - 351 26 74

Van Zuylen van Nyeveltstraat 95
2242 AL Wassenaar
Tel. 070 - 514 21 41
Fax 070 - 511 69 57

Leidseweg 37
2252 LA Voorschoten
Tel. 071 - 561 46 84
Fax 071 - 561 78 06

www.reichmanenrommelaar.nl

Chapter 2

Housing

Of all the decisions that you must make about moving to the Netherlands, the one that will have the most subtle impact on your feeling "good" about your move is the choice of where to live. Finding and getting settled into the right home is therefore a priority. It is a process of weighing options, thinking about the way your family works, and thinking about the kind of "Dutch" experience that you want to have. In the process, you may have to alter your life-style somewhat, but with patience and perseverance you should not have to compromise in any area that is truly important to your family's needs.

Looking for a home takes time. The market here is very competitive and the number of "available" houses changes almost daily. Be prepared to spend a period of time in a hotel until you find a suitable residence or your household goods arrive. It is inconvenient, but it is short term. You will be grateful when you do move into the "right" place.

Finding a Home

Factors to Consider

- Is there easy access to public transportation?
- Will you have a second car?
- Do you want/need to be near the office?
- Do you want/need to be near the schools?
- Do you want to live in a village or in a big city?
- How much can you spend on housing?

Discuss these things with your family and ask for suggestions from colleagues in the office and parents at school. Make a list of what is important to you, and then prioritize. You can use this list to weigh the pluses and minuses for each house.

Location Location Location

Most expatriates settle in the Randstad, the name for the area that encompasses Amsterdam, Haarlem, Leiden, The Hague, Rotterdam and Utrecht. Many international corporations are located in this region, as well as international schools, shops, churches and social clubs. Within the Randstad and in other parts of the country, like Maastricht and Eindhoven, there are many options for styles of living. A Dutch saying is "You make your money in Rotterdam, spend it in Amsterdam and talk about it in The Hague." This is a rough flavor of each of these cities, but it doesn't really give you a sense of the options within each, the suburbs around each or the flavor of the cities further out.

As you start to think about location, when you prioritize what is important to you, you will find yourself easily excluding certain locations such as:

- I want to live close to the train, because we don't want a second car.
- I want to live within 10 kilometers of the school we have chosen for our children.
- I want to live in a rural farm village.
- I want to live in Amsterdam.

Making the initial choices may be the easy part; finding a home that feels right to you that you can afford can be more difficult.

Dutch Housing is Compact

Space is efficiently used to optimize the number of people who can live in one area. About 75% of the nation lives on 25% of the land. Public spaces are highly regarded—even in an apartment building there is always some green space available. A result of having so much of living space "shared" is that privacy is highly valued. Though everyone seems to live on top of each other, there is respect for the privacy of each family. When you look for housing, you will need to look at the options available to you through "Dutch" eyes.

Single family houses are a rarity; if you are lucky enough to find one, it will be called free standing (*vrijstaand*). The duplex houses are known as *twee onder een kap* meaning "two under one roof." The majority of Dutch families, however, live in multiple family houses and apartment complexes. A multiple family can be six or more houses connected; like town houses in the U.S. or row houses in the U.K., they share one or two walls with neighbors. They usually have a private small garden in the front and also in the back (the Dutch love gardens). Apartments can be on one level or multistory. The ground floor apartments (*begane grond* or *maisonnette*) will be on one level. Multistory (*bovenwoning* or *twee ops*) apartments have entry on the ground floor with living accommodations on the first and/or second floors.

Common to all of them is a utilitarian design. Things you will find common to Dutch houses:

- Small efficient kitchens.
- Central, multipurpose rooms (dining and living) which have large windows or French doors in the front (to the street) and back (to the garden).
- Steep often winding stairways.
- Toilets separated from the bathrooms known as "water closets."
- No built-in closets. Closets are considered furniture, not a part of the house.

Furnishings

When a home is described as:

- **Unfurnished (*ongemeubileerd or kale huur*):** This home will normally not have light fixtures, water heaters, bathroom cabinets, appliances, window coverings, or floor coverings of any kind. Expect an unfurnished house to be literally stripped clean.
- **Partly furnished (*gestoffeerd*):** This home rarely has furniture, closets or storage chests. When you look at a partly furnished home, be sure to ask if what you see will still be there if you move in. You can expect a partly furnished home to have carpeted or parquet floors, window coverings throughout, ceiling lights, and major kitchen appliances.
- **Fully furnished (*gemeubileerd*):** means the home will have just about everything: furniture, pots, pans, china, silverware, major appliances (except perhaps a clothes dryer and dishwasher) and sometimes linen. When considering a furnished house, make sure you understand exactly what is included and ask for an inventory.

If the house comes with appliances, you will find them to be smaller than those in the U.S. Refrigerators have a smaller capacity and often little or no freezer. Washers usually front load to conserve and heat their own water. Dryers can only take a few pounds of wet laundry at a time. Dishwashers are standard sized, but might not be a part of a kitchen. Ovens are smaller, sometimes not much bigger than an American microwave.

If you need furniture temporarlly or for the duration of your stay, you can often rent it. One company offering this service is:

IN-Lease Netherlands BV
August Janssenweg 7, 3742 RX Baarn
☎ +31 (0)35 542 66 95
www.in-lease.com

Dutch Housing is Expensive

Rental properties in desirable areas may have very high rents. An apartment on one of the inner canals in Amsterdam or a freestanding house in 't Gooi area (suburbs of Amsterdam off the A1) are priced at a premium. To find lower cost housing, you will have to consider exactly what makes a place a home to you. There are lots of lovely communities where the housing is not as competitive. The choice is up to you. Do not be surprised if you see something with a For Rent (*Te Huur*) sign, and then find out that you can't view it. Many Dutch qualify for housing subsidies, and this gives them access to different living spaces than what you as a foreigner (*buitenlander*) will have access to if you are here on a temporary basis.

▸ Additional Costs to Consider

When reviewing the costs of living in the Netherlands there are many extra expenses in addition to your housing expense. A few of these to consider are:

- Utilities: gas, electricity, water, telephone, Internet, cable TV
- Property tax (if you buy a house)
- Garbage and sewer tax
- Environment tax
- Maintenance: cleaning of central heating system, chimney cleaning, gardening
- Dog tax
- Auto expenses: parking permits, road tax, APK (annual car inspection fee)
- Insurance: auto, rental or homeowners, personal liability, medical
- BTW (*Belasting Toegevoegde Waarde*): VAT – Value Added Tax which is 19% on goods and services and 6% for books, food and other items

▸ Internet Search for Housing

Whether you plan to buy (*te koop*) or rent (*te huur*), if you would like to get an idea about housing in the Netherlands before arriving, you can do your own Internet search at *www.funda.nl*. Funda is an organization of realtors and contains essentially all available housing. This site is mostly in Dutch, but this is a good opportunity to find out what Dutch words you will use when house hunting (see the vocabulary list at the end of the chapter).

At the Funda site you can search by city (*locatie*) or post code and specify your price range (*prijsklasse*). You can narrow your search by specifying the number of rooms (*kamers*), square meters required (*woonoppervlakte*), whether you want a garden (*tuin*) or if you'd like to live on the water (*aan water*). The main headings you will see on a listing are:

- Overview (*Overzicht*): House and lot size, year built and type of home such as apartment or free standing (*vrijstaande woning*) as well as photos.
- Description (*Omschrijving*): Floor-by-floor layout of the house.
- Characteristics (*Kenmerken*): Outline including the type of heating.
- Photos (*Fotos*)
- Neighborhood (*Buurt*): Photos of the surrounding houses.
- Map (*Kaart*)

If you decide to buy or rent directly from the owner or owner's agent, don't forget to negotiate the price. Often the final price is about 10% less than the asking price. You will also want to ask for all contracts to be in English.

Professional House Hunting Assistance

To find a house or apartment, you will probably choose to have some help.

▸ The Real Estate Agent

Dutch law doesn't require that you use a real estate agent (*makelaar*), but renting or buying can be quite a complicated process and you may save yourself a lot of time and frustration by doing so. Be careful: The law in the Netherlands is such that anyone can call themselves a *makelaar*. Be sure to use a real estate agent registered with the Dutch Association of Real Estate Brokers (*Nederlandse Vereniging van Makelaars or NVM*). Members of this association are generally reputable, very well trained and offer free financial advice. They also share a computerized multiple-listing system. This means that you only need one agent in order to see all available housing in one region or area.

NVM agents adhere to a standard commission scale. Whether real estate is being rented or sold, both parties to a transaction pay a commission, each to his or her own agent. For rental properties, this commission amounts to approximately one month's rent. Should you have any problems with or questions about a *makelaar* who is a member of the NVM, you can contact:

NVM (Nederlandse Vereniging van Makelaars)
Fakkelstede 1, 3431 HZ Nieuwegein
☎ (030) 608 51 85
www.nvm.nl

Real estate agents are generally only available during normal business hours, but this is changing. Homes for sale can often be seen in the evenings and on Saturdays, but rental properties, especially if occupied, are mostly shown only during weekdays.

To Find a Real Estate Agent:

- Ask your associates and friends for recommendations.
- Ask the human resources manager of your company for advice.
- Call the agent listed on a For Sale (*Te Koop*) or For Rent (*Te Huur*) sign.

Once you have selected a real estate agent, and before he or she begins to show you around, be sure you have a clear understanding of the fees, as you may be asked to sign an agreement.

▸ The Relocation Agent

Relocation agencies offer a number of services to expatriates as they move into the country. A relocation agency may be on contract with the company that brought you here, or you may hire their services directly. In any case, a relocation agent can be a godsend in terms of knowing exactly what you need to do and helping you to adjust to life in the Netherlands.

If your company contracts with the agency, they will have predetermined the scope of support that the agency will provide. If you are privately contracting with the agency, then you have the choice to use them as little or as much as you need and can afford. Typically a relocation agent charges a package price for his/her services.

Services Offered by Relocation Agencies:

- Show you around and introduce you to the area.
- Help you find and negotiate for your housing, utilities, etc.
- Help you find and get registered with the right school for your children.
- Help you establish a relationship with a bank and set up needed accounts.
- Arrange the import of your household goods/automobile to the Netherlands.
- Ensure that you have all the proper forms and registrations to be able to work and live here legally.
- Assist with settling in (health care, transportation system, driving licenses, shopping, social clubs, finding a place of worship, sport options, etc.).
- Provide support for establishing a business here.

Of course, you can do all of these things on your own. However, you will find that the insight an agent can provide, as you try to set yourself up in this country, can be invaluable. All relocation agents are bilingual (Dutch, English) and most can provide additional language support if it is required. Various relocation agents are listed at the end of this chapter.

▸ Negotiations

Once you have found the ideal house, you can expect some negotiations both in the asking price and condition of the property whether you are purchasing it or renting it. For instance, if there is no dryer in a rental house, your desire for one can be used as a negotiable item. To have your own agent is always wise, and you can negotiate with him about his fee and what kind of service you expect to have. When discussing rental fees or housing prices, it is best to let your real estate agent do the talking.

Real estate deals were previously agreed orally and were binding, but that is no longer the case. There is now a "thinking it over" period. The time to think the matter over (*bedenktijd*) is three working days after the receipt of the copies of the signed deed of the purchase. Negotiations can be done verbally, so don't commit yourself orally or with a handshake agreement until you are absolutely certain.

Renting Versus Buying

Consider how long you will be staying in the Netherlands. If it is for less than three years, then you should probably rent. Even if you know you are staying longer, it is often wise to rent for a year to get to know the market and neighborhoods that interest you before you buy.

Real estate agents are helpful to get the best value for your money. Nonetheless, resident foreigners can still expect to pay top prices for housing, since they generally expect to live in housing that is large and luxurious by Dutch standards, and they need it quickly. The yearly rental price usually reflects the sales value of houses in the Randstad area—8% to 10% of the value.

The western part of the Netherlands, you will quickly notice, is very densely populated. There is also a shortage of low income housing. If you are going to stay for a long period of time (more than three years) and you qualify for this type of housing, you can enroll on a waiting list in your municipality. It should be emphasized that subsidized housing comes unfurnished (unless you make arrangements with the previous tenants).

Renting

▸ The Finances of Renting

Rent is paid one month in advance and is due on the first of each month. It may be adjusted yearly based on the cost-of-living index. Ordinarily, rent is exclusive (*exclusief*) meaning it does not include utilities and cable TV. The owner pays the property tax and this amount is not included in your rent. Renters are responsible for municipal taxes such as garbage and sewer, animal taxes, etc., which are paid separately from your rent. You can expect to pay a deposit in the amount of one or two month's rent. It should be refunded when you leave if everything is as you found it, normal wear and tear excepted.

▸ Your Rental Contract

Read the fine print. Most NVM real-estate agents will provide you with an English contract/lease:

- **Diplomatic Clause:** Be sure your lease contains the standard diplomatic clause allowing you to vacate—without penalty—should the family bread winner be transferred. If your job takes you out of the Netherlands, you may legally break the rental contract by giving two full calendar month's notice.
- **Reverse Diplomatic Clause:** You should be aware that the rental contract might bear a clause giving the lessor the right to re-occupy with three month's notice.
- **Term of Contract:** When leaving, you will also need to give notice within the time specified in your contract. Unless otherwise noted, a contract will continue on a silent agreement (*stilzwijgende verlenging*) making you liable for an additional year.

- **Damages:** Does your contract state who is responsible for damage caused to your belongings as a result of structural defects of the building? For example, if the roof leaks and the ceiling caves in on all your expensive bedroom furniture, who pays? It is advisable to purchase insurance for your personal belongings (*inboedel verzekering*). The landlord's insurance wouldn't cover the replacement of your items due to fire or theft.
- **Household Inventory:** You may want to make sure that your real estate agent makes an inventory of all furnishings, indicating their true condition. Have a duplicate made and signed by you and the owner, one for you and one for the landlord. If there are valuable items in the house, you might be wise to engage the services of an Appraiser (*Taxateur*).

Buying

▸ Thinking About Buying?

Many foreigners have bought homes in the Netherlands and you can, too. Furthermore, the mortgage interest is tax-deductible; this applies also for those with the 30% rule. However, it is not easy, so a word of caution is in order: proceed slowly and with care. By law, the seller is obligated to inform you of any defects that aren't immediately recognizable. Nonetheless, before tendering a bid, you should carefully inspect the condition of the property. While it isn't a tradition to use an independent surveyor in the Netherlands, it is highly recommended.

When purchasing a house, you will sometimes need housing authority approval called a *woonvergunning*. The criteria for such a permit vary from municipality to municipality.

A deposit of 10% to 15% of the purchase price must be paid approximately two weeks after acceptance of your purchase offer. A special kind of lawyer called a *Notaris* will keep the deposit until the official date of transfer. Alternatively, it's possible to acquire a promissory note from your bank or a *bankgarantie* that guarantees you will be granted a loan.

Other costs amount to approximately 10% to 12% of the purchase price:

- Property transfer tax of 6%
- Notary costs are negotiable (an apartment is about € 1,100, a house €1,400 and large houses/villas €2,500)
- Real estate agent fees are also negotiable (0.75% to 1.85%)
- Mortgage initiation fee called a *afsluitprovisie*

An offer on a house should always be dependent on receiving financing. It is useful to first check with your bank or mortgage lender about how much you will be approved for. If you make an offer on a house and then decide that the down payment PLUS tax PLUS registration fees, etc., are more than you can handle, you will have to pay a sizable penalty to break the contract—your 10% deposit!

If you are considering making alterations or additions to the house or garden, consult your real estate agent. You may have to have municipal approval for exterior alterations and for the removal of trees larger than a certain diameter. It's useful to determine any restrictions before you buy.

▸ The Attorney or *Notaris*

The law requires both the buyer and the seller to use the services of a *Notaris* who is an independent attorney specializing in the drawing up of legal documents. The choice of a *Notaris* is up to the buyer.

The *Notaris* will have the title searched, write up and record the deed, and disperse funds at the closing. First you will be sent a draft of the deed of transfer together with a statement showing how much is required to complete the purchase. This statement includes the purchase price, the transfer tax, land registry fees, *Notaris* fees, the commission on a possible mortgage loan, the real estate agent's fees, etc. If there is a mortgage loan, you will receive a draft of the mortgage deed. Your real estate agent will also receive a copy and review it for you. Remember, all legal documents are presented in Dutch so be sure to request a translation of all terms.

The *Notaris* will take care of the financial settlement of the transaction and ensure that the deed of transfer is entered in the public registers. Later, you will receive a copy of the deed, which is your proof of ownership (*eigendomsbewijs*).

In Amsterdam, a *Notaris* can also write your offer to buy (*voorlopig koopcontract*) in English if you like, and advise you of the proper contingency clauses. In other municipalities, this may be done by the seller's real estate agent, who will then send it on to the *Notaris*. Don't forget to request this.

The asking price gives an indication of the price the seller wants to get. The actual purchase price might be 10% less, but this is not a rule. Your real estate agent can help you decide on a reasonable offer. Sometimes a house is even sold at a higher price, such as in a seller's market when people will bid well above the asking price in order to secure the property.

If your price is non-negotiable, have your real estate agent indicate this clearly since this is quite out of the ordinary in the Netherlands. Keep in mind, also, that if your offer is insultingly low, you may not get a chance to make a counteroffer. A Dutchman's home is his castle and one of the unwritten rules is that you never point out the flaws and shortcomings in an effort to get the price down. It just won't work. In general, the Dutch don't fix up their houses before putting them on the market. Like the Dutch, let your money do the talking.

An Offer to Buy Should Include:

- Specify the date for taking possession.

- List all appliances, light fixtures, curtains, etc., which you think you are buying, in an attachment.
- Include all contingencies. Specification of contingencies protects the buyer. If they can't be fulfilled, then it should be possible to break the contract without penalty.
- State that the contract will go through provided you can obtain a mortgage at the current rate within a specified time period, usually three weeks.

▸ Financing

The first rule is persistence. Don't give up if the first bank you visit won't give you the loan you want—the second or the fifth might. Your real estate agent should be able to give you a great deal of help with this step. Ask about the possibility of a mortgage guaranteed by your municipality (*gemeente garantie*). Such a loan is generally accompanied by a more favorable interest rate. Your bank may require you to buy life insurance equal to the value of the home.

Mortgages *(Hypotheken)*

Four types of mortgages are described below:

- **Endowment Mortgage (*Leven Hypotheek*):** There's no repayment of capital during the mortgage term. Interest is paid on the full amount of the loan all the time. Also, there's a premium to pay for an endowment policy. This premium is used for life insurance coverage and also is invested to guarantee payment of the loan. Regular payments of interest and premium remain the same during the fixed interest rate period.
- **Annuities Mortgage (*Annuiteiten Hypotheek*):** Regular installments of principal and interest are made. The amount of the annuities remains the same, but the composition changes. Payments are at first mainly interest with very little capital repaid. As the balance falls, the interest decreases and more principal is repaid.
- **Non-Repayment Mortgage (*Aflossingsvrije Hypotheek*):** The principal is repaid at the end of the loan. During the course of the mortgage, only interest is paid in a level amount.
- **Repayment Mortgage (*Lineaire Hypotheek*):** Regular installments of a fixed percentage of the original principal plus interest. Over a 30-year mortgage, the repayment is $3\frac{1}{3}$% of the principal per year. The payment of principal remains the same. As interest is paid on the outstanding principal, the interest gradually decreases, thus payments decrease.

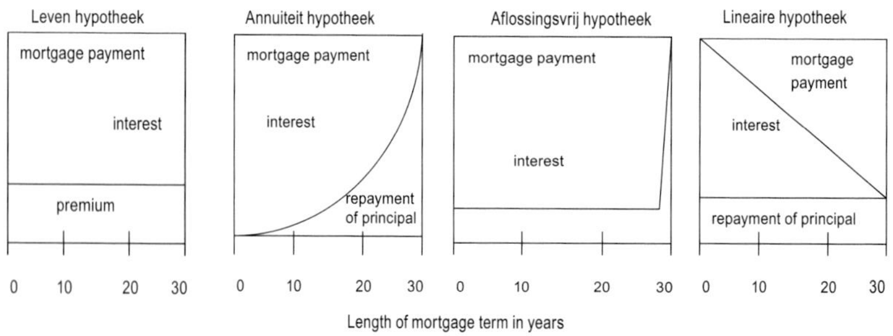

Inspect the Premises

Complete an inspection of the home or apartment you are considering before making a final decision:

- Check for leaks and cracks in the roof and walls, around the plumbing and appliances, and inspect the rain gutters. If renting, be sure it is clear who is financially responsible for inside and outside repair costs.
- Call the local power company (*gemeentelijk energiebedrijf*) to request a check on the wiring and gas connections. The power company performs this service free of charge. If all isn't in order, the house will have to be rewired or repaired at the new owner's expense.
- Be sure the house has adequate central heating (*centrale verwarming*.) Heating a house here is expensive. Be warned that double glazed windows aren't always found in older houses.

- Ask for an estimate of the monthly utility bill.
- Locate meters, main switches, fuses, cutoff valves and drains; they are often found in unexpected places. All family members should have this information in case of an emergency.
- If the house includes appliances, security systems, etc., inquire about use. If the instruction manuals aren't in English, do a Google search on the model name and number to see if free downloads are available.

▸ Vereniging Eigen Huis

If you buy (or are considering buying) a home, it might be wise to join the *Vereniging Eigen Huis* (United Homeowners). It costs about €30 per year as of January 2009. It is a consumer advocacy bureau that will give you an unbiased evaluation of a property that you own or are seriously considering buying. This service costs money (like getting a second opinion on a used car from the ANWB). However, it can give you the analysis you need to be an informed purchaser of a house and they can provide guidance if, after you own the house, you find problems that you think you should have known about before. They don't provide repairs nor do they recommend service providers. They do, however, have a high reputation within the legal community if you need to litigate for misrepresentation. Check their website for current information.

Vereniging Eigen Huis
Displayweg 2, 3821 BT Amersfoort
☎ (033) 450 77 50
www.eigenhuis.nl

House-Hunting Vocabulary

There are several Dutch terms and phrases that you will see during the house-hunting phase, and the most important ones are listed below. The first two are vital and frequently misunderstood.

Kosten koper, k.k.	*Notaris* and registration fees paid by buyer
Vraagprijs	Asking price; it is negotiable
Badkamer	Bathroom; usually without a toilet
Benedenwoning	House on the ground floor only of a building
Bijkeuken	Room off kitchen (pantry or laundry)
Bungalow	Bungalow, a free standing one-floor house
Centrale verwarming	Central heating
Dakkapel	Dormer
Dakraam	Skylight
Dubbele bovenwoning	Two story house on 2nd and 3rd floors of building
Douche	Shower

Eetkamer	Dining room
Eetkeuken	Kitchen with space for eating
Garage	Garage
Gemeentelijk energiebedrijf	Regional or municipal power company
Gemeubileerd	Including furniture
Gestoffeerd	Including curtains, carpeting, ceiling lights
Halfvrijstaand/twee onder een kap	Half of a duplex
Hoekhuis	Corner row house
Hypotheek	Mortgage
Inbouwapparatuur	Built-in appliances
Kamer	Room
Keuken	Kitchen
Ligbad	Bathtub
Makelaar (adviseur onroerend goed)	Real estate agent
Notaris	Attorney of real estate and wills
NVM	Dutch Association of Real Estate Agents
(Goed) onderhouden	Well maintained, in good condition
Open haard	Fireplace
Serre	Sun room
Slaapkamer	Bedroom
Taxateur	Appraiser
Te huur	For rent
Te koop	For sale
Trap	Stairs
Tuin	Yard, garden
Verhuurd	Rented
Verkocht	Sold
Villa	Large freestanding house with grounds
Voorlopig koopcontract	Offer to buy (binding)
Vrijstaand	Completely detached or freestanding
Wastafel	Washbasin, sink
Woonkamer	Living room

First Floor, Please: The *eerste etage* or *eerste verdieping*, literally translated as first floor, is what Americans call the second floor. You may see the abbreviation for the first floor – 1e – in elevators and staircases. The floor on the ground level is referred to as the *begane grond* or BG.

Relocation Agencies in the Netherlands

Dutch Relocation
Willem Alexanderplantsoen 12,
2991 ND Barendrecht
☎+31 (0)18 062 02 21
www.dutchrelocation.nl

Dutch Living Services
Rendementsweg 24/M,
3640 AH Mijdrecht
☎+31 (0)29 728 34 55
www.*dutchlivingservices.nl*

Primacy Relocation B.V.
Frans van Mierisstraat 89,
1071 RN Amsterdam
☎+31 (0)20 573 60 70
www.primacy.com

Identity & Company B.V.
P. O. Box 9665, 1006 GD Amsterdam
☎+31 (0)20 619 95 56
www.identity-company.com

Link'O B.V.
Dorpsstraat 227, 1531 HE Wormer
☎+31 (0)75 642 67 00
www.linko.nl

The Partners in Relocation
Loosdorp 4, 4143 LT Leerdam
☎+31 (0)34 558 03 81
www.pir.nl

Relocation Advisers B.V.
Jan Willem Brouwersstraat 16, 1071 LJ Amsterdam
☎+31 (0)20 664 74 70
www.relocationadvisers.nl

Relocation Services Holland B.V.
Herengracht 10a, The Hague
☎+31 (0)70 387 17 15
www.relocation-holland.nl

Georgia Regnault, REMAS Nederland
Van der Aastraat 6, The Hague
P.O. Box 416, 2240 AK Wassenaar
☎+31 (0)70 324 85 82
E-mail: *remas237@yahoo.com*

Settle Service B.V.
Van Eedeustraat 18, 20112 EM Haarlem
☎+31 (0)23 534 41 88
www.settleservice.com

References

Here are some websites with articles on housing in the Netherlands:

- *www.justlanded.com*
    - Choose *Netherlands* and English, then *Need Housing?*
    - For additional articles, go to *Tools*, *Articles*, then *Property*
- *www.hollandsouth.angloinfo.com*
    - Click on *INFOrmation* then *Property & Real Estate*

Chapter 3

Banking

Figuring out the banking system in a foreign country can be a daunting task. Fortunately, it's getting much easier to navigate the banking system in the Netherlands thanks to an increasing number of services offered in English.

This chapter gives you an overview of the range of banking options available, as well as a primer on the euro (€), how to pay bills, transfer money, use a "smart card" and much more. If you keep in mind that bank accounts are never free, debit cards are the norm, and electronic bank transfers (not checks) are used to pay bills, you'll be on your way to managing your money like you've lived here for years.

Euro Coins and Bank Notes

The euro is the official currency of the European Union and is now the single currency for 320 million Europeans. The "€" symbol means euro in the same way "$" means dollar and "¥" means yen. Like the U.S. dollar, the euro is based on the decimal system with 100 eurocents equal to one euro. Coins are issued in denominations of 1, 2, 5, 10, 20 and 50 eurocents, as well as 1 and 2 euros. In the Netherlands, the 1 and 2 eurocent coins are no longer used in shops, so don't be surprised when the cashier rounds the amount due to the nearest 5 eurocents. Paper notes are issued in denominations of 5, 10, 20, 50, 100, 200 and 500 euros. Each denomination is a different color and size, ranging from smallest to largest. Many shops won't accept bank notes higher than €50. For the current exchange rate, try *www.xe.com/ucc* or check the *International Herald Tribune*.

Writing Numbers: The convention for the Dutch number notation is to use a comma where Americans would use a decimal and a period instead of a comma to separate thousands and millions. For example, 5 euros and 25 eurocents is written €5,25. Five thousand euros is € 5.000.

Bank Services

Banking is quite sophisticated in the Netherlands. Most banks offer general banking services like euro and foreign currency accounts, debit and credit cards, online banking and overdraft protection as well as savings accounts. In addition, many banks offer investment accounts, personal loans, safety deposit boxes, mortgages, foreign currency exchange and insurance.

You can choose from a number of banks including:

- **ABN AMRO** (*www.abnamro.com*)
- **Rabobank** (*www.rabobank.com*)
- **ING** (*www.ing.com*)
- **Postbank** (*www.postbank.nl*)

Several of these banks are preparing to merge as this edition goes to press, so websites and bank names might change. Services are being targeted to expats and Internet banking in English is gaining in popularity. Some banks will assign a preferred banker to you, who will be your contact person for any questions that arise about your account. Usually, a phone call or email can resolve most problems that may occur.

Opening a Bank Account

When you are ready to open a bank account, you will need your passport, your employment contract and an idea of what your monthly deposit amount will be. You will be asked to sign a signature card to verify your identity. If you open a joint account, your spouse will also need to bring a passport and sign all agreements.

Other things to consider include:

- **English Communication:** Not all banks offer bank statements and communications in English, so don't forget to ask.
- **Account Features:** Options include credit cards, branch office locations, online banking, telephone banking and overdraft protection to name a few.
- **Banking Fees:** Make sure to ask about fees for every service you request, including fees for credit and debit cards, interest rates for overdraft protection and account fees.

Bank Hours and Holidays

In general, banks are open from 9:00 a.m. to 5:00 p.m. Monday through Friday. Some banks open late on Mondays and some are open Saturday mornings. Some will even stay open during the late night shopping evening (*koopavond*) each week. Banks are closed for the following holidays:

- New Year's Day (*Nieuwjaarsdag*)
- Good Friday (*Goede Vrijdag*)
- Easter Monday (*Tweede Paasdag*)

- Queen's Day (*Koninginnedag*)
- Ascension Day (*Hemelvaartdag*)
- Pentecost Monday (*Tweede Pinksterdag*)
- Christmas (*Kerstdag*)
- Boxing Day (*Tweede Kerstdag*)

Foreign Currency Accounts and Transfers

If you decide to open a foreign currency account (USD, CAD, GBP, etc.), keep in mind that these funds are converted to euros only if withdrawn from the account and there will be a fee. You can also deposit euros into the account, which will then be converted to the foreign currency. When you transfer money from your home country to your foreign currency account, charges are usually applied by your home bank and by your Dutch bank. You may chose to arrange with your home country to electronically transfer funds on a regular basis. You will find it helpful to keep a bank account open in your home country to pay expenses there and for visits home. You can also access your Dutch bank account in your home country by using your Dutch PIN card along with a special card reader.

Paying without Cash

You will not be issued checks when you open a bank account. The Dutch don't write checks to pay for goods or services. Instead, the Dutch use a combination of debit cards, "smart cards" and electronic bank transfers. Credit cards are used sparingly.

PIN Cards

The most common form of noncash payment is the debit or PIN card (*pinkaart*). The PIN card is issued by your bank and all payments are instantly deducted from your account. Your bank assigns you or you choose your own PIN (Personal Identification Number), which you enter at the cash register (*kassa*) into the point of sale keypad after you've swiped your debit card. After your PIN is accepted, you press "*Ja*" (yes) to confirm your purchase. If you enter the incorrect PIN code more than three times, your PIN card will be blocked as a security precaution and you must contact your bank to have it reactivated or replaced. Stores that accept debit payments will display the blue and white PIN logo. Most shops and many restaurants accept PIN cards, but it's wise to double check. Be sure to take your receipt as proof of payment and to compare to your bank statement.

PIN cards can be used to withdraw money in the Netherlands as well as in other countries as long as the logos on the card match those on the foreign ATM machine; there will likely be a service charge to use ATMs from other banks. Your home country ATM card can also be used to withdraw cash in Europe, but you will pay higher fees and you won't be able to use it as a debit card in shops.

Chipknip or Chipper

The Chipknip is an electronic chip that makes your PIN card a "smart card." You can use this electronic cash to pay for small purchases like parking, movies or trams without having to enter your PIN code. To load the chip with money from your account, look for the Chipknip Machine (*Oplaadpunt*), usually next to the ATM (*Geldautomaat*). The instructions are in Dutch, so grab a friend or ask someone from your bank branch for help. As you make purchases, the amount of the purchase is deducted from the balance embedded on the chip. You can "load" and "unload" these chips indefinitely. As with any prepaid card, keep in mind that if your card is lost or stolen, the money on the Chipknip is also lost or stolen.

Credit Cards

While many smaller stores in the Netherlands don't accept credit cards, if you like to travel, having a euro-based credit card will come in handy for purchasing airline tickets online and making hotel reservations. A European credit card is useful to avoid the extra fees added to a U.S.-issued card for euro-based purchases. Your bank here should offer you a Eurocard, Mastercard or VISA. Make sure to ask about all fees as well as payment options. Some credit cards automatically deduct the balance from your bank account as soon as 7 days after the purchase. Others offer the option of paying after receiving a monthly bill. American Express (*www.americanexpress.com*) also offers a euro-based credit card issued in the United Kingdom with all correspondence in English.

▸ Paying Bills with Electronic Bank Transfer

Electronic bank transfer is the preferred method of bill payment in the Netherlands. Transfers from your bank account to the payee's bank account are requested either online or using an *acceptgiro* form. *Acceptgiros* are usually sent to you when you receive a bill for non-recurring expenses such as medical services or household repairs. Most utilities prefer that you pay automatically by providing them with your account information, but some will still send out *acceptgiros* per your request for an extra service charge.

The yellow *acceptgiro* form is printed with the name and account number of the company to whom you owe money. You can process an *acceptgiro* in the payments section of online banking or do the following:

- Fill in the amount due in euros
- Fill in your bank account number
- Sign where it says *handtekening*
- Drop off at your bank in the box for *acceptgiros*

Sometimes a company will send an *acceptgiro* with the amount due, your name and bank account number already printed on it. In this case, all you have to do is sign it where it says *handtekening*. Detach the small stub for your records before dropping it off at the bank. Payments will be processed by the bank by the following day. Other times a company will send you an invoice without an *acceptgiro*. In those cases, their bank account information will be provided so you can do an online bank transfer directly into their account.

Standing orders *(automatisch overschrijven)* for automatic payments of fixed amounts from your account can be arranged for recurring bills such as utilities and rent. When you open a utility account it is common for you to sign a document authorizing an automatic payment from your account. For other recurring expenses, such as rent, you can set up a standing order using online banking. Keep track of all of your automatic payments so that you can easily stop them when you move by using online banking or calling your bank.

Online Banking

After you have opened your bank account, you will need to have access to it online. To access your account online:

- You will need your PIN card.
- You will also need a card reader, which is supplied by your bank for extra security.
- Go to your bank's website.
- Enter your account number.
- Place your PIN card in the card reader.
- Enter your PIN code.
- The bank will provide you with a code to enter into the card reader.

- The card reader will respond with an access code that you use to complete the log-in to your account.

You will need the card reader again to confirm bank transfers. This may sound confusing, but once you get used to it you'll never want to write another check. Once online, you can check your balance, transfer funds within your own accounts, pay bills from companies and pay individuals, all instantly and without paper.

Some banks offer an English version of their online banking. If yours doesn't, someone at your bank should be able to help you figure out what to do. If there is more than one person on your account, make sure the bank activates both PIN cards for online access. You might also want a card reader for each account holder. Remember, if you want to check your balance or make payments while on vacation, you will need access to a computer as well as your card reader and your PIN card.

Automatic Teller Machines (ATM)

The Dutch ATM machine is called the *Geldautomaat*, and many of them offer an English-language option. If your bank does not offer English, ask someone from the bank to help you the first time or enlist the help of a Dutch friend. While each bank has a different set of screen instructions, here are some common phrases that may help:

Welkom	Welcome
Voer uw pas in AUB	Please put your card in
Toets uw pincode AUB	Please enter your pin code

You will then have two options:

1) *Geld opnemen*	Withdraw money
2) *Saldo informatie*	Account balance information

If you choose *Geld opnemen*, a screen with various amounts will appear. Choose an amount or press *Ander bedrag* to enter a different amount. It may also give you the option to choose what denomination of bills you will receive by choosing *biljetkeuze*.

Wilt u een transactiebon?	Would you like a receipt?
Transactie voltooid	Transaction completed
Neem uw pas terug AUB	Please remove your card
Tot ziens!	Goodbye! (See you later!)

If you choose *Saldo informatie* you may see these instructions:

Een moment geduld AUB	Please wait
Uw saldo is:	Your balance is:
U kunt maximaal opnemen:	You can withdraw a maximum of:

Wilt u doorgaan?	Would you like to continue?
Ja/Nee	Yes/No

You can access your home country accounts via an ATM if the logos on your debit card match those on the Dutch ATM, which means they are part of the same system such as Cirrus, Plus or Maestro. You will be charged a fee for withdrawing euros, but it will be far less than if you use a credit card for a cash advance.

Banking Vocabulary

Acceptgiro	Collection form
Adres	Address
Bestedingsruimte	Spending limit
Betaalkrediet	Overdraft amount
Betalen	Payments
Contant	Cash
Factuur	Bill/Invoice
Geblokkeerd	Blocked
Geld	Money
Geld opnemen	Withdraw money
Geldautomaat	ATM machine
Handtekening	Signature
Internet bankieren	Internet banking
Internet sparen	Internet savings
Kassa	Cashier
Naam	Name
Naam begunstigde	Name of payee
Oplaadpunt	Chipknip machine
Pas invoeren	Insert your card
Port betaald	Postage paid
Prive rekening	Personal account
Rekening	Account
Rekeningnummer	Account number
Saldo	Balance
Spaarrekening	Savings account
Telefonisch bankieren	Telephone banking
Toegangscode	Access code
U heeft betaald	You have paid
Verzekering	Insurance
Woonplaats begunstigde	Town of payee
Zakelijke rekening	Business account

Chapter 4

International Education

One of the critical decisions you have to make if you have children is where they will go to school. The Netherlands offers many educational opportunities from preschool for your toddler to advanced studies for your teenager (or even yourself). Children can attend international schools or schools directed at the needs of specific religions or nationalities. Your choices are many.

Your first choice is between English language or other language programs. If you decide on English language, the options range from some of the Dutch public schools to international private schools. If you choose other language programs, your options include the Dutch public schools and private schools in French, Japanese, German, etc. There is no single school that is right for everyone.

Choosing the Right School

As an English speaker in the Netherlands, you may find that the Dutch educational system doesn't seem to fit your child's needs. Maybe you want to continue with the British system, as your daughter will be in her last year before university. Perhaps your son needs the structure of the French system so he fits back in when he returns to it in two years time. Perhaps your daughter has a learning disability. You need to make some decisions about what path to put your children on and you need to know your options.

If you are lucky enough to have "the company" pay for the education of your children while you are here, a private international school will give your child an experience which may be hard to match in the public school system of your home country when you return there.

If you are paying for education costs, be assured that there are wonderfully varied options before you. The Netherlands has schools that can fit the needs of every family. Before you begin your search, you must first think about your expectations of education for your child.

What Do You Need to Consider?

As you look at the experience you want your child to have, there are several dimensions to take into account such as:

- The age of the child
- How long you expect to be in the Netherlands and where you plan to go next
- The type of educational system you are leaving at your last place of residence
- The kind of experience you and the child are looking for
- The cost and who is paying
- Proximity of your new home to the school

Why Are These Dimensions Important?

Primary school children shift educational systems more easily than students in the final years of secondary school. Children who have a fluent second language will have a lifetime advantage.

An example:

- Your son is 15, your family is moving from the U.K. for the first time, and you expect to be here for two years. In this case you might think seriously about continuing the "British education model" at a British school. Your son will continue in the structure and classes which are a part of a familiar educational system. On return to the U.K. for his last year, he will have had the exams that he should have taken and can be a part of the university application process without having to make up any time.
- On the other hand, a totally different option would be to place him in an English language program in a Dutch school which would give him the exposure to a different educational system and the benefits it brings. However, it might mean that he has to repeat a year when he gets back.

Another example:

- Your child is 4 and you have moved here for an indefinite period. You may decide that your daughter really should have the advantage of attending the local Dutch schools and learning the Dutch language so that she has pals in your neighborhood. She, and you, would really have a taste of the experience of living in the Netherlands.

Another example:

- Your daughter is 10 with a learning disability. In the U.S. the public educational system provided special help for her, but the private international schools in the Netherlands don't have the resources you need. You have to find the outside independent educational support she needs.

From the above examples, you can see that you need to determine what is best for you and your children.

Dutch Education

Some people recommend that you choose the school first, and then find a home nearby, so that you need not be so involved in the transportation of your child(ren) after hours. But at times, that may not be possible.

Below you will find a description of the options you have as you think about schooling here. At the end of this chapter, there is an index by city of potential schools. It is a partial listing and doesn't give an evaluation of the "quality" of education offered – that is up to you to determine for yourself.

A large number of Dutch schools have been set up by private bodies and institutions and are called "private" schools. Nonetheless, the majority of their funding comes from the federal government, which by law may not discriminate between educational philosophies or against religious ones. If you are coming from the U.S., you will find that this system is very different from the U.S. educational model for students over age 12. If you are coming from a European country, you will find that it is more similar to the educational system of your home country.

Dutch School Helpline: Complete search of Dutch schools
☎ (0800) 50 10
www.scholenlijst.nl

▸ Infants and Toddlers

Day nursery schools, crèches and *kinderdagverblijven* are available in the Netherlands. However, there is usually a waiting list to get in. Preschools for children from age two to four are called *Peuterspeelzalen*. Check with your local *gemeente, afdeling onderwijs* for information or look in the Yellow Pages under *Peuterspeelzaal*.

Play groups and Mother-Toddler groups exist for speakers of French, English and other languages. Phone ACCESS or see the listings in our **Children** chapter for further information.

▸ Primary School *(Basis School)*

Children in the Netherlands must attend school from the age of four. Primary school covers ages 4 through 11. The Dutch primary education (*primair onderwijs*) policy is inclusive of children with special needs. All Dutch children are obliged to start school on the first day of the month following their fourth birthday. Full-time education is compulsory until the school year in which a young person turns 16. The young person must, however, continue attending school at least part-time for another year. In principle, education is free, but schools may ask parents to make a contribution.

Some schools offer alternative educational philosophies:

- Montessori Schools (*www.montessori.nl*): Children's work is very self-directed
- Free Schools (*www.vrijescholen.nl*): Emphasizes imagination and mysticism (anthroposophy)
- Dalton and Jena Plan Schools (*www.dalton.nl*): Emphasizes contact between children of different ages, which they believe more accurately reflects real life
- Standard Public-Authority Schools (*www.voo.nl*): *vereniging voor openbaar onderwijs*

Secondary Education (*Voortgezet Onderwijs*)

At age twelve, children finish primary school and take the CITO exam, which tests for proficiency in three areas: Dutch language skills, mathematics and problem solving. The CITO exam is a standard test given nationally and will influence the type of secondary school that your children can attend. There are two main tracks to follow: one is university oriented and the other is professional/technical school oriented. There is a one-to-three year bridge period (*brugperiode*) during which both tracks are combined. The student then makes a "choice," based on the results of tests and performance in school, about the direction of his/her career.

Secondary Tracks: The tracks that they follow after the "bridge period" are:

- VMBO (*Middelbaar Algemeen Voortgezet Onderwijs*): Pre-vocational secondary education; this track provides for technically trained employees in a range of fields.
- HAVO (*Hoger Algemeen Voortgezet Onderwijs*): General secondary education; this track lasts five years after which the student is finished with school and may go into the workforce. He/she may choose to get a more advanced certificate, HBO (*Hoger Beroeps Onderwijs*) which would allow entrance into a university. This track also prepares technicians for employment; however, they have greater opportunities for further study and greater job responsibility.
- VWO (*Voortgezet Wetenschappelijk Onderwijs*): Pre-university education; this track takes six years after which the student may head on to university. The students choose a subject (*vakkenpakket*) on which to concentrate during their third year.

Higher Education

This is equivalent to a Master's Degree in the U.S. Dutch higher education comprises higher vocational and university education from about age 18. There are eight public universities; five *hoge scholen*, which are equivalent to undergraduate universities; and seven theological colleges, as well as private institutions. Students must have a VWO or HBO certificate or the equivalent to qualify for admission. A standard course of study takes about four years, and it is possible to continue on for a doctoral degree. Introductory courses in the Dutch language are compulsory for non-Dutch speaking foreign students.

International Education

More than half of the international schools in the Netherlands are located in or near the cities of Amsterdam, The Hague, Rotterdam and Utrecht. The fees for American, British and some other international schools are very high because they aren't underwritten by the Dutch government. Many schools offer English as a Second Language (ESL) training for international students who need help with speaking, reading or writing English.

International Programs in Dutch Schools

- **English Stream Programs:** Several Dutch schools in the Netherlands offer an opportunity for children to be educated in a truly mixed environment in the "English Stream" or English-speaking department of their regular primary and secondary schools. This program is available to non-Dutch families and to repatriating Dutch families whose children have received schooling abroad. Contact the Dutch Ministry of Education and Science (*www.minocw.nl*) to see if there is such a school in your area.
- **International Stream:** If your child is well motivated and has a suitable academic record, an additional alternative within the Dutch System is the International Stream (IS) Program, available to students ages 11 to 16, and the International Baccalaureate (IB) Program for students ages 16 to 19. The IS program is designed to give intellectual mobility to students living in a truly international world and who are consequently required to adjust to varied socio-cultural settings. These schools often offer the IB track.

International (Country Specific) Language Education

It is possible to find schools which teach in any one of several languages, and which follow the educational model of specific countries such as American, Japanese, British, French and German (see the list at the end of this chapter). The goal of these schools is to make it easier for a student to move back into their home country's educational system without disruption. These are also places for a long term expatriate family to give their child an education with continuity, regardless of where they live in the world.

International English Language Schools

These schools are taught in English and follow a curriculum which allows students to transfer from country-to-country without disruption in education. They offer a "lifetime" expatriate family the chance to have consistency as they move around the world. In the Netherlands, the student population is extremely multicultural, giving the children real insight into the lives and cultures of their peers. These also offer Dutch language courses. These schools offer the International General Certificate of Secondary Education (IGCSE) and also the International Baccalaureate (IB) track. They usually offer the exams needed to place in the universities of English language countries.

Special Needs Education

Private international schools have limited resources for children with special needs. While Dutch public education does offer resources and can provide a caring environment, their services tend to be rather dated by American and British standards. Both the American School of The Hague and the International School of The Hague offer on-site educational psychologists and speech therapists. They will help refer you to a school psychologist in your area that offers assessment and counseling in English.

There are several organizations throughout the Netherlands that can help you better cope with the challenges facing your child with special needs. You'll find additional special needs resources in our chapter on **Children**.

ACCESS: Provides list of special needs practitioners and resources.
☎ (020) 423 32 17 Amsterdam
☎ (070) 346 25 25 Den Haag
www.access-nl.org

Autism Association for Overseas Families Network in the Netherlands (AAOF): An English-language group serving the international community, consisting of parent/family members and professionals, offering support and information to families of individuals with autistic spectrum disorders.
www.aaof.info

Lighthouse Special Education: Serves children, ages 3–12, in the international community who have special educational needs including those with severe behavioral and/or educational problems. Offers opportunities for these children to be mainstreamed into a traditional school.
Amalia van Solmsstraat 155, Den Haag
☎ (070) 338 7070, *www.lighthousese.nl*

Parents United: For children who learn differently. This group at the American School of The Hague has assembled a library of resources that you can use to determine what your options are.

International Primary/Secondary Schools

Almere Area

International School Almere:
English. Ages 11–16.
Sas Van Gentlaan 6, 1324 CT Almere
☎ (036) 845 35 00
www.internationalschoolalmere.nl

Amsterdam Area

Amsterdam International Community School: English. Ages 4–18. IB.
Prinses Irenestraat 59, 1077 WV Amsterdam
☎ (020) 577 12 40
www.aics.espritscholen.nl

British School of Amsterdam: Ages 3–15.
Antonie van Dijckstraat 1,
1077 ME Amsterdam
☎ (020) 679 78 40
www.britams.nl

International School of Amsterdam, ISA: English. Ages 4–18. U.S. high school diploma, IB.
Sportlaan 45, 1185 TB Amstelveen
☎ (020) 347 11 11
www.isa.nl

Japanese School of Amsterdam: Japanese. Ages 6–15.
Karel Klinkenbergstraat 137,
1061 AL Amsterdam
☎ (020) 611 81 36
www.jsa.nl

Lycée Français Vincent Van Gogh: French. Ages 3–12.
Uiterwaardenstraat 60A, 1079 CB Amsterdam
☎ (020) 644 65 07 w
www.lyceevangogh.nl

Arnhem

Arnhem International School
Dr. Aletta Jacobs School: English. Ages 4–12.
Slochterenweg 27, 6835 CD Arnhem
☎ (026) 323 07 29

Lorentz Lyceum: English. Ages 12–18.
Groningensingel 1245, 6835 HZ Arnhem
☎ (026) 320 01 11
www.arnheminternationalschool.nl

Assen

British School in the Netherlands – The Helen Sharman School: Ages 3–11.
Epe 83, 9406 HK Assen
☎ (059) 234 45 90
www.britishschool.nl

Bergen

European School: English, German, Dutch, French, Italian. European Baccalaureate. Ages 4–18.
Molenweidtje 5, Postbus 99,
1860 AB Bergen NH
☎ (072) 589 01 09
www.europeseschool.nl

Budel

Deutsche Schule Budel: German.
Europalaan-Noord 16, 6021 EH Budel
☎ (049) 549 17 76

Brunssum

AFNORTH International School: English, German. Ages 4–19. Sponsoring nations: Canada, Germany, the U.K. and the U.S. Curricula appropriate for each of these nation's requirements.
Ferdinand Bolstraat 1, 6445 EE Brunssum
☎ (045) 527 82 21
www.afno-is.eu.dodea.edu

Eindhoven

International Secondary School Eindhoven: English. Ages 11–18. IGCSE, IB. Bilingual VWO.
Venetiestraat 43, 5632 RM Eindhoven
☎ (040) 242 68 35
www.issehv.nl

Regional International School: Dutch, English. Ages 4–12.
Humperdincklaan 4, 5654 PA Eindhoven
☎ (040) 251 94 37
www.riseindhoven.nl

Groningen

International Department of Groningse Schoolvereniging: English, Dutch. Ages 4–12.
Sweelincklaan 4, 9722 JV Groningen
☎ (050) 527 08 18
www.g-s-v.nl

Maartens College International School: English. Ages 11–18. IGCSE, IB.
Postbus 6105, 9702 HC Groningen
☎ (050) 534 00 84
www.maartenscollege.nl

The Hague

See also under the headings, Voorschoten and Wassenaar.
American School of The Hague (ASH)
See under the heading: Wassenaar

British School in the Netherlands (BSN): Ages 3-18. GCSE, IB.
Admissions Office: Tarwekamp 3, 2592 XG Den Haag
☎ (070) 315 40 77
www.britishschool.nl

Deutsche Internationale Schule: German. Ages 3–18.
van Bleiswijkstraat 125, 2582 LB Den Haag
☎ (070) 354 94 54
www.disdh.nl

Haagsche School Vereeniging, International Stream (HSV): English. Ages 4–11.
Nassaulaan 26, 2514 JT Den Haag
☎ (070) 363 85 31
Koningin Sophiestraat 24a, 2595 TG Den Haag
☎ (070) 324 34 53
www.hsvdenhaag.nl

International School of The Hague (ISH): English. Ages 4–18. IGCSE, IB.
Wijndaelerduin 1, 2554 BX Den Haag
☎ (070) 338 45 67
www.ishthehague.nl

Lycée Français Vincent Van Gogh: French. Ages 3–18.
Scheveningseweg 237, 2584 AA Den Haag
☎ (070) 306 69 20
www.lyceevangogh.nl

Hilversum

International School Hilversum: Dutch, English. Ages 4–18. IGCSE, IB. Bilingual VWO Dutch.
Emmastraat 56, 1213 AL Hilversum
☎ (035) 672 99 31
www.klg.nl/ish/

Violenschool International Primary School: English. Ages 4–12.
Rembrandtlaan 30, 1213 BH Hilversum
☎ (035) 621 60 53
www.ipsviolen.nl

Leiderdorp

Elckerlyc International School: Dutch, English. Ages 3-12.
Klimopzoom 41, 2353 Leiderdorp
☎ (071) 589 68 61
www.elckerlyc.net/main.html

Maastricht

International School Maastricht: English. Ages 11–18. IGCSE, IB.
Nijverheidsweg 25, 6227 AL Maastricht
☎ (043) 367 46 66
www.ismaastricht.nl

Joppenhof International Department: Dutch, English. Ages 4–11.
Kelvinstraat 3, 6227 VA Maastricht
☎ (043) 367 13 35
www.joppenhof.nl

Oegstgeest

Het Rijnlands Lyceum International School: Dutch, English. Ages 11–18. IB.
Apollolaan 1, 2341 BA Oegstgeest
☎ (071) 519 35 55
www.isrlo.nl

Ommen

International School Eerde: English. Ages 4–18 boarding school. Special education. IGCSE, IB.
Kasteellaan 1, 7731 PJ Ommen
☎ (052) 945 14 52
www.eerde.nl

Rotterdam

The American International School of Rotterdam: English. Ages 4–18. IB.
Verhulstlaan 21, 3055 WJ Rotterdam
☎ (010) 422 53 51
www.aisr.nl

De Blijberg International Primary School: Dutch, English. Ages 4–12.
Graaf Florisstraat 56, 3032 CJ Rotterdam
☎ (010) 448 22 66
www.blijberg.nl

Rotterdam International Secondary School (RISS): Dutch, English. Ages 11–18. IGCSE, IB. Dutch-English VWO.
Bentincklaan 294, 3039 KK Rotterdam
☎ (010) 890 77 45
www.wolfert.nl/riss/

Voorschoten

British School in the Netherlands–Senior School: GCSE, A Levels, IB. Ages 11–18.
Jan van Hooflaan 3, 2252 BG Voorschoten
☎ (071) 560 22 22
www.britishschool.nl

Wassenaar

American School of The Hague (ASH): Ages 4–18 . U.S.-style university preparatory program. AP, IB, TOEFL, SAT, ACT, GMAT.
Rijksstraatweg 200, 2241 BX Wassenaar
☎ (070) 512 10 60
www.ash.nl

Indonesian School in the Netherlands: Indonesian. Ages 6–18.
Rijksstraatweg 679, 2245 CB Wassenaar
☎ (070) 517 88 75
www.sekolahindonesia.nl

Further Information About International Education

Look in the Yellow Pages under Schools (*Scholen*). Also check the following resources:

- The Dutch Ministry of Education, Culture and Science: *www.minocw.nl*
- European Council of International Schools (ECIS): *www.ecis.org*
- Eurydice, the Information Network on Education in Europe: *www.eurydice.org*
- Foundation for International Education in the Netherlands (*Stichting Internationaal Onderwijs*): *www.sio.nl*
- International Baccalaureate Organization: *www.ibo.org*
- Netherlands Organization for International Co-operation in Higher Education (NUFFIC): *www.nuffic.nl*

Advanced Education

Erasmus University
Burgemeester Oudlaan 50, 3062 PA Rotterdam
☎ (010) 408 11 11
www.eur.nl

Institute of Social Studies: MA and PhD degrees in development-related studies.
Kortenaerkade 12, 2518 AX Den Haag
☎ (070) 426 04 60
www.iss.nl

Leiden University
Rapenburg 70, 2311 EZ Leiden
☎ (071) 527 27 27
www.leidenuniv.nl

Leiden University School of Management
Pieterskerkhof 6, 2311 SR Leiden
☎ (071) 527 46 48
www.lusm.leidenuniv.nl

The Open University
Open Universiteit Studiecentrum
Lange Houtstraat 11, 2511 CV Den Haag
☎ (070) 360 74 43
www.open.ac.uk

Open University Business School
Brederodestraat 80-1,
1054 VE Amsterdam
☎ (020) 412 19 62
www.oubs.nl

Tilburg University
Warandelaan 2, 5037 AB Tilburg
☎ (013) 466 91 11
www.tilburguniversity.nl

University of Amsterdam
Binnengasthuisstraat 9,
1012 ZA Amsterdam
☎ (020) 525 33 33
www.english.uva.nl

University of Phoenix
Rivium 1e Straat 1,
2909 LE Capelle a/d Ijssel
☎ (010) 288 63 40
www.uop.nl

Webster University
Boommarkt 1, 2311 EA Leiden
☎ (071) 516 80 00
www.webster.nl

Chapter 5

Essentials to Bring

When you are planning your household shipment to the Netherlands, remember that the Dutch survive quite well on local products. You can too, if you choose. Nevertheless, having an initial supply of the items that you and your family are accustomed to using will make your initial adjustment period easier. As you run out of these things, you'll learn how to find local equivalents or substitutes.

You will eventually find that your shopping list for friends and family going back home becomes shorter and shorter. When we note that some items are expensive, we are speaking from an American perspective. You might come from a country where it is just the opposite. The important thing to remember is that, except for a few items, almost everything you need or desire is now available in the Netherlands. If you can't find what you are looking for, remember that things are changing very quickly. What you can't find one day may be there the next.

Read through our suggestions and evaluate your own lifestyle. If you regularly use an item that is unavailable or very expensive, you will be happy you brought some along. Bringing canned pumpkin and green chilies in your household shipment is easier than hauling suitcases of canned food back from vacation. Don't forget, however, Dutch homes are small and you may have less storage space than you are accustomed to. Don't go overboard!

We have listed items you probably already own and wish to remind you not to forget those holiday decorations tucked away in your attic or the gardening tools out in your garage. You don't want to have to buy a second set of something just because the first set is in storage. A sense of humor is the single most important thing to bring with you. A sense of adventure helps, too. Many times you will feel like you are totally inadequate, which you are not; totally illiterate, which you know is not true; a failure as a cook, which is impossible; or an awful driver, which may or may not be the case! Just hold onto a positive attitude with both hands, and keep going. Others have made it and so can you. If you skate through your stay in the Netherlands without any of these doubts, then you are an exception.

Appliances

Please refer to the chapter on **Housekeeping and Maintenance** for information about using specific appliances in the Netherlands and also where to buy dual-voltage or European standard appliances. If you have a video/DVD collection, consider buying a multi-system TV and VCR/DVD player before leaving home. Remember that you may have to pay Dutch customs duties if you have owned an item for less than six months. If you bring a U.S. electrical appliance unequipped with dual voltage, it must be used with a transformer. Most people find it easier to buy small appliances in the Netherlands. Kitchen scales with metric and imperial measurements are available and the charts in the chapter on **The Dutch Kitchen** will make conversions easy. If vacuuming with an upright model suits you best, you might be advised to purchase a 220V model from an appliance store that carries overseas models. If you decide to bring your own, remember that you will be forced to lug a heavy transformer from room to room. Remember to bring appropriate bags and belts. Be aware that some appliances (typically ones that generate heat) may not work or may break, even with the proper transformer. Look for product labels or check with the manufacturer.

Backyard Pleasures

If you like to barbecue, by all means, bring your grill. Charcoal is available, as is gas to refill your tank. However, you may need to change the coupling on your gas hose, which is available at sport and camping stores. If your housing budget is generous enough for you to afford a home with a garden, then bring along your outdoor furniture. Even small homes have terraces, and you will want to be outside in nice weather. Garden furniture is also available in all price ranges.

Computers

Please refer to the chapter on **Communications** for more detailed information. Don't be afraid to bring your computers unless they are older models. Most newer computers will have built-in frequency converters and will only need a plug adapter, which is easily purchased here. A large variety of computer supplies and equipment such as paper and toner cartridges are available, although an initial supply would be handy to bring. New computer equipment and software are available in the Netherlands several months after they appear in the U.S. Keep in mind that some types of software or user instructions are available only in Dutch, French, and German.

Cosmetics and Skin Care Products

Many familiar brands of cosmetics and skin care products are available, but may take a while to locate and may also be more expensive. Bring a small supply of your favorite toiletries, soaps, deodorants, lotions and hair color. If you have an allergy or a strong brand preference, stock up in advance.

Drug Store and Pharmacy Items

Please refer to the chapter on **Health Care** for more detailed information. Many items that are sold over the counter elsewhere will require a doctor's prescription in the Netherlands. Cortisone creams, cold medicines and anti-bacterial lotions are examples of such items. They are becoming more readily available, but you may want to have familiar brands. The list we have included contains items that are easy to obtain in the U.S., but difficult to obtain here. You may want to bring them with you. Be sure to take note of the expiration dates.

- **Acetaminophen** (Tylenol): It is available as paracetamol, but you may want familiar brands, especially children's chewable tablets or liquid for infants.
- **Allergy medications**
- **Antihistamines:** Many, mostly homeopathic, are available over the counter.
- **Antiseptic lotions and sprays** (Bactine)
- **Aspirin:** It is available, but more expensive than in the U.S.
- **Athlete's foot medication**
- **Baby ointment** (Desitin): Brand names may not be available, but the non-toxic Dutch marigold creams (*calendula zalf* or *sudocreme*) are recommended.
- **Burn medications** (Aloe vera gel)
- **Children's & infant's cold medicines** (Pediacare & Baby Tylenol)
- **Contact lens solution:** Available, but can be more expensive.
- **Contraceptives** (prescription and/or favorite brand)
- **Cortisone creams**
- **Cough syrups:** Available but you may prefer familiar ones. Europeans often use thyme syrup (*tijm stroop*). It is natural and actually tastes quite good.

- **Decongestants and cold medication:** Bring familiar ones. Try using the OTC Dutch drug *antigrippine* which contains 500 mg of paracetamol, caffeine, and vitamin C.
- **Eye drops**
- **First aid creams** (Neosporin antibiotic ointment)
- **Ibuprofen** (Advil & Motrin): It is available, but may be expensive.
- **Mosquito repellents:** Readily available here and necessary, but you may want to bring a favorite one.
- **Motion sickness and nausea medications** (Dramamine & Emetrol): These are available under different brand names.
- **Pedialyte**
- **Pepto Bismol**
- **Thermometers:** Generally only Celsius thermometers are available. The Braun Ear Thermometer has both Fahrenheit and Celsius, but directions are in Dutch.
- **Vitamins:** Available, but may be more expensive.

Note: It might be a good idea to have your doctor write you a prescription for an antibiotic, fill it and bring it with you to have on hand.

Food

Note: Consult your moving company before packing any food in your shipment since restrictions might apply. Some have "No Food or Drink" policies due to tightening restrictions worldwide.

If you are allowed to include food, you might want to continue to enjoy the familiar tastes of home and may want to bring a supply of the following items. Adjust this list to your own preferences. Most of these products are available in the Netherlands (although they may be only seasonal) if you know where to look and are willing to pay the higher prices. Also, expat shopping stores may be able to special order items for you. The starred items, however, are generally unavailable:

American salad dressings
Baking powder and soda
Cake mixes
Campbell's soups
Canned pumpkin
Candy canes
Chocolate and other types of baking chips
Crisco
Dip mixes
Flavoring extracts
Gatorade*
Grape jelly
Green chilies
Karo syrup
Kosher dill pickles*
Liquid smoke*
Low-fat and low-salt products
Maple flavoring* and syrup
Matzo meal
Onion salt*
Pickle relish*
Pure vanilla extract*
Sugar-free products
Spices with English labels

Some low-cholesterol products are available, such as the ever-expanding Becel line of margarine and salad oils. Health food and nutrition stores may carry vitamins, protein-fortified products and nutrition bars. See **The Dutch Kitchen** chapter for more information on expat shopping and alternative food stores.

Hobbies and Recreation

Many of us enjoy hobbies and there is no reason why we should not enjoy them while living in the Netherlands. The Dutch are very fond of hobbies and most enthusiastically pursue at least one. There will undoubtedly be people who share your hobby interests.

If your hobby requires a great deal of equipment, then you will have to weigh the pros and cons of bringing it all along and then finding storage space. In some cases, it may be possible to rent equipment or to join a club. Below is more specific information on what to expect here:

Bicycles: Most people that move to the Netherlands will use a bicycle. It may end up being your main mode of transportation! It is well worth it to bring a bicycle with you, or you may purchase new or used ones in the Netherlands. You probably don't want to bring fancy, expensive bicycles since theft is a problem. Bicycles have to meet equipment guidelines, see the **Transportation** chapter for details. Bicycles here do look different, so if your student will be riding to school, buy your sturdy Dutch bicycle from a shop or expat website when you arrive. Some stores will buy them back when you move, and usually used bicycles are easy to sell.

Crochet and knitting instructions and needles: Instructions will probably be in Dutch, and the needles sized in millimeters. You will really enjoy the selection of yarns.

Fishing equipment: Why buy it all new?

Games and puzzles: Great for your stay in the hotel or just for fun anytime. If you buy them in the Netherlands, there is no guarantee that included directions will be in English, although it does frequently happen and directions can be found online. American-type playing cards are available. However, if you buy a Dutch set, you will have to get used to A, H, V, B instead of A, K, Q, J, which stand for *Aas* (ace), *Heer* (man), *Vrouw* (woman) and *Boer* (farmer).

Golf clubs, racquet ball racquets and balls and tennis racquets and balls: All are available, but are generally more expensive than in the U.S.

Handicrafts: If you enjoy a craft, such as jewelry-making, you may want to bring your own tools and supplies. Good craft stores are scarce.

Ice skates: You can, of course, try the long-bladed metal or wooden Dutch skates (they really do work) but you might be more comfortable in your boot-style ones.

Models and craft sets: Instructions are in Dutch.

Needlework: Embroidery floss and cross-stitch fabric are available. Patterns and instructions in English are difficult to find.

Patterns: Some are available in English, but do not forget to calculate yardage in meters. You may want to bring your own patterns to help you through the transition period. Think in particular of children's Halloween costumes. Fabrics are generally more expensive than in the U.S., but some fabric shops have beautiful selections.
Skateboards and roller blades: Very popular with youngsters everywhere, and life is just more fun if they can join in with the other kids. Dutch skateboards are quite expensive, so bring one with you if you can.
Skis: Skiing in the Netherlands? No mountains, but there are clubs with simulated hills for skiing and the Alps are a day's drive away.

Holiday Decorations

Remember your special holidays may go unnoticed unless you bring some special things from home. The American Women's Club of The Hague carries some seasonal items in its Gift Shop and at its Holiday Bazaar, but you will certainly want to have a small supply of decorations, paper, napkins, plates, etc., for special events like birthdays, religious holidays or national days specific to your home country. More and more Christmas decorations are available in the Netherlands. Christmas trees can be purchased, but bring your artificial tree if you have one. Christmas lights are available, and reasonably priced. Many garden centers (*tuincentra*) carry a huge, and beautiful, supply of decorations. Also consider buying some European decorations at the outdoor Christmas markets to take home as souvenirs.

Kitchen Supplies

Though most products are readily available, others still are scarce. Some wholesalers also carry these supplies but membership is required.

Angel food cake pans: Not available.
Baking pans: 9 in. x 13 in. baking pans and baking racks for roasts are not available.
Bread loaf and quick bread pans: A little different in size.
Cookie sheets: Dutch ovens are often 16 in. x 16 in. square so bring small cookie sheets.
Griddle pans: Not available.
Large stainless steel thermoses: Available, but expensive.
Lunch boxes: Your children may want their own familiar lunch boxes, so bring a few along.
Measuring cups and spoons: Measuring utensils are usually only metric and you may prefer more familiar measuring devices with English and metric measures.
Muffin tins: Available, but the sizes may be different and selection may be limited.
No-spill "sippy cups": Available for babies and toddlers.
Pie pans: Only ceramic, not metal, are available here.
Pitchers: Large juice and iced tea containers are not readily available here. Once you have seen Dutch refrigerators, you will understand the storage space limitations.
Plastic wrap and aluminum foil: Available here, but may not be the heavy duty variety.

Roasting pans or pans: Those for grilling in the oven are not available. Be aware that these very large pans may be too big for ovens here.
Thermometers: If you prefer Fahrenheit oven, meat and candy thermometers to those in Celsius, bring them with you.
Tupperware and Rubbermaid: These products are international institutions and readily available here, though possibly a bit different since they cater to a local clientele.
Zip-Lock bags: Available, but usually limited in sizes.

Lamps

Lamps deserve special mention because the Netherlands has many overcast days and few daylight hours in the winter. You can use U.S. lamps in the Netherlands by replacing the light bulbs with European bulbs and by using plug adapters or replacing the plugs (see the chapter on **Housekeeping and Maintenance**). It is also possible to buy plug adapters at electrical supply shops (*Electrische Artikelen*) or in do-it-yourself shops (*Doe-het-zelf*).

Passport Size Photos

It is a great time-saver to have several passport size photos on hand when you arrive, however, these can be inexpensively and easily made in the Netherlands at many train stations and at *Pasfoto* shops. You will need several soon after arriving for residency permits, driver's licenses, school identification cards, etc. Photo booth pictures are not acceptable for residence applications and some other official documents. You will need about ten per person. Standard U.S. size is a bit larger than Dutch size (3x4 cm), but they can, of course, be trimmed.

Reading Materials

Consider bringing along your favorite books, in particular reference works, and subscribing to your favorite magazines. Books in English are readily available, but are considerably more expensive than in the U.S., and the selection is limited. Dutch public libraries are actually quite well-stocked with novels in English that you may borrow for a small annual fee. The American Women's Club of The Hague's library contains a wide variety of books. See the chapter on **Hobbies and Recreation** for more ideas. However, you may find the following types of books especially helpful during your stay.

Cookbooks: Bring the ones you use the most and also try to bring some ethnic ones on Chinese, Turkish and Moroccan food, as it will be easy to find the proper ingredients.
Dictionaries: Bring your favorite English-language dictionary and an English-Dutch dictionary. Both English-French and English-German dictionaries are also useful.
"How-to" books: Again, this information may come in handy.
Medical guides & child care books: In the event of an illness, you may feel better having a book in English.
Travel guides, atlases and maps: Travel guides in English will be more expensive.

Stationery

Hanging folders are readily available, however manila folders are not. For projects started using American binders and hole-punched paper, note that standard paper and binders used in the Netherlands are different. Paper is A4 (8.27 in. x 11.69 in.) and most binders are 2-hole.

Other Items

If you feel that these items are important to you and to your lifestyle, bring them along. Many items can be purchased in the Netherlands, but those we have starred (*) have yet to be found.

Anti-static spray*
Baby- and child-proofing hardware and devices: These are available, but not easily purchased. You will want to install child-proof protection right away; gates for blocking steep staircases are essential in the Netherlands.
Brown paper lunch bags
Card table and chairs: These are handy to have.
File cabinets and folders: Standard European format (A4) is 8.27 in. x 11.67 in.
Gardening tools: These are available but different in design. However, buy hoses and sprinklers here as taps are metric.
Greeting cards: Consider bringing some along for special holidays not celebrated in the Netherlands.
Ironing board covers: Need to be brought to fit your U.S. ironing board if you bring it along. Dutch covers will not fit.
Lawn mowers: Many gardens need only a push mower.
Plug adapters: Needed for lamps and other small appliances.
Refills: Think of pens or other items which may vary in size.
Rulers and tape measures: Inches as well as metric conversions will be helpful.
Sewing machine: Those of 110V will need transformers.
Sheets: Needed for any beds you bring with you—sizes are different in the Netherlands and top sheets are NOT available.
Short-wave radio: Bring it if you have it.
Sleeping bags: These are handy for overnight guests.
Smoke alarms: For added security, but available here.
Transformers: Often available from people leaving the Netherlands. Available at some electronic stores, but more expensive.
Wrapping paper: Stores will often wrap your purchases if they are gifts (*cadeau*) or you can bring or buy paper and wrap them yourself. Cellophane is readily available, but tissue paper may be hard to find.

We Wish We Had Not Brought

As mentioned at the beginning of the chapter, Dutch houses usually don't have much storage space. You will have to weigh the convenience of bringing something against the fact that there are only so many things you can squeeze under the bed. Dutch kitchens can be very small. Many don't have space for a kitchen table, let alone the numbers of drawers and cuboards you may be used to. Many homes have attics, and sometimes cellars, but they might not be easily accessible, dry or large enough. Consider whether you really need to bring the following:

Garden hoses: Couplings are different.
King-size beds: Although they may fit in a bedroom, they may be impossible to get up staircases. Sheets are not available.
Large roasting pans, baking pans and cookie sheets: They may not fit in your oven.
Large Tupperware containers: They may take up too much space in small cupboards.
Loads of knickknacks: Do not assume that you will have built-in shelving.
Multiple sets of dishes: However, many people wish they had brought good dishes because of increased entertaining at home.

OCTAGON
Professionals
recruiting beyond borders
As one of the first companies established in The Netherlands providing talented international professionals for international organizations, Octagon has gone from strength to strength and country to country providing our clients with the best on the market.
Our multicultural team of consultants understands the importance of diversity in the current global marketplace. Combined with our market-knowledge and dedication, we make sure our clients are provided with the best suited internationals.
These professionals are offered the career they seek, not just a job.
For more information regarding our company's activities, please refer to our website or contact our consultants on +31(0)70-324 93 00 / recruitment@octagon.nl
WWW.OCTAGON.NL

Chapter 6

Legal Matters

It can be overwhelming to try to understand the legal complexities of a foreign country. This chapter will help you by highlighting some of the most common rules and regulations that might affect you while living in the Netherlands. The information contained in this chapter is current as of January 2009. Immigration, tax, residence and citizenship laws are, however, always subject to change. Therefore, it is best to inquire through the company which transfers you, or an attorney or an accountant specializing in immigration or residence law to assure that you are in compliance with current legal requirements.

Please note: The American Women's Club of The Hague provides the following information as a guide and cannot provide constant updates; therefore, the American Women's Club of The Hague cannot be held responsible for the consequences of a failure to conform to Dutch and/or U.S. laws and regulations.

You should familiarize yourself with your rights and obligations under the Dutch legal system. For example, under Dutch law, foreigners with resident status are required to carry their resident alien card (*vreemdelingen document*) at all times as proof of their right to be in the Netherlands. Tourists or temporary visitors are required to carry their passports with them. Failure to comply with these rules could, theoretically, result in your arrest.

You are strongly advised to request an English translation of any documents, leases, contracts, etc., before signing. If no translation is available, ask a Dutch friend to read the document and translate the small print for you. Standard clauses for the Dutch may not be "normal" for you. If you need to have documents translated into or out of Dutch, then you will need to find a certified translator (*beëdigd vertaler*). Look in the Yellow Pages under *Vertaalbureaus* or *Vertalers*.

In all circumstances involving the law, when you are not sure about something—ask questions. It is far better to ask what you might consider to be a stupid question than to find yourself enmeshed in a legal tangle. And remember, although the Dutch generally speak good English, words can mean different things to different people, especially when they involve legalities. A verbal agreement may be legally binding in the Netherlands, so be certain of your understanding of a verbal commitment. Many troubles begin with a simple misunderstanding in communication.

When You First Arrive – Be Aware

Your employer or relocation agent may help you go through the registration procedure, obtain your work permit, register with the town hall (*gemeentehuis*) and clear your household goods through customs (*douane*). In any case, the following procedures for residence and employment registration must be followed. If you need a law firm specializing in Dutch immigration law, contact:

Everaert Advocaten Immigration Lawyers
Rokin 69, 1012 KL Amsterdam
☎ (020) 752 32 00
www.everaert.nl

▸ Registering With the *Gemeentehuis*

To apply for a residency permit, you need to follow this procedure:
Go to the Population Registry (*Bevolkingsregisster*) at the *Gemeentehuis* of the town in which you will be residing. The entire family must be present for this registration process. Take the following with you:

- Passports for each member of the family (with at least one year validity)
- Birth certificates
- Marriage certificate
- Divorce certificate (if applicable)
- One full-face color passport picture (it is best to have it made in the Netherlands)
- Work permit (non-EU citizens)
- Employer's Declaration (the form is available at the Town Hall)
- Proof of medical insurance

All birth, marriage and divorce certificates must be validated with either double legalization or an *apostille*, which is a statement on a separate sheet of paper affixed to the original document verifying the signatures on the original document. Documents issued in the United States and Great Britain require an *apostille*, whereas Canadian documents require double legalization. For other countries, please refer to your country's Embassy or Consulate in the Netherlands or the Dutch Embassy in your country of residency.

For information on applying for an *apostille* for U.S. documents, go to: *http://amsterdam.usconsulate.gov*. Choose U.S. Citizens Services then Other Services. There you will find an example of an *apostille* as well as the addresses of each state authority where you can obtain such an *apostille.*

British documents must be sent to the Legalisation Office for the *apostille*:
Norfolk House (West)
437 Silbury Boulevard, Milton Keynes MK9 2AH
☎ +44 01908 295 111
www.fco.gov.uk

If you are already living in the Netherlands and have a spouse or common law partner who is a Dutch citizen, an EU citizen or a foreigner with residence status, he/she may apply to sponsor you for your residency permit. For details, please contact the *gemeente* where you are residing.

Once you have completed the registration at the town hall, you will be issued a BSN (*Burger Service Nummer*), formerly known as the SoFi number. This is necessary for opening a bank account as well as health insurance.

You must be prepared to pay the fees for a residency permit at this time. For current fees, please check *www.ind.nl*.

For all matters involving immigration requirements for Entry Clearance Visas (MVV) to the Netherlands from other countries not listed below, please refer to the Dutch Immigration and Naturalization Service (IND) at *www.ind.nl* or ☎ +31 20 889 30 45 or the Dutch Ministry of Foreign Affairs *www.minbuza.nl* ☎ +31 70 348 47 87 (mornings only).

Countries NOT Requiring an Entry Clearance Visa or MVV: All EU countries and Australia, Canada, Japan, Monaco, New Zealand, Vatican City, U.S. and Switzerland. Be aware that if you or your spouse requires an entry clearance visa, you will have to obtain the clearance visa in either your country of origin or your country of last legal residence.

▸ Other Administrative Matters at Your Local *Gemeentehuis*

Certificate of Registration: This can be issued immediately when you first register and is necessary for the Customs Clearance of your household goods. Make sure it states which country you have moved from.

Proof of Residency: This can be issued only after your registration has been completely finished (7-10 days) and is often necessary for other organizations or transactions such as buying a car, getting a cellular phone, etc.

Driver's License: If you plan to drive in the Netherlands, you are required by Dutch law to get a Dutch driver's license. You may not drive here for more than six months using a foreign license. No one under 18 years of age may drive in the Netherlands even with a valid foreign license. You may be eligible to exchange your foreign driver's license for a Dutch license, otherwise you will be required to take proficiency exams. You must first have your *vreemdelingen document* or alien registration card before you apply. You can obtain the forms necessary for application in the *gemeentehuis*. Please see the **Transportation** chapter for more details.

Gemeente Gids: All *gemeentes* publish an informative and free guide for their residents. In some cases these are in English as well. Most *gemeentes* also now have websites with sections in English. If you don't know your city's web address, try *www."insert name of town here".nl* (for example: *www.wassenaar.nl*).

▸ Arranging for a Work Permit

If you are not from a European Union (EU) member country, your employer must obtain a work permit (*tewerkstellingsvergunning*) for you prior to your arrival in the Netherlands. It must be submitted with your application for residency for you and your family.

Your company will need the following documents from you to complete the application for your work permit:

- Curriculum Vitae (CV/Resume) showing educational and professional background
- Copies of professional certificates/qualifications (includes college/university degrees)
- Employment contract

If the labor market must be tested for a position, the employer must be able to show that there are no Dutch people or other EU nationals able to fill the position before the Dutch District Labor Office will approve hiring a non-EU citizen for the position. The process is similar to the procedure for obtaining an alien resident card or "green card" in the United States, and is best undertaken with the advice and assistance of an immigration attorney in the Netherlands or relocation advisor knowledgeable in immigration. As of January 1, 2005 the requirement for work permits eased somewhat for "highly skilled migrants," defined as employees (non self-employed) whose income lies above a certain level. Instead of having to apply first for a work permit through the Labor Office–Center for Work and Income (CWI) and then a residency permit with the IND, the process is centralized via the IND.

A spouse of a non-EU citizen may work, provided he/she finds a job and an employer who is willing to apply for a work permit. The process for obtaining work authorization in the Netherlands normally requires posting the job vacancy and advertising the position. In 1998 an exception to this process was instituted whereby an accompanying spouse of an intracompany transferee may obtain a work permit for employment without the necessity of a Dutch employer testing the labor market for his/her position. The accompanying spouse's work permit will be issued for the same expiration period as the intracompany transferee. Thus, partners, spouses and dependent children of accompanying principal intracompany transferees may obtain work permits without the vacancy registration and EU priority recruitment generally required for testing the labor market in the Netherlands. A spouse of a highly skilled migrant may work without a work permit.

In addition, there are employment agencies that specialize in recruiting foreigners to work in the Netherlands. Check our *Index of Business Resources* in the chapter on **Church and Community** for websites of such organizations. District Labor Offices also give advice about work permits. If you wish to find the District Labor Offices, look in the pink pages of the telephone book under *Arbeidsbureau*.

Customs for Your Household Goods

If you intend to live in the Netherlands, all your household goods may be imported duty-free provided you have owned and used the goods for at least six months before arriving in the Netherlands, and provided further that they have had their domicile outside the European Union for at least twelve consecutive months preceding their arrival in the Netherlands. If you try to import a car that you have owned for even one day less than exactly six months, you will probably be heavily taxed on it. You will need to complete an application for exemption from import duties (*aanvraag voor vrijstelling*) before your shipped goods will clear Customs. See our chapter on **Transportation** for more information about importing cars.

The Dutch Tax Office (*www.belastingdienst.nl*) and Dutch Customs Authority (*www.douane.nl*) publish a number of pamphlets in both Dutch and English on tax issues, customs and moving to the Netherlands. Consult the customs website for more information about the customs office nearest your city of residence where your application for an exemption must be filed.

Insurance

Insurance (*verzekering*) is widely available in the Netherlands, frequently through banks. However, the procedures may differ from those you are accustomed to and may take longer. It is advisable to check in your home country before arrival, and work with an insurance adviser (*verzekerings-adviseur*) to determine which, if any, additional policies you need. See our **Health Care** chapter for medical and dental insurance information.

If necessary, you may obtain a temporary request for insurance coverage (*voorlopig verzoek om een verzekering*). The insurance company will require that you are registered at the town hall. The problem with seeking insurance coverage in the Netherlands is that an insurance company may require proof of residence status before they will issue a policy. It becomes a problem because the IND will require proof of health insurance (*ziektekosten-verzekering*) coverage before resident alien status will be granted. So be sure you have interim insurance coverage before leaving home!

Here are some other types of insurance policies you may want or need to have:

- Building — *Opstal-verzekering*
- Glass — *Glas-verzekering*
- Legal Aid — *Rechtsbijstands-verzekering*
- Medical & Hospitalization — *Ziektekosten-verzekering*
- Motor Vehicle — *Auto-verzekering*
- Passengers Accident — *Ongevallen-verzekering inzittenden*
- Personal Liability — *WettelijkeAansprakelijkheids verzekering*
- Personal Property — *Inboedel-verzekering*
- Travel — *Reis-verzekering*

Further information you will need to ask or gather:

- Does your present policy cover you and your family?
- Will coverage change or stop while residing abroad?
- Will you need additional insurance?
- How you get reimbursed from abroad?
- Get written answers from your agent.
- Obtain a letter from your insurance agent stating your years of no claim with regard to auto insurance.

Taxation

Tax laws are constantly changing; therefore, it is advisable that you refer your questions to the local tax office listed under *Belastingdienst* in the pink pages of your telephone book, go to the *Belastingdienst* website at *www.belastingdienst.nl* or engage the services of a reputable tax adviser (*belastingadviseur*). A person taking up residence in the Netherlands is subject to several types of taxes including:

- Dividend Withholding — *Dividendbelasting*
- Dog — *Hondenbelasting*
- Municipal — *Gemeentebelasting*
- Net Wealth — *Vermogenbelasting*
- Personal Income — *Inkomstenbelasting*
- Real Estate — *Onroerend goedbelasting*
- Road — *Wegenbelasting*
- Social Security Contributions — *AOW*
- Value-added — *BTW (Belasting op Toegevoegde Waarde)*
- Income Tax — *Loonbelasting*

Tax Tips:

- All mail having to do with taxes (*belasting*) comes in blue envelopes.
- You will be required to file a Dutch income tax return prior to April, although extensions are easily obtained.
- You do not pay your taxes with the return, but wait for an assessment.
- Save the receipts from your large purchases. You may need them for tax purposes, as well for insurance claims, evaluation of your household goods and for Customs.

▸ Citizen Service Number (*Burger Service Nummer* BSN) – (formerly known as Social Fiscal Number SoFi)

Everyone who resides in the Netherlands is issued by the Municipal authorities a BSN number. This is imperative for opening a bank account, setting up health insurance and being put on a Dutch payroll.

▸ Miscellaneous Dutch Taxes

It is assumed by the Dutch tax authorities that you are aware of and will comply with the following:

Road Tax (*Wegenbelasting*): This tax is based on the weight of your car and the type of fuel your car uses. Obtain the appropriate form from the post office. For information, call the *Belastingdienst*: ☎ (0800) 07 49.

Dog Tax (*Hondenbelasting*): You are required to register your dog at your *gemeentehuis* and pay an annual tax for each dog you own. See the **Pets** chapter for more details.

Value-Added Tax (BTW): VAT is a general consumer tax added to all goods and services at either 6% or 19% depending on type. If you buy goods when traveling outside the EU, you may be able to secure a refund of the value-added tax (*belasting op toegevoegde waarde* or BTW) on your purchases. Inquire at the place of purchase or at the border.

For more information about various tax administration and collection concerns, go to *www.belastingdienst.nl*. Free contact numbers for *Belastingendiensten*:

☎ (0800) 05 43 Anonymous helpline for individuals
☎ (0800) 04 43 Companies
☎ (0800) 01 43 Customs inquiries
☎ (0800) 07 49 Car tax information

Children's Allowance

Children's Allowance (*Kinderbijslag*) is an intrinsic part of the Dutch social welfare system. Instead of receiving a tax deduction for each child, Dutch parents receive quarterly cash payments for each of their children. Eligibility does not depend upon citizenship, but rather tax status and other factors. Furthermore, a "child" is interpreted as one who is economically dependent. Therefore, a child up to age 27 might be working on a master's degree at a foreign university and still be eligible for *kinderbijslag*.

Some companies require non-Dutch employees to sign over *kinderbijslag* rights because the company is paying their Dutch taxes. Although the ability to qualify for a *kinderbijslag* is becoming increasingly difficult, you may be eligible and entitled to quite a few euros, but only if you apply. Application forms are available at the post office. For more information, contact:

Sociale Verzekeringsbank
☎ (020) 656 56 56
www.svb.nl

Legal Dilemmas

If you encounter personal legal problems in your family life, your relationship with your landlord or with your employer, please be advised that the legal situation might take you by surprise. Some legal aspects in the Netherlands might be treated more advantageously than in your home country, such as the protection of employees, tenants and children. Some other legal aspects might seem unexpectedly complicated, such as the legislation for wills and testaments. Being a foreign national might complicate these matters even further.

For reliable advice when faced with a difficult legal dilemma, contact:

GMW Advocaten
Scheveningseweg 52, 2508 CG Den Haag
☎ (070) 361 50 48
www.gmw.nl

▸ Divorce

A divorce is always a difficult situation to go through and living abroad makes it even more complicated. The divorce laws in the Netherlands might be different from your home country. For example, the decision on how the assets should be split or how much alimony should be paid doesn't depend on who is at fault. The website *www.echtscheidingswijzer.nl* is a useful resource which explains the divorce process and allows you to fill out a form for help finding a divorce lawyer or mediator. Unfortunately this website is currently available only in Dutch. A helpful English source is *www.gmw.nl*.

In general, there are five steps to follow:

1) **Look for a lawyer or a mediator** (*echtscheidingsbemiddelaar*)**.** The two parties have the option of choosing their own lawyers, or finding a mediator who will work with both of them to agree on a "collaborative divorce."

2) **Apply for divorce** (*vraag de scheiding aan*)**.** This must be done either by your *echtscheidingsbemiddelaar* or your lawyer.
3) **Make a financial plan.** Your finances must be in order before you go to court. The financial plan should include the following:
   i) value of your household goods
   ii) value of your properties
   iii) salaries and other income
   iv) mortgages and loans
   v) investments and pensions
   vi) alimony
4) **Make a plan for custody (*zorgplicht*).** This includes making decisions related to who will take care of the children and of visiting rights.
5) **Go to court (if necessary).** Going to court is now only a formality as all the details have already been discussed and decided upon.

Wills and Testaments

If you do not already have a will, or if you need to update or make out a new one, a Dutch *notaris* can assist you. This is a lawyer who specializes in the drawing up of contracts and deeds. If you are not a Dutch citizen and you already have a will that was made according to the laws of the country in which it was drawn up, your will is also valid in the Netherlands; however, it must be registered in the Netherlands.

One is also well advised to check if a previously formulated will is complying with the new host country's inheritance law. Your wills made before moving to the Netherlands will be recognized as long as the formalities required by the law of the country where the will was drawn up were fulfilled.

Special Note: If you are a legal resident in the Netherlands for more than five years, Dutch custody law will apply to your children of minor age. This means that in the case of the death of both parents, the guardianship of the children will go automatically to the Dutch state. In order to rule out that special Dutch law, you will have to have a registered Dutch will and designate guardians for your children accordingly.

It is advisable to employ a *notaris* who is familiar with the registration and execution of foreign wills. The society of *notaris'* in the Netherlands may be contacted for referrals:

Koninklijke Notariele Broederschap
☎ (0900) 346 93 93 (€0,25/minute)
www.notaris.nl

The registration procedure requires the following:

- Take your existing will to a *notaris*
- Sign the will in front of four witnesses
- Place it in an envelope, simply stating, "This is my will."

The will is then filed with the Dutch Central Register of Wills. It is considered to be a totally new will, and you can be assured of its recognition as valid in the Netherlands.

You may want to consider including the following in your will:

- The name of a designated guardian for your children. Be sure that each of your children has his or her own passport for each country of which they are a citizen, i.e., they are not included in the passport of either parent. Then, if the need arises, the citizenship of the child is protected and custody of the child can then pass to the designated guardian with fewer complications.
- Your choice of funeral arrangement: cremation or internment.

Filling Out Dutch Forms

When an American must mark an option on a form, the natural response is to either circle or to put an "X" through the appropriate item. It just so happens that the Dutch do the opposite. Below is an example of a very simple Dutch form.

Dutch/English translation:

Naam ________________	Name ________________
Leeftijd _______ jaar M/V*	Age_____ years M/F*
**doorhalen wat niet van toepassing is*	*cross out whatever does **not** apply

Dutch Law in Brief

Dutch law is based on the Napoleonic Code that finds its roots in the Justinian Code. The legal system as we know it in common law countries is completely different here and, generally speaking, the Dutch are not litigious.

Abortion: Abortion is legal in the Netherlands up until the 13th week of pregnancy. The Dutch attitude is quite pragmatic.

Drugs: Soft drugs, such as marijuana and hashish, are sold in authorized places.

Euthanasia: Euthanasia is now legal, but is limited to terminally ill patients who have undergone extensive psychiatric and family counseling and request euthanasia.

Lawsuits: The Dutch don't routinely file lawsuits, but this is changing. They have a procedure similar to small claims courts in the U.S. Claims of less than €5,000 go to the *Kanton-*

gerecht. Amounts contested above €5,000 go to the Dutch equivalent of U.S. District Court. For further explanation of the court system in English, go to *www.rechtspraak.nl*.

Lawyers *Notaris*: This is a specialized lawyer who deals with wills, deeds for real estate transactions, marriage contracts and the like. A *notaris* never appears in court and is not the same as a Notary Public in the United States. These lawyers are known for their independence and impartiality, and thus do not engage in litigation.

Lawyers *Advocaat*: This is a lawyer who can help you in all legal matters other than what a *notaris* handles as mentioned above.

Legal Aid Societies: Dutch Legal Aid Societies (*Bureaus voor Rechtshulp*) offer free legal advice to those who cannot afford a lawyer. Law students practice inexpensively at *Wetswinkels*. These legal aid societies are located in most major cities:

Bureaus voor Rechtshulp
Spuistraat 10, 1012 TS Amsterdam
☎ (020) 665 86 99
www.rechtshulpnederland.nl

Moving: If you move during your stay in the Netherlands, even if it is only next door, you must notify the Population Registry (*Afdeling burgerzaken/afdeling bevolking*) of your *gemeentehuis* of your new address.

Verbal agreements: Verbal agreements can be legally binding. Watch out! Unlike the U.S., if you orally agree to rent or purchase property, you might have a contract.

For U.S. Citizens

This section focuses on rules and regulations that are of concern to U.S. citizens.

▸ American Government Abroad

U.S. Consulate General: The U.S. Consulate General is responsible for all U.S. consular services in the Netherlands. Visit their website at *http://amsterdam.usconsulate.gov*, and click on the link for U.S. Citizen Services. The site is constantly being updated and provides the most current information and requirements. It also lists a general information guide for U.S. citizens residing in the Netherlands which you may find useful.

It is strongly recommended that U.S. citizens register with the Consulate on their website. Registration provides a permanent record of citizenship and is helpful in the event of an accident or emergency. All pertinent information will be recorded, thereby making it easier for you to apply for a replacement if your passport is lost or stolen. Registration information is confidential and will not be released without your authorization.

Services Rendered by the U.S. Consulate General:

- Issuance, amendments, and extensions of U.S. passports
- Issuance of Reports of Births and Reports of Deaths of U.S. citizens
- Providing information regarding the acquisition, retention, loss and transmission of U.S. citizenship
- Assistance in death and welfare/whereabouts cases involving U.S. citizens
- Assistance in estate cases when the deceased was not residing in the Netherlands
- Assistance to U.S. citizens incarcerated in the Netherlands
- Absentee voter registration and balloting information
- Selective Service registration
- Shipping and Seamen Services
- Notarial and related services
- Assistance in setting up depositions
- Issuance of Immigrant Visas and providing information on U.S. Permanent Resident status, Alien Registration Cards, re-entry permits and refugee documentation
- Issuance of Non-Immigrant Visas for visiting, working, studying, and investing in the United States of America

Services NOT Rendered by the U.S. Consulate General:

- Renewal or replacement documents issued by State authorities such as: driver's licenses, birth, marriage, and death certificates, etc.
- Issuance of visas for foreign countries
- Performance of marriage ceremonies
- Cashing of checks or loaning of money
- Procurement of residence permits, work permits, driver's licenses and employment
- Processing of mail for private individuals

The U.S. Embassy: The U.S. Embassy provides some services to American citizens, but it is first and foremost concerned with the relationship between the U.S. and the Netherlands. The role of the **Community Liaison Office (CLO)** is specifically to assist Americans attached to the U.S. Embassy. The CLO officer maintains contact with local organizations with significant American membership, and is available to assist individual American citizens in a limited way. The CLO officer, for instance, will know on which dates an IRS representative will be in the Netherlands, and will have FPCA forms available for you to request an absentee ballot. The U.S. Embassy Community Liasion Office can be reached at ☎ (070) 310 92 37.

Since passage of the State Department Authorization Bill in 1991, it is now possible for American citizens who are not Foreign Service dependents to be hired for some positions at

U.S. Embassies and Consulates. There must be a job opening, and applicants must meet all job requirements and be competitive with other candidates.

Selected American Citizen Services

U.S. Birth Certificate and Citizenship for Children Born Abroad: Even if both parents are U.S. citizens, transmission of U.S. citizenship to children born abroad is **not** automatic. Children born in the Netherlands who are entitled to U.S. citizenship should be documented by means of a Consular Report of Birth Abroad (CRBA). This certificate is documentary evidence that the child is a U.S. citizen and provides the basis for entitlement to a U.S. passport., Make sure to review the detailed information on obtaining the CRBA online at *http://amsterdam.usconsulate.gov*, under U.S. Citizen Services and then under Birth and Citizenship.

The procedures for obtaining U.S. Citizenship for children born abroad and registration of births with local Dutch government authorities is as follows:

1) **International Birth Certificate:** You must register at the Population Registry at the *gemeentehuis* the birth of a child born in the Netherlands within three working days of the date of birth. If this is can't be done by one of the parents, then it must be done by someone who was present at the birth, i.e., the doctor or midwife. To obtain an International Birth Certificate you need:
   i) Certificate or statement supplied by the hospital, doctor, or midwife
   ii) Marriage License – original or certified copy with apostille
   iii) Passport
2) **Register the Birth at the U.S. Consulate General.** For this process you will need:
   i) International birth certificate
   ii) Marriage certificate – original or certified copy
   iii) Proof of citizenship of parent(s) – passport or birth certificate
   iv) Divorce certificate (if applicable) – original or certified copy
   v) Two passport-size photos of baby, four if you want to get a passport immediately for the child

6 Legal Matters

While at the U.S. Consulate General, also obtain a Social Security Card application form for your baby. You will need two identical photos, either color or in black and white. These must meet certain specifications, namely they must be 4.5 cm high x 3.5 cm wide, the full face should show and the size of the face excluding hair should be 2.5 cm high. The background of the photo should be light. Below the age of 18, a U.S. passport is valid for 5 years. Both parents must sign the application for their child's U.S. passport application.

Registering a Birth with the IND: If two U.S. citizens have a baby in the Netherlands, the baby is not entitled to dual citizenship and thus needs to be registered with the IND (*www.ind.nl*).

Death Certificates: The death of an American citizen should be reported immediately to the U.S. Consulate General. This office provides assistance in death cases 24 hours a day, 7 days a week. It will issue a Report of the Death of an American Citizen Abroad, which is usually required to settle estate and other matters in the United States.

Immigration to the U.S.: For current information regarding immigration to the U.S., visit the Consulate General's website at *http://amsterdam.usconsulate.gov*. Click on Visas to the U.S. to find out immigration rules, requirements and answers to frequently asked questions.

Marriage, Citizenship and Dual Nationality: Marriage between an American and a Dutch citizen does not automatically confer citizenship to either of the two parties. Information on the acquisition of Dutch citizenship can be found at *www.ind.nl*. Information on dual nationality can be obtained from the Consulate General website at *http://amsterdam.usconsulate.gov* under U.S. Citizen Services and then Dual Nationality under Birth and Citizenship.

Notarial Services: Notarial and related services are provided at the U.S. Consulate General. More detailed information can be obtained from the website at *http://amsterdam.usconsulate.gov* under U.S. Citizen Services and then Other Services.

U.S. Passports: Passports can be issued, renewed or replaced at the Consulate General in Amsterdam, and in some cases by mail. Other passport matters, such as name changes and extra pages can also be processed. An appointment is necessary and can be made at *http://amsterdam.usconsulate.gov* under U.S. Citizen Services and then Passports.

Selective Service: Almost all male U.S. citizens and male alien residents living in the U.S., who are age 18 through 25, are required to register with Selective Service. Dual nationals of the U.S. and another country are required to register, regardless of where they live, because they are U.S. nationals. For general information on Selective Service and how to register see the Consulate website *http://amsterdam.usconsulate.gov* under Other Services.

▸ Compliance with American Tax Laws

As a U.S. citizen or lawful permanent resident of the United States (green card holder), you are required to file a U.S. Tax Return, reporting your worldwide income. U.S. citizens residing abroad must file their U.S. Federal Income Tax returns even though their income earned outside the U.S. may be exempt from U.S. tax.

The Internal Revenue Service (IRS) provides detailed current information on tax requirements, publications and forms for International taxpayers on their website. Go to *www.irs.gov* then click on Individuals, then International Taxpayer.

In the spring of each year, an IRS representative visits the Netherlands to provide taxpayers assistance. Details of these visits and on making appointments are listed on the Consulate's website *http://amsterdam.usconsulate.gov* under U.S. Citizen Services and then under Public Services. This link also provides a list of tax consultants and IRS websites where you can download tax forms and other information.

The IRS office servicing U.S. Citizens residing in the Netherlands is:

U.S. Consulate General Frankfurt
Internal Revenue Service
Giessener Str. 30, 60435 Frankfurt/Main
Germany
☎ +49 69 7535 38 34
Email: *IRS.Frankfurt@irs.gov*

Important Dates for American Taxpayers

April 15: If you owe money to the government, it is due on this date.
June 15: Residents abroad receive a two-month extension for filing tax returns by attaching a statement to their return. Payment is still due on April 15, so you will be charged interest if you owe money and file after that date.

Voting in U.S. Elections

Living abroad doesn't mean you can't or shouldn't vote. You don't have to reside in the U.S. to vote, nor is it required to have lived in the U.S. in the recent past. U.S. citizens residing abroad can vote in federal elections via an absentee ballot. You are eligible to vote in your legal state of residence, which is the last state or territory you lived in prior to leaving the U.S. For complete up-to-date voting information, contact:

Federal Voting Assistance Program
☎ (800) 438 86 83 toll-free from the U.S.
☎ (0800) 022 82 13 toll-free from the Netherlands
www.fvap.gov

Absentee Ballots: You must request a ballot for each election, and this should be done at least 1½ to 2 months prior to the election. Even if you are registered to vote in your home state, you might not automatically receive a ballot.

The Federal Post Card Application (FPCA) is the form used to request an absentee ballot and/or register to vote. It can be obtained from the U.S. Consulate General and U.S. military bases as well as from representatives of Republicans Abroad and Democrats Abroad. It can also be obtained online through the Federal Voting Assistance Program at *www.fvap.gov*.

If you request a ballot with the FPCA and it does not arrive in timely fashion, you may still vote. A Federal Write-In Ballot is available to voters who have requested a ballot, but who have not received it.

For more information about absentee voting, contact the U.S. Consulate General at *http://amsterdam.usconsulate.gov*. The FAWCO committee (Federation of American Women's Clubs Overseas) of The American Women's Club of The Hague also has a copy of the *Voter's Guide*.

Helpful Vocabulary

Annuity Premiums	*Lijfrente premies*
Appeal	*Beroep/Cassatie*
Assessment	*Aanslag*
• Preliminary Assessment	*Voorlopige aanslag*
• Additional Assessment	*Navorderings aanslag*
• Final Assessment	*Definitieve aanslag*
Child Allowance	*Kinderbijslag*
City Hall	*Stadhuis/Gemeentehuis*
Computation of Tax	*Berekening van belasting*
Customs	*Douane*
Depreciation	*Afschrijving*
Dog Tax	*Hondenbelasting*
Driver's License	*Rijbewijs*
Employee	*Werknemer*
Employer	*Werkgever*
Employment	*Dienst betrekking*
Entrepreneur	*Ondernemer*
Extension of Filing Period	*Uitstel indiening aangiftebiljet*
Fiscal or Financial Year	*Boekjaar*
Foreign Tax Relief	*Verrekening buitenlandse belasting*
Gift and Succession Tax	*Schenkings en Successierecht*
Housing Authority	*Gemeentelijke Dienst Volkshuisvesting*
Immigration and Naturalization Service	*Immigratie en Naturisaliedienst (IND)*
Income Tax	*Inkomsten belasting*
Inspector of Customs and Excise	*Inspecteur der Invoerrechten en Accijnzen*
Insurance	*Verzekering*
Insurance Adviser	*Verzekerings adviseur*
Interest	*Rente*
Land and Property Tax	*Onroerend goedbelasting*
Lawyer	*Notaris, Advocaat*
Net Wealth Tax	*Vermogens belasting*

Non Taxable Base Income	*Belastingvrije som*
Old Age Tax Reserve	*Fiscale oudedags reserve*
Owner's Tax	*Eigenaar's belasting*
Periodic Payment	*Periodieke betaling*
Population Registry	*Bevolkingszaken*
Preliminary Assessment	*Voorlopige aanslag*
Professional Expenses	*Beroepskosten*
Profit	*Winst*
Property Tax	*Onroerend goedbelasting*
Road Tax	*Motorrijtuigen/Wegenbelasting*
Shares	*Aandelen*
Taxable Income	*Belastbaar inkomen*
Taxes	*Belastingen*
Tax Adviser	*Belastingadviseur*
Tax Group	*Tariefgroep*
Tax Liability	*Belastingschuld*
Tax Office	*Inspectie der Rijks belastingen*
Tax Refund	*Belasting teruggave*
Tax Return	*Aangiftebiljet*
Tax Treaty	*Belastingverdrag*
Third-party Liability	*W.A. Verzekering*
Transfer Tax	*Overdrachtsbelasting*
Users' Tax	*Gebruiker's belasting*
Value-Added Tax (VAT)	*Belasting op Toegevoegde Waarde (BTW)*
Wage Tax	*Loonbelasting*
Work Permit	*Werk-vergunning/Tewerkstellingsvergunning*

May Peace Prevail On Earth
Moge vrede heersen op aarde

Chapter 7

Health Care

Dealing with an illness may be cause for anxiety under any circumstance, and can be compounded by being away from the support systems in your home country. Fortunately, despite clear cultural differences, you may find that when it comes to the health care system and practitioners in the Netherlands, the standard quality of care and medical technology rate highly. In fact, statistics have shown that Dutch health care is among the best in the world.

Under the Health Insurance Act (*zorgverzekeringswet*), all residents of the Netherlands are obliged to take out a basic health insurance policy. Insurers are obliged to accept everyone for the standard package. Persons under the age of 18 do not pay any premium. Most expatriates living in the Netherlands are insured through their employers. However, it is always wise to ascertain what type of coverage is offered for outpatient care, hospitalization and life insurance before being faced with an illness. Each individual or family should have a family physician (*huisarts*), who not only acts as a general practitioner for routine medical care, but also serves as the source for referrals to specialists.

A significant cultural difference in the Dutch health care system is one of attitude. In general, the Dutch practitioner is more likely to allow the body to heal itself and less likely to administer medical treatments, such as antibiotics for infections and pain medications during childbirth and dental care. Although times are changing, the Dutch patient is still less likely to question the physician about medical conditions and treatment options and more likely to take a trusting, watchful "wait-and-see" approach.

In this chapter you will find a brief description of the Dutch health care system, including *huisarts* and specialist care as well as hospitalization. Pay particular attention to the "In Case of Emergency" section. This chapter also addresses other issues such as pregnancy and childbirth, children's health programs, mental health services, blood donation, organ donation, and dental and eye care. It also describes the Dutch drugstore (*drogisterij*) and pharmacy (*apotheek*) and lists the types of items to be found in each. Finally, at the end of this chapter you will find a body temperature Celsius/Fahrenheit conversion chart, a list of several organizations offering further information or specific medical help and an abbreviated Dutch-English medical vocabulary.

If you wish to read more detailed discussions about any aspects of Dutch health care, ACCESS publishes an excellent book called *The ACCESS Guide to Health Care in the Netherlands*.

Before You Arrive

If you have not yet relocated to the Netherlands, the following suggestions may be useful.

- Get a complete physical and dental exam before you leave home, including a mammogram and a thorough gynecological exam, if applicable.
- Bring copies of medical histories, including your children's immunization history, any important x-rays and information about any ongoing medical treatments.
- Ask your doctor or pharmacist to give you the generic name of all medicines you use regularly. This will help your Dutch physician find a local equivalent.
- Pack a 2-to-3 month supply of familiar medications for the family to use until you find local substitutes. It is wise to bring a 6-to-12 month supply of favorite over-the-counter remedies, particularly cold and cough syrups, antihistamines and antacids. Be sure to check the expiration dates on any prescription or over-the-counter medications.
- Consider bringing an extra pair of prescription eyeglasses. It can take a week or more for certain lens prescriptions to be filled, and can also be quite costly. You should be aware that some opticians quote the price per lens.

Upon Arrival in the Netherlands

Your Family Doctor, the *Huisarts*

Once you have arrived and settled into your housing, look for a *huisarts* in your neighborhood (postcode). Dutch *huisartsen* make house calls when necessary; thus they generally accept only individuals who live within a reasonable distance from their offices. Your *huisarts* will virtually be the center of your family's health care while living in the Netherlands. It is uncommon to change to a different *huisarts* once you have been accepted as a patient, and so it is important to choose carefully and feel comfortable with whom you select.

To Help You Choose a *Huisarts*:

- Ask your neighbors and colleagues for recommendations.
- Call ACCESS for names of English-speaking doctors in your area.
- Ask at a local club (e.g., American Women's Club, British Women's Club, International Women's Club or sports/fitness clubs) for suggestions.
- A listing of doctors in your area may be obtained by asking your neighborhood pharmacy (*apotheek*), checking the Yellow Pages (*Gouden Gids*) under *Artsen-huisartsen*, or at *www.kringhaaglanden.nl* (choose *huisarts zoeken*, then enter your postcode).

The Role of the *Huisarts*:

- Provides you and your family with all routine medical care.
- Sends you to a specialist. (This is particularly true if your insurance requires a *huisarts* referral letter (*verwijs brief*) before paying for the specialist visit and any treatment.)
- Calls an ambulance for you in the case of a NON-life-threatening emergency.
- Arranges for you to be seen in a hospital emergency room in the event of a NON-life-threatening injury.
- Arranges for your admission to a hospital in NON-life-threatening situations.

Once You Have Selected a *Huisarts*

It is a good idea to have an introductory meeting with your family doctor and bring in any copies of pertinent medical records before you are faced with an illness. Each *huisarts* has a different daily routine which includes making hospital visits, house calls, answering phone calls, and seeing patients on an appointment-only or drop-in (*spreekuur*) basis. Therefore, it is also important to get your doctor's schedule.

When you visit the office, do not be surprised if it is in a residential street. It may in fact be your *huisarts*' home! It is polite to arrive slightly before the scheduled time, and to greet those already in the waiting room with a simple "good day" or "*goede morgen*" before noon, "*goede middag*" after noon. Keep a mental note of those already there and those who arrive after you, because you will generally be called from the waiting room in turn. Roughly ten minutes are scheduled for each visit, so if you have many questions or several health issues to address, you should let the assistant know in advance when making your appointment. You may find that you often deal with your *huisarts*' assistant who answers the phone, makes appointments, answers certain medical questions, prepares referral letters and handles prescriptions. Some assistants may even give injections or carry out laboratory tests.

Both your *huisarts* and the assistant have been specially trained. A Dutch *huisarts* completes six years of theoretical and clinical training in medical school followed by three years of additional training in family medicine. The *huisarts*' assistant has also followed an appropriate course of study.

When Your *Huisarts* is Unavailable

When your doctor is unavailable, there will be another *huisarts* in the neighborhood who is on call. Usually the on-call physician's name and telephone number are left on a taped message on the answering machine of your *huisarts*. Sometimes these messages are only in Dutch. It is helpful to learn the sounds of numbers in Dutch and have pen and paper ready. The local paper is also a good source for the names and numbers of the doctors on-call. There you can find a list of the doctors responsible for urgent night duty, weekend care and even those who are unavailable due to a planned vacation.

▸ Changing Your *Huisarts*

While it is very uncommon to leave one *huisarts'* practice for another, particularly within the same neighborhood, it is possible. If for some reason you decide to change your family doctor, notify your former physician. It is considered impolite not to do so. At the same time, ask for your medical records to be forwarded to your new *huisarts*.

Paying Medical Bills

Although some *husiartsen* may require that you pay at each visit, it is common practice to wait to pay until you are billed. Expect to receive your bill on a monthly, quarterly or annual basis. Ask your *huisarts* about his or her billing system. You may be charged for telephone consults, prescriptions and refill orders telephoned to the pharmacy as well as a quarterly fee for being a patient.

▸ Health Insurance

You will be required to provide information about your health insurance when seeing a health care practitioner. If you are insured with a private carrier unknown in the Netherlands, you will likely be asked to pay your own bills and request reimbursement from the insurance company. The United States Medicare Program does not apply outside of the U.S. under any circumstance, and the U.S. Champus Program covers only U.S. military retirees under 65 years of age.

In Case of Emergency

Dial ☎ 1-1-2 when you need emergency response by an Ambulance, the Fire Department or the Police Department. If you have a life-threatening emergency, every second counts! Other emergency telephone numbers (*alarmnummers*) are listed on the back cover of the local telephone book.

▸ The Emergency Room

Emergency rooms are identified by the initials *E.H.B.O. (Eerste Hulp Bij Ongelukken)* which means "First Aid for Accidents." They are located in many but not all hospitals, and are only for patients who:

- Experience a life-threatening injury
- Allergic reaction or poisoning
- Have been referred by their *huisarts* for urgent treatment in a non-life-threatening situation

It is prudent to learn the name and address of a nearby hospital (*ziekenhuis*) in the event you need to get there on your own. See www.*zeikenhuis.nl* for general information and links to all hospitals in the Netherlands. It is also wise to know which local hospitals have Emergency Rooms and which are equipped after hours to treat children. However, be aware that the emergency health care system works differently here. In case of a life-threatening medical emergency, dial ☎ 1-1-2, the national emergency number, and an ambulance will be sent to your location. If you require urgent care, but the situation is not life-threatening, you should call your *huisarts* immediately. In non-life threatening situations, Dutch hospitals can, and probably will, refuse to help you if you are not first referred by a *huisarts*. Additionally, you will be charged a fee if you call an ambulance on your own in a non-emergency situation. Your *huisarts* will contact an ambulance for you, and will then call the hospital and tell them to prepare for your arrival.

SMASH (*stichting mobiele artsen service Haaglanden*) is a cooperative effort of *huisarts* in The Hague, Leidschendam, Rijswijk, Voorburg, Voorschoten and Wassenaar providing after hours, weekend and holiday urgent care. Call ☎ (070) 346 9669 to reach a doctor's assistant who can provide advice and consult with the *huisarts* to determine the best course of action. You can read more about this after-hours service in English at *www.smashaaglanden.nl.*

The Specialists

Your *huisarts* will treat you and your family for common illnesses and medical problems. However, if your problem is beyond the scope of his or her abilities, you will be referred to a specialist. In addition, if you do not feel comfortable with the level of care your *huisarts* is giving you, ask to see a specialist. In this event, you will likely be asked to carry a referral letter (*verwijs brief*) to the specialist yourself. Occasionally, this pertinent medical information will be given to you in a sealed envelope by your *huisarts* or the assistant. Certain insurance policies will only cover the cost of the visit to a specialist if your *huisarts* has written you a referral letter. However, you may always take responsibility for the bill and see a specialist of your choice on your own. While this is seldom done in the Netherlands, it is possible.

Specialists' offices are generally housed in the Outpatient Clinic (*Polikliniek*) section of a hospital. Few specialists have private practices, although physical therapists, chiropractors and homeopathic practitioners sometimes work out of their homes. Be aware that some specialists may expect to make the medical decisions for you. Be sure you understand and agree with the treatment plan.

▸ Second Opinions

Asking for a "second opinion" is unusual in the Netherlands. However, if you are not confident that your medical condition is being accurately diagnosed and treated by either your *huisarts* or the specialist, you should seek another opinion. You may ask your *huisarts* for another physician's name or you may find another doctor independently. If your *huisarts* is reluctant to give a referral, call a specialist yourself and ask to make an appointment. Remember to check your insurance coverage. After all, you are your own primary health advocate, and you know your own body better than anyone.

The Hospital *(Ziekenhuis)*

The first time you go to a hospital, whether it is for x-rays or for admission, you will need to arrive a few minutes early to register. The hospital will issue you an identity card. This identity card contains pertinent information about you and your insurance coverage. You will need this card each time you go to the hospital.

If your *huisarts* or specialist feels you need to be hospitalized, he or she will call ahead and request a bed. You will be notified when the bed is available. Inform your insurance company immediately that you plan to enter the hospital. Many insurance plans require pre-certification approval before you are admitted or treated. While you are a patient in the hospital, your specialist will visit you daily and your *huisarts* will probably drop in for a friendly visit, usually at no charge, once during your stay.

▸ Hospital Admissions

If you are admitted to the hospital you should take along:

- Passport or Netherlands residency card.
- Your insurance card or your doctor's information for admittance.
- Any medicines you currently take (show these to the admitting nurse).
- Night clothes, robe and slippers.
- Toilet articles like soap, brush, toothbrush, toothpaste, etc.

A few tips:

- Visiting hours vary; be sure to ask.
- There are very few private rooms. If you want a private room, request it in advance and be prepared to pay extra.
- Rest assured—the hospital staff does speak English, although they may tease you about your poor Dutch.

▸ The Children's Hospital *(Kinderziekenhuis)*

If your child needs to be hospitalized, ask to have him/her placed in the children's section or in a Children's Hospital. You may be permitted to stay with your child in some hospitals.

Pregnancy (*Zwangerschap*)

If you are planning to have children while in the Netherlands, be assured that according to the World Health Organization, the Netherlands is one of the safest places in the world in which to give birth.

The Dutch consider pregnancy and childbirth as very natural conditions, and believe the less intervention, the better. At least half of Dutch women give birth at home with the help of their *huisarts* or midwife (*verloskundige*). The majority of the remaining women give birth in a hospital with the help of a *huisarts* or midwife. A minority of babies are delivered by obstetricians. In all settings, women generally give birth without the use of pain medications. If the delivery is in a hospital and is uncomplicated, the mother and baby can expect to go home the same day or the following day. Sometimes the entire hospital stay can last only twelve hours.

▸ The *Kraamzorg*

As an extension of hospital care, a baby nurse (*kraamzorg*) visits each new mother's home from four to eight hours per day for approximately one week after the birth. This nurse checks on the health of the mother and baby, and assists parents with the care of their newborn. Expatriate new mothers may find this especially helpful living far from family. If there are other children, the *kraamzorg* will help care for them, and she may even help with household chores. In order to reserve a baby nurse, either contact your local Cross Association (*Kruisvereniging*) or call a private nursing agency (*kraamverzorging*) when you find out that you are pregnant. Indicate if you prefer to speak in English. The cost of this service is often covered by insurance, and it is truly one of the special features of having a baby in the Netherlands.

▸ When You First Become Pregnant

Decide whether you will want to have your baby delivered in your home (*thuisbevalling*) or in the hospital, and whether you prefer utilizing a midwife, your *huisarts* or an ObGyn specialist (*vrouwenarts*). Your decision will determine which health care professional will care for you throughout your pregnancy.

Ask your *huisarts* or friends for recommendations in order to find the right professional to deliver your baby. You can also contact a hospital near your home and ask for a list of midwives and doctors who are affiliated with the hospital. If your *huisarts* will not be the one to deliver your baby, he/she should be informed as to who will be caring for you during the pregnancy and labor. Make an appointment with the *verloskundige* or *vrouwenarts* right away. Some midwife practices in particular get very busy, and you may not get your first choice of health practitioner. Remember that many midwives and physicians work in groups, and your baby may be delivered by anyone in that group. In addition, in some hospitals, routine deliveries during the evenings are attended by junior physicians. If you have concerns, discuss them in advance. If your pregnancy develops complications or your labor and delivery are anticipated to be unusual, your practitioner may decide to refer you to a specialist, and you may require an in-hospital delivery.

Pain medication during childbirth is generally not offered. If you feel strongly that you may want pain control during labor, discuss the options with your doctor or midwife and be persistent about your preferences. Pain management during in-hospital births may be requested, but because anesthesiologists are not generally available after normal business hours, anesthesia such as epidurals and spinal blocks can't be guaranteed.

▸ During Pregnancy

Good prenatal care is standard in the Netherlands, but you may find some differences from what you know to be offered in your home country. The first prenatal visit usually occurs when you are about three months into your pregnancy. In keeping with the concept of pregnancy as a natural state, certain laboratory tests and examinations are not routinely performed. Again, the Dutch believe that the best outcome in normal situations is expected with little to no intervention. When you are seen for prenatal care, your blood pressure and the fetal heart beat are regularly checked. Blood work, urine exams, ultrasound exams (*echoscopie*) and internal examinations, however, are not routine. If you are 36 years of age or older at the time of conception, you may be offered genetic testing such as the "triple marker" blood test or an amniocentesis. If you are younger than 36 and wish to have genetic tests done, you must discuss them with your practitioner.

▸ Once Your Baby is Born

Either your *huisarts* or a midwife will come to your home within the first days after delivery to do the postnatal follow-up (*nacontrole*). If there are stitches to be removed, he/she will take care of them. If you delivered in a hospital with an OB-Gyn specialist, it is likely that you may have been expected to make arrangements with your *huisarts* to perform the *nacontrole*. You will need to register your baby's birth with several local Dutch authorities within the first three days. When you inform your local town hall (*gemeentehuis*) of the birth, the information will then be passed on to the local well-baby clinic (*consultatiebureau*). A well-baby clinic nurse will then contact you for a home visit. This nurse will perform the heel stick for PKU/CHT and will schedule your first *consultatiebureau* appointment (see below). If you delivered the baby in a city other than where you reside, you need to register the birth at that *gemeentehuis* as well. For more information about registering births and citizenship, please refer to the chapter **Legal Matters**.

If your baby is a boy and you are interested in having him circumcised (*besnijdenis*), you should know that the procedure is not routinely done. If you want to have your son circumcised, you will need to make special arrangements.

The Dutch Cross

It is a good idea to join your local Cross Association (*Kruisvereniging stichting thuiszorg*) early in your pregnancy. For a small annual fee, the *kruisvereniging* offers prenatal and postnatal exercise classes, home maternity nursing care, maternity and baby equipment rental, and dietitian services. Most importantly it enrolls your baby in the well-baby clinic (*consultatiebureau*). Some of these services are only offered once you have been a member (*lid*) for a few months.

The Well-Baby Clinic

The *consultatiebureau* is where you will take your infant for regular health checks, advice on feeding, growing and development and standard immunizations. The *consultatiebureau* offers well-baby health services only; if your child is sick, you need to call your *huisarts*. Your children will be cared for at the *consultatiebureau* until the age of four, after which public health maintenance services are offered through the school health departments. You should note that these services are not provided at most private schools.

The vaccination schedule in the Netherlands may differ from that in your home country. In addition, certain vaccinations you may expect are not routinely given, such as, the Hepatitis B vaccine, BCG (Tuberculosis) vaccine and Varicella (chickenpox) vaccine. It is essential to keep good records of which vaccinations your child receives—and does not receive—while living in the Netherlands.

The *kruisvereniging* distributes a baby care booklet *het Groeiboek* that has space for recording the immunizations, as well as documenting your baby's growth and development. Also published in English as *The Growth Book*, it should accompany you to all *consultatiebureau* visits, so the doctor or nurse can make appropriate entries. You will likely receive your copy of this booklet when you register your child as having been born in the Netherlands.

▸ Breastfeeding Information

If you would like information about breastfeeding or would like to rent breast pumps, several support groups and resources exist:

La Leche League
☎ (011) 141 31 89
www.lalecheleague.nl

Vereniging Borstvoeding Natuurlijk (Dutch Breastfeeding Association)
An English speaking representative is available to answer questions by phone
☎ (035) 542 28 56.
www.borstvoedingnatuurlijk.nl

▸ More Information for Parents-To-Be

In addition to their book on health care, ACCESS publishes a regularly updated and thorough guide for expectant parents called *Babies and Toddlers – The ACCESS Guide to Having and Caring for Children in the Netherlands*. ACCESS also offers childbirth preparation courses, postnatal exercise and baby massage classes, and a wealth of information about pregnancy support services, child care providers, mother-toddler groups and help for parents of children with special needs. They can also provide local information on adoption and infertility counseling and treatment.

The Dentist *(Tandarts)*

You can choose your dentist in much the same way you selected a *huisarts*. Ask friends, neighbors and colleagues for recommendations. You don't need a referral from your *huisarts*. Many dental schools in the Netherlands also offer excellent less expensive dental care. Don't expect to receive a reminder phone call about an appointment you made six months ago. If you don't show up for an appointment, you will be charged a cancellation fee.

Dutch dentists perform a full range of services from cleanings and fillings to cosmetic dental care. Dentists tend to take the same approach to pain medication as do other Dutch physicians, so if you want local anesthesia, you should request it. Fluoride is not added to the Dutch water system, so you may want to give children under twelve years of age non-prescription fluoride tablets and give babies fluoride drops. Ask your *tandarts*, *huisarts* or *consultatiebureau* for advice. Other dental professionals, such as hygienists *(mondhygienist)*, oral surgeons *(specialisten kaakchirurgie)* and orthodontists *(orthodontisten)* can also be found.

▸ Dental Insurance

Dental insurance can be more complicated than regular health insurance. You must have your teeth checked and any needed repairs performed by a dentist at your own expense before an insurer will consider granting you dental coverage. Some insurance is granted for a minimum of three years, so if you expect to stay in the Netherlands for a shorter period, discuss your options with the insurer. You may also be required to have your teeth checked every six months in order to maintain your dental insurance. Request your insurance information in English. If you have insurance coverage through an employer, you will likely have to bring your claim form and ask the dentist to complete it so you can file the claim yourself. Children are usually insured for free when their parents purchase insurance. Sometimes they can receive dental care through their schools. Inquire with the school's director.

Eye Care *(Oogheelkunde)*

Eye care is carried out by opticians *(opticiens)* and ophthalmologists *(oogartsen)* in the Netherlands. The former can perform basic eye examinations, including glaucoma screening, fill eyeglass and contact lens prescriptions, and repair eyeglasses. The latter is a physician and surgeon with a specialization in the diagnosis and treatment of eye disorders. If you have an ongoing medical condition requiring regular eye care, or an acute problem with your eye, you should seek a referral from your *huisarts* to an *oogarts*. Also look in the Yellow Pages *(Gouden Gids)* under *Artsen – specialisten oogheelkunde*, but consider whether or not your insurer will cover the visit if you are not first referred by your *huisarts*.

For refractions and glasses prescriptions, you can ask friends or colleagues for the name of a good *opticien* in the neighborhood.

Mental Health

If you feel that you or a family member may be suffering from a mental illness, discuss with your *huisarts* if you need a referral for psychiatric specialist care. Be certain that the referral is to someone who communicates fluently in English. If what you seek is a professional English speaking counselor or psychologist, you can obtain a list by calling ACCESS. The counselors available through ACCESS are either native English speaking practitioners or have an excellent command of the English language. They are committed to confidentiality and your privacy is ensured. Fees are based on ability to pay and no one is turned away for lack of funds.

Additionally, there are local Dutch mental health facilities that offer counseling services. These are listed in the telephone book under RIAGG (Regional Institution for Ambulatory Mental Health) and also offer special services for youths between the ages of 15 to 25. Counseling at the RIAGG Centers is very inexpensive, but there is often a waiting list for their services. You should get a referral from your *huisarts* to begin the process. Emergency services are available 24 hours a day, but you must also request them via your *huisarts.*

The Pharmacy *(Apotheek)*

In the Netherlands, there is a significant difference between a drugstore (*drogisterij*) and a pharmacy (*apotheek*). When you need to fill a prescription, you do so in an *apotheek*. It is generally expected that you use the same *apotheek* for all of the prescriptions given to members of your family. Your information will be entered into their computer, and the pharmacist can monitor for any possible drug interactions and advise you accordingly. In addition, because your insurance information will be recorded in the computer, some pharmacies may be able to bill certain Dutch insurers directly. If you carry private insurance, you will probably need to pay the pharmacy and keep your original receipts to send with your insurance claims.

Medication prices are controlled, and are nationally uniform. If you need to fill a prescription urgently and your pharmacy is closed, check the window for the duty roster (*dienstrooster*), a sign indicating which pharmacy in the area has after-hours duty. In heavily populated areas of the Netherlands, there is always a pharmacy responsible for emergency duty for the neighborhood. The roster is published in the local newspapers. You should also be able to obtain a copy of the night duty schedule for the year at your *apotheek*. If no local pharmacy is open and obtaining the medication cannot be postponed, there is often a service bell (*dienstbel*) at the entrance of the pharmacy. Ringing this will summon the pharmacist or an assistant within thirty minutes. In some rural areas, physicians themselves may also dispense medication.

Note that the instructions for proper use of your medications will be written in Dutch, so be sure to clarify any questions you have regarding the medication with either the pharmacist or your *huisarts*. The pharmacist will also assist you in choosing the proper over-the-counter remedy as these are normally kept behind the counter.

Items Found in the Pharmacy:

- Prescription medications
- Certain over-the-counter remedies, such as pain medicine (*pijnstillers*), cough syrup, Zantac, Rogaine, and many items that can also be found in the drugstore (*drogisterij*)
- Vitamins and certain homeopathic treatments that can also be found at a health food store (*reformhuis*)
- Non-prescription birth control preparations
- Certain cosmetic lines, primarily body lotions and creams
- Hydrogen peroxide (*waterstof peroxide* 3% or H2O2)
- Rubbing alcohol (*isopropyl alcohol*)
- Acetone and other agents for spot removal
- Bandages, sport braces, hot/cold packs, insulin and syringes, and specialized medical products
- Information folders on a variety of diseases (in Dutch)

The Drugstore *(Drogisterij)*

Your neighborhood drugstore contains a plethora of items ranging from over-the-counter remedies to toilet articles, cosmetics, cleaning products, baby supplies, seasonal items and candy. You can't, however, fill a prescription at a *drogisterij*. Major *drogisterij* chains include Etos (*www.etos.nl*) and Kruidvat (*www.kruidvat.nl*).

Items Found in the Drugstore:

- Allergies (*allergien*) or hay fever (*hooikoorts*): Polaramine, Allerfre (no drowsiness), Triludan
- Athlete's foot (*voetschimmel*): Dermacure, Canesten
- Bandages (*pleisters*)
- Cold and sinus relief (*verkouden*): Paracetamol (similar to Tylenol), Anti-grippine, Nurofen, Bayer Aspirin, Coldrex, Citrosan
- Constipation (*verstopping*): Dulcolax tablets and suppositories Prunasine, Nourilax. For children: Microlax
- Cough (*hoest*): Dextromethorfan *siroop*, Broomhexine *siroop*, Acetylcystine, Bexedijl. For children: Thijm Siroop
- Dental care (*tandenverzorging*): (Zymaflor) Fluoride drops or tablets, toothbrushes, floss, toothpaste, fluoridated rinses and many periodontal aids
- Diarrhea (*diarree*): Imodium, Tannalbin
- Earache (*oorpijn*): Otalgan drops
- Eye drops (*oogdruppels*): Vidisept
- Eye wash (*oogwassingen*): Oculine, Optrex

- Foot ailments (*voetklachten*): Dr. Scholl's products, Trannonsan Foot Bath Tablets, Decylon and topicals for athlete's foot
- General tired feeling (*vermoeidheid*): Biovital or Tai Ginseng
- Headache (*hoofdpijn*): Aspirin-containing Bayer, Chefarine. Aspirin-free Hedex, Saridon, Advil, Panadol, Nerofen, Sanalgin. For children: Sinaspril, Finimal
- Hemorrhoids (*aambeien*): Sperti (Preparation H), Zwitsanal, Anusol
- Indigestion (*maagzuur*): Rennie, Alka Seltzer, Gaviscon, Pepcid, Regla PH
- Inhalants (*inademing, inhalatieproducten*): Vicks
- Insect bites (*insekten* bijten): Azaron Cream, Nestosyl Cream
- Menstrual discomfort (*menstruatiepijn*): Nerofen, Femex, Femapirin, Saridon (aspirin-free)
- Motion sickness (*reisziekte*): Dramamine, Marizine. For children: Primatour
- Muscle aches (*spierpijn*): Finalgon, Midalgan, Deep Heat Mentholatum: Algesal
- Nose drops (*neusdruppels*): Otrivin nebulizer, Vicks Sinex. For children: Otrivin. For babies: baby Otrivin (isotonic saline)
- Pregnancy tests (*zwangerschapstest*): Predictor, Clear Blue
- Skin antiseptic (*antisepticum*): Betadine, Sterilon
- Sore throat (*keelpijn*): Lozenges: Strepsils, Hibitane
- Thermometers (*Koorts thermometer*): Generally in Celsius
- Vitamins (*Vitaminen*)
- Wart removal (*wratten*): Formule W

Public Health Programs

The *G.G. en G.D.* (*Gemeentelijke Geneeskundige en Gezondheidsdienst*) are public health centers responsible for the prevention of communicable diseases, standard immunizations, etc. They issue vaccination packets for babies seen in the *consultatiebureau* and send notices for immunizations, dental care and preventative care for older children via Dutch schools. They also send registered female residents notices for PAP smears and mammograms when age appropriate. The telephone numbers for your local agency can be found in the White Pages. However, you may want to ask your *huisarts* to advise you on its applications—if and when they are necessary.

Blood Donation

If you are between 18 and 70 years of age and would like to donate blood, this generous and important act is possible in the Netherlands. First, you will be interviewed and your blood tested. Once you are approved as a donor (*goedgekeurd*) you may be called one to three times yearly to donate. Evening donations are also possible. Go to *www.sanquin.nl* or look under *Bloedbank* or *Bloedtransfusiedienst* in the White Pages.

Organ Donation

To be listed in the donation registry, you must be 12 years of age or older and fill out a donation form available online at *www.donorvoorlichting.nl*. Your name is held in the donor registry only for the duration of your stay in the Netherlands. While no one wishes to imagine a situation which could ensue in organ donation, it is easy to imagine the gratitude you would feel if you or a loved one were given such a precious gift. For information please contact:

Stichting Donor Voorlichting
☎ (045) 567 92 00
www.donorvoorlichting.nl

Body Temperature Conversion Chart

Use the following body temperature conversions as a guide:

Oral Temperature	C	F
	36.5	97.7
"normal" Celsius*	**36.6**	97.9
"normal" Fahrenheit*	37.0	**98.6**
slight fever	37.5	99.5
	38.0	100.4
fever	38.5	101.3
	39.0	102.2
high fever	39.5	103.1
	40.0	104.0
very high fever	40.2	104.4

* Note: "normal" temperature in Celsius is slightly lower than "normal" temperature in Fahrenheit

General Medical & Support Group Information

ACCESS
☎ (070) 346 25 25 or ☎ (020) 423 32 17
www.access-nl.org

Alcoholics Anonymous
☎ (020) 625 60 57
www.AA-Netherlands.org
24-hour answering service, English-speaking meetings every day in Amsterdam and The Hague

Cancer Information Line (*Nederlandse Kankerbestrijding*)
☎ (020) 570 05 00 or ☎ (0800) 022 66 22
www.kwfkankerbestrijding.nl

AIDS/STD Information Help Line
☎ (0900) 204 20 40 (toll call)
Anonymous advice in English and Dutch

Medical Vocabulary

English	Dutch
Abdominal pain	*Buikklachten*
Abortion	*Abortus*
Admission	*Opname*
Anesthesiologist	*Anesthesist*
Anti-diarrheal	*Diarreemiddel*
Adhesive bandage	*(Hecht) pleister*
Bandage, gauze	*Verband, gaas*
Bill/account	*Rekening*
Birth	*Bevalling*
Birth control	*Geboortenregeling*
Blood	*Bloed*
Blood pressure	*Bloeddruk*
Burn	*Brandwond*
Cardiologist	*Cardioloog*
Chest pain	*Borstpijn*
Children's hospital	*Kinderziekenhuis*
Chiropodist	*Podotherapeut*
Chiropractor	*Manueeltherapeut*
Constipation	*Darmverstopping*
Contagious	*Besmettelijk*
Cotton	*Watten*
Cough	*Hoest*
Cough medicine	*Hoestsiroop*
Cross Association	*Kruisvereniging*
Dentist	*Tandarts*
Dermatologist	*Huidarts*
Diarrhea	*Diarree*
Dietician	*Dietiste*
Drugstore	*Drogisterij*
Ear infection	*Oorontsteking*
Ear, Nose & Throat Doctor	*Keel, Neus en Oor-specialist (KNO arts)*
Emergency	*Spoedgevallen*

English	Dutch
Emergency department	*E.H.B.O. afdeling or Eerste Hulp*
Eye hospital	*Oogziekenhuis*
Faint, pass out	*Flauwvallen*
Family doctor	*Huisarts, Dokter*
Fever	*Koorts, verhoging hebben*
First aid	*E.H.B.O., Eerste Hulp Bij Ongelukken*
Flu	*Griep*
Give birth	*Bevallen*
Gynecologist	*Gynaecoloog, Vrouwenarts*
Have a cold	*Verkouden zijn*
Headache	*Hoofdpijn*
Head lice	*Hoofdluis*
Hospital	*Ziekenhuis*
House calls	*Huisbezoek*
Iodine	*Jodium*
Immunizations: DPT & MMR	*Inentingen: DTP & BMR*
Diphtheria	*Difterie*
Tetanus	*Tetanus*
Polio	*Polio*
Mumps	*Bof*
Measles	*Mazelen*
German measles	*Rode hond*
Insurance	*Verzekering*
Insurance/identity punch card	*Ponsplaatje*
Internist	*Internist*
Itch	*Jeuk*
Laboratory	*Laboratorium*
Medicine	*Medicijn*

English	Dutch	English	Dutch
Menstruation	*Menstruatie*	Referral	*Verwijzing*
Midwife	*Vroedvrouw/ Verloskundige*	Rehabilitation	*Revalidatie*
		Salve	*Zalf*
Midwifery	*Verloskunde*	Sanitary napkin	*Maandverband*
Miscarriage	*Miskraam*	Social worker	*Maatschappelijk werkster*
Mother's helper	*Kraamverzorgster*		
Municipal Health Dept.	*G.G. & G. D.*	Sore throat	*Keelpijn*
Nurse, female/male	*Zuster/Broeder*	Specialist	*Specialist*
Obstetrician	*Vrouwenarts*	Stomach ache	*Maagpijn*
Office hours	*Spreekuur*	Surgeon	*Chirurg*
Ophthalmologist	*Oogarts*	Syrup	*Stroop (drankje)*
Orthopedic surgeon	*Orthopedisch chirurg*	Temperature	*Temperatuur*
Outpatient department	*Polikliniek*	Thermometer	*Thermometer*
Pain Medication	*Pijnstiller*	Toothache	*Kiespijn*
Pediatrician	*Kinderarts*	Tuberculosis, TB	*Tuberculose, TBC*
Pharmacy/Pharmacist	*Apotheek/Apotheker*	Ulcer, sore	*Zweer*
Physiotherapist	*Fysiotherapeut*	Unconscious	*Bewusteloos*
Plastic surgeon	*Plastisch chirurg*	Undertaker	*Begrafenis-ondernemer*
Podiatrist	*Podotherapeut*		
Powders	*Poeders*	Urologist	*Uroloog*
Pregnancy	*Zwangerschap*	Visiting hours	*Bezoekuren*
Prescription	*Recept*	Vomit	*Overgeven, braken*
Psychiatrist	*Psychiater*	Wound	*Wond*
Psychologist	*Psycholoog*	X-Ray department	*Röntgen afdeling*
Rash	*Uitslag*		

Chapter 8

Transportation

The world of transportation in the Netherlands is like no other. You will be amazed at the timeliness of the train, tram and bus systems, and dazed by the speed of automobile traffic on narrow streets. You will be dazzled by the number of bicycles on the road and marvel at the ease by which you can move around the country without a car. What's more, when you drive you will find yourself quickly doing things you initially condemn: making U-turns in the middle of the street, parking on the sidewalk and driving faster than you believed possible.

Bicycles

In many countries, bicycles are used primarily for recreation or for exercise. In the Netherlands, bicycles (*fietsen*) are an unbelievably popular form of transportation. Statistically there are more bicycles than people in this country.

▸ Buying a Bicycle

While bicycles are easily rented from bicycle shops and train stations, if you intend to stay in the country for a while, you should either bring one with you or buy a new or used bicycle here. You can get a good used bicycle from the bicycle rental/storing place associated with your train station. Most bicycle shops also carry some and can help fit you with the correct size. A good used bicycle can cost approximately €250. You can also check at the *Kringloop* stores for cheaper ones.

▸ Cycling Rules

Cycling is the easiest way to get around the cities of the Netherlands. Special bicycle lanes (*fietspad*) are marked by a blue circular sign containing a white bicycle and are often paved in red. These lanes have separate paving markings (such as shark's teeth indicating the necessity to yield) and often their own traffic signs and lights. These lanes are mandatory when they are present and cyclists may not use the regular roadway. The bicycle lanes are also shared with invalid vehicles and motorized bicycles (*bromfietsen* or *brommers*). Bicycle paths marked with a black rectangular sign that says "*Fietspad*" are for bicycles only. The sign

"Geen Rijwielen Hier Plaatsen" means that the building owner does not want cycles of any kind parked there and has the right to have them removed. **Required:** All bicycles (even children's bicycles) are required to have the following equipment in good working order:

- Headlight and rear light
- Rear reflector
- Bell
- Brakes
- Side reflectors on the wheels and pedals

If you are missing any of these mandatory items, the police may fine you. With all the rain in the Netherlands, fenders are also a good idea.

Bicycle Theft

The biggest problem you will face with a bicycle will be keeping it safe from theft. Ask for advice from the bicycle shop regarding the best locks as well as special bicycle insurance. To prevent theft and speed recovery of stolen bicycles, you should have a bicycle shop engrave your zip code (*post code*) and house number on your bicycle's frame. You can get a bicycle registration form (*fietsregistratiekaart*) from the police on which to record a very detailed description of your bicycle for your own records. Finally, there are special guarded bicycle parking garages (*bewaakt*) in cities and at most train stations that will keep your bicycle safe for the small fee of approximately €1 per day.

▶ Bicycles on Trains

Bicycles may be taken on trains in the specially indicated cars, provided you buy an appropriate ticket for them (the price is approximately €6 per day and the maximum allowed is one bicycle per person). However, bicycles are not allowed on trains during the weekday rush hours (from 6:30–9:00 a.m. and from 4:30–6:00 p.m.) This restriction does not apply on holidays or during the months of July and August. Folding bicycles can be taken for free and are not restricted to the special bicycle car or times of day.

▶ Renting a Bicycle

Even if you own a bicycle, you may find it more convenient to rent one at a distant train station for a day. Rental costs are dependent on the location and type of bicycle, but start at approximately €7 per day with a deposit of approximately €50. Although it is not mandatory, it is a good idea to reserve a bicycle in advance. The telephone numbers of rental shops at train stations can be found at *www.ns.nl* under *Fietsverhuur*. They are also listed in the yearly booklet Er-Op-Uit!, which has many suggested train-and-bicycle day tours in all areas of the country. These tours include train ticket, bicycle rental, and a detailed map of the bicycle route. (You can find these books at train stations, the VVV and ANWB stores.)

Public Transport

Public transportation (*openbaar vervoer*) in the Netherlands, as well as in most of Europe, is efficient and convenient. Public transportation needs are met by an extensive network of easily-located trams, buses, metros and trains. The national telephone number for Public Transportation Information (*Inlichtingen Openbaar Vervoer*) is ☎ (0900) 92 92. There is a charge of €0,70 per minute for this service. You can provide them with the address where you are and the one you want to go to, and they will give you all the information you need to use the system. This same information can be accessed on the Internet at *www.9292ov.nl* to show you fare information and alternative ways to get where you are going by combining trains with trams and/or buses.

Trains

The Dutch train system (*Nederlandse Spoorwegen or NS*) is clean, comfortable and reliable, providing safe, modern transport with frequent schedules to most destinations within the Netherlands and the rest of Europe. This is a great way to see the Netherlands with no worries about traffic jams or parking. In most cases the stations are very near the old center of town as well as the VVV tourist office. With special tickets and passes, trains are not only convenient and relaxing, but economical as well.

Intercity trains service 30 large and medium-large Dutch cities providing the quickest travel times and fewest stops. They also tend to have the newest equipment. *Sneltreinen* stop at a few stations along each route, while *Stoptreinen* stop at every station. Sometimes it is necessary to transfer trains (*overstap*) at a connecting station in order to get from point A to point

B. In most cases, this is quite simply a walk across the platform and a short wait for the connecting train. For example, to get from Voorschoten to Amsterdam, the fastest way is to take a *Stoptrein* to Leiden (only *Stoptreinen* stop at small towns like Voorschoten), then an *Intercity* or *Sneltrein* to Amsterdam.

▸ Planning Your Train Trip

While the ticket agents at the train station are very helpful, it pays to do some homework on your own. There are several ways to determine the best route to take:

- **Internet:** By far the easiest method you can use to plan a trip by train is to access the NS web site on the Internet at *www.ns.nl*. This site has an English option and guides you step-by-step through the process. You simply enter your starting and ending points (stations, addresses, attractions, airports or museums), any intermediate stations you wish to include, and your preferred departure or arrival time. Not only does the site give you several options to choose for your trip, it provides all necessary track numbers, connections and prices for the combined trip including trains, buses and trams. It is worthwhile to browse the site for special day excursions. International trips are also covered.
- **Telephone Advice:** You may call ☎ (0900) 92 92 for train advice for €0,70 per minute.

▸ Purchasing Train Tickets

Note: Prices quoted in this chapter are current as of December 2008, so you should only use them as an approximate guide.

Only the larger stations still have ticket agents. If you wish to purchase tickets from an agent, go to the *Nederland* line for domestic trips and the *International* line for trips outside the Netherlands. There will be a surcharge of a minimum €3.50 per transaction at the ticket window. Keep in mind that unlike some other European countries, tickets may NOT be purchased onboard the train in the Netherlands. If you are on the train and cannot show that you have a valid ticket, you will be fined approximately €35.00 plus the cost of the fare. The fastest way to get a domestic ticket is to use the ticket machines that are in the station. These machines are bright yellow with “Tickets” written at the top in blue. All ticket machines accept PIN cards and some accept coins, but no machines accept bills.

The NS ticket vending machines use touch screens and are very easy to use; press on the British flag to switch to English. Much of the screen should be self-explanatory, such as choosing your destination and class of travel. You must choose *Full Fare* unless you have a valid *Discount* Card (see below). If you are traveling that day, choose *Valid Today*. If you are buying tickets in advance of the date you want to use them, choose *Open Date*. However, don’t forget that undated tickets must be date-stamped on the train platform in the *stempelautomaat* on their day of use BEFORE getting on the train. A round trip ticket is approximately 10 percent cheaper than two one-way tickets.

▸ Special Train Discounts

The Dutch train system has a number of special discounts (*korting*) which are worth mentioning:

- ***Voordeelurenabonnement*:** This card gives significant discounts during "off peak" hours defined as after 9:00 a.m. on non-holiday weekdays. If you leave after 9:00 a.m., the fare is reduced 40 percent. This same reduction applies to holidays, weekends and all of July and August without the 9:00 a.m. restriction. The cardholder is also allowed to take up to three persons with him/ her who may also travel at the 40 percent discounted rate provided that they all travel together, which comes in very handy when hosting visitors. The cost for the *Voordeelurenabonnement* is approximately €55 annually. Applications for this card are available at the NS counter at large stations. A completed application can be mailed to NS along with a recent Dutch-size passport photo or submitted to a NS ticket agent who will issue a temporary card. The permanent card will arrive in the mail. Always show the card when buying tickets or press discount or *korting* on the ticket machine in order to get your full savings. You must present both your ticket and your *Voordeelurenabonnement* to the conductor on the train when asked.
- ***Dag Kaart* (Day Card):** Purchase of this ticket permits the purchaser to travel throughout the Netherlands for one day at the following prices: second class is approximately €42 or €25 with a *Voordeelurenabonnement*, first class is €71 or €43 with a *Voordeelurenabonnement*. For an additional €5 you can purchase an **OV Dagkaart** which allows you to use all other forms of public transport as well.
- **5-Retourkaart:** This is a set of 5 undated round trip tickets to the same destination. The set costs the same as buying the tickets individually, but saves time. Since the tickets are undated, they must be date-validated in the stamping machine on the platform BEFORE entering the train.
- **Railrunner:** Children three and under are always free on the train. Up to three children ages 4 to 11, inclusive, can accompany a paying adult of 19 or older for the day for €2 in first or second class with Railrunner tickets. Children in this age range traveling alone qualify for the *korting* ticket, i.e., 40 percent off, but do not need a *Voordeelurenabonnement*. Railrunner tickets are independent of destination.
- **Yearly and Monthly Passes:** If you commute regularly by train, you'll want to consider purchasing a yearly or monthly pass for unlimited travel on your specific route. It is possible to add trams, buses and metros to these passes for an additional fee. Applications are available at major train stations.

Other Train Tidbits: Small dogs and other pets that fit in a carrying bag may ride the train free, but larger pets require a ticket for approximately €3 per day. International train tickets can be purchased at the larger train stations, travel agencies such as *www.treinsreiswinkel.nl* or online at *www.nshispeed.nl*.

Buses, Trams and Metros

Buses are available everywhere in the Netherlands, even in remote areas. Trams are common in the bigger cities, but subways/metros are limited to a few lines in Amsterdam and Rotterdam. While buses, tram and metros are operated by different companies in different cities, they are all paid using the same national system. A new national payment system is currently being developed using smart card technology called OVChipKaarts (see *www.ov-chipkaart.nl* with English available) that will work on buses and trams as well as trains. This system has been delayed nationally due to security concerns, but is being tested in Amsterdam and Rotterdam. The remainder of the country should be phased in when those security issues are solved.

As of December 2008, fares for much of the country are paid with strip cards called *strippenkaarten*, meaning "ticket of strips." At every tram stop (*tramhalte*) and bus stop (*bushalte*), the numbers of the bus and tram lines that stop there are posted, along with many of the stops they will make and their ultimate destination. This is helpful when you want to verify that you are going in the right direction. Timetables for that particular stop are usually posted, and you may find a route and zone map as well. Timetables for buses and trams in a particular region are available for sale at major bus stations.

Doors on buses are operated by the driver, but you need to push the "*deur open*" button next to the door on most trams. All doors close automatically. When your stop is approaching, push one of the Stop buttons located throughout the vehicle; a red light goes on in the front to alert the driver to stop at the next stop on the route. You should exit at the side or rear of buses and trams.

▸ The *Strippenkaart*

Strippenkaarten are tickets used for public transport (buses, trams, and metros) across the country. The *strippenkaart* looks a bit like a thin, cardboard bookmark, and is divided into skinny rectangular boxes, or strips. There are several types of *strippenkaarten*. Those available from a tram or bus driver include 2, 3 and 8-strip cards, plus the *dagkaart*. Children under four always ride free. For significant savings, purchase *strippenkaarten* at train stations, VVV's, cigar shops, supermarkets, post offices, newsstands and certain bookstores. The 15-strip blue card for adults is regular rate (*vol tarief*) for approximately €7,50. If you use public transportation frequently, it will be convenient to buy a 45-strip blue card for approximately €21,50. The 15-strip pink card is reduced rate (*gereduceerd tarief*) for children age 4–11, PAS-65 holders and dogs for approximately €5. Small dogs and other pets that are small enough to be carried in a bag or basket may ride free.

Zones: All public transport routes are divided into numbered zones. For example, The Hague *Centrum* is zone 5400 and is posted on all *tramhalte* and *bushalte* signs within the zone. Each journey costs one strip for the basic fare plus another strip for each zone traveled.

Local zone maps are posted at tram and bus stops, and are available for sale at major bus stations. To determine how many strips you need for your trip, each zone costs one strip and there is a starting fee of one strip. Thus, the minimum used will be two strips for a trip within a single zone. Likewise, a 2-zone journey will cost 3 strips and a 3-zone will be 4 strips. Keep in mind that failure to stamp your *strippenkaart* the correct number of times will result in a fine.

Using a Strippenkaart: It is helpful to know in advance how many zones your trip will cross. On buses, the driver will stamp your *strippenkaart* for you. Just tell him/her your final destination or the number of zones you want to cross. When you board a tram, you can stamp your *strippenkaart* yourself with the yellow stamping machine near each door or ask the driver for assistance. To prevent fare dodgers, some trams in Amsterdam require entry through the very last door where agents sell tickets or stamp *strippenkaarten*.

It is not necessary to stamp every single strip, but rather just the last strip for your number of zones needed. To use the stamping machine, count the correct number of strips, fold your ticket at the bottom of the correct strip, and then insert the card with the fold forwards into the stamping machine until you hear a click, which means that your strip has been time-zone-and-date-stamped.

It's possible for more than one person to travel on the same *strippenkaart* as long as you stamp the correct number of strips for each person. For example, if you and a friend are going to cross two zones, stamp the last one of three strips for yourself and then do the same for your friend. The stamp includes the time to the next quarter hour. Depending on the number of strips "paid," you are allowed a certain amount of time to complete your journey. For example, if you stamp 2 or 3 strips, you will have an hour to travel within the zones you've paid for. You can transfer to another bus, tram or metro, and even get off and back on again as long as you travel within those zones. If you plan well and are quick with your errands, it is possible to make a round trip journey on the original stamp.

On a journey that requires more strips than are left on your old card, simply stamp the last strip on the old *strippenkaart* and as many more strips as you need on the new one. Inspectors may ask to see your cards either on or after you get off the tram or metro, so keep them until your trip is finished. If you are caught without a *strippenkaart* or an insufficient number of strips stamped, you will be asked to produce identification when they fine you, so be sure to carry an ID. On the 45-strip blue card, you must stamp the last strip on the first side before continuing on the back side even if it is for the same journey (just as if it were two separate cards).

If you are planning a journey that requires a bus trip and then a tram, keep in mind the final destination and have the full journey stamped at the beginning to save strips. If you have stamped the full amount of strips on a tram and then enter a bus, you only have to show the driver the stamp so he knows you have already paid the fare. When there is a fare increase (typically in January of each year), old *strippenkaarten* are valid for 12 months past the date of the increase. A date will be announced when *strippenkaarten* will be phased out, so you'll want to use up your supply by then.

▸ Bus Passes

If you travel regularly by tram and/or bus, monthly or yearly passes (*abonnementen*) may save time and money. These are available at transit offices. You will need your passport or driver's license and one Dutch-size (3 x 4 cm) passport photo. The price will depend on how many zones you wish to include. To use your pass on a bus, simply show it to the driver. On a tram with stamping machines, you just need to have your pass available if transit inspectors ask to view it.

Airplanes

Amsterdam's Schiphol Airport (*www.schiphol.com*) is Europe's 5th largest airport and is a major hub for travel all over the world. There are lots of ways to make reservations for travel. The ANWB has an in-house travel agency to assist with trips. Most towns have at least one travel agency. There are travel agents in the major cities which specialize in serving English-language speakers. Most airlines have offices in major cities or at the airport from which you can schedule and pay for flights.

▸ Air Travel and the Internet

There are a large variety of websites available to assist with checking airfares and making reservations. One such website is *www.kayak.com* which is easy to use and allows you to book directly with the airlines. Many airlines have electronic newsletters which contain special offers, so consider signing up with airlines that you frequently use. In addition, *www.travelocity.com* offers a service called "Fare Watcher Plus." You can select up to ten destination cities you would like to permanently track and whenever you log on, the site updates you with information on the best available fares to those cities. You may also choose to have them e-mail you if the fare to a certain city drops below a target amount. Finally, several websites allow you to compare prices among low-cost European carriers such as *www.wegolo.com* and *www.skyscanner.net*. For arrival and departure information, you can check the individual airline websites or the airport websites.

Ferries

Before the Chunnel was completed, travel by ferry was the only way to travel to England with your car. Now you can drive to Calais, get your car on the train, and be in Folkestone in 35 minutes. If you want to go to Ireland, the north of England, Iceland or Scandinavia, ferries are still a great way to travel. It is good to have a reservation for a ferry, especially at holiday times. Traveling by ferry in the winter months can be a little unsettling as the North Sea is rough, so plan your itinerary carefully. You can find the ferry company you need by doing a Google search or looking in the Yellow Pages under *Ferrydiensten*.

Automobiles

The rules of the road are somewhat different in Europe than in the U.S., and also differ within each European country. You can comfortably drive in all of them. You just need to know what to do.

In Germany, the speed signs posted on the *Autobahn* are the minimums (some stretches also have maximums posted)—get out of the passing lane if you aren't going that speed. However, in the Netherlands, the posted speed is the maximum speed and you will get an expensive ticket if you ignore it—there are cameras everywhere. In Belgium, the yield to the right rule in traffic circles means that drivers enter without looking, creating a gridlock as no one can get in or out, but in the Netherlands, the "yield to the right" rule at traffic circles is shifting to yield to people already in the rotary. In England and Ireland, you drive on the left-hand side of the road, but in the rest of Europe you drive on the right. If you drive your English car in the Netherlands or your Dutch car in England, because the headlights aim to the incorrect side, so you will find yourself being flashed by oncoming drivers who assume you have your high-beams on.

▸ Driving in the Netherlands

The Netherlands has one of Europe's finest highway systems. The roads are well maintained and frequently marked with road signs which clearly indicate the direction of your destination. Highway signs direct you, however, by specifying the major towns and cities along the route rather than the compass direction of east, west, north or south; so until you learn where the towns are, you will find that maps are critically important. You can obtain maps just about everywhere: ANWB, book stores, gas stations and VVV tourist offices. Once you arrive at your destination, whether in a city or village, there is usually a street map (*platteground* sign marked with a small black "i" for information on a white base) with index, to help you find the rest of your way. *Het Shell Stratenboek* is a handy guide that includes maps of most of the towns in the Netherlands with streets listed and is available at ANWB, gas stations and some book stores. A navigation system can also be purchased to make finding your way worry free. Before purchasing, you should consider if you want a deluxe system that includes maps of the U.S.

maximum speed

end 50km/h

recommended speed

priority road

side street must yield

direction of traffic

direction of traffic

closed in both directions

do not enter

you have right of way

you must yield

rotunda

keep to the right

no passing

autos prohibited

end any prohibition

mopeds/bikes prohibited

yield to pedestrians

maximum width

residential max 15 km/h

no parking

no parking or stopping

permit required

parking disc required

Understanding the Signs

The following are some signs you will frequently see and really need to know:

Bestemming Delft, *volg pijlen*	Destination Delft, follow arrows
Denk aan uw lichten	Remember your headlights
Doorgaand verkeer	Through traffic
Doorgaand verkeer gestremd	Not a through road
Fietspad	Bicycle path—no cars
Inrit	Entrance
Invoegend werkverkeer	Construction traffic entering
Let Op!	Caution! Watch Out!
Lichten ontsteken	Turn on your headlights
Matig uw snelheid	Slow down!
Niet Parkeren	No Parking
Omleiding	Detour
Ongeval / Ongeluk	Accident
Pas Op!	Caution! Watch Out!
Rijwielpad	Bicycle and moped path—no cars or motorcycles
Uitrit (Uit)	Exit

Uitrit Vrijlaten	Do not block driveway
Verkeerssituatie gewijzigd	Traffic pattern change
Voetpad, Wandelpad	Footpath—pedestrians only
Verboden te ...	It is forbidden to....
Zachte berm	Soft shoulder

Rules of the Road

Everyone new to the Netherlands needs to understand the basic rules of the road to drive safely. You should study the booklet of traffic regulations obtainable from the KNAC (*Koninklijke Nederlandse Automobiel Club*) or ANWB (*Algemene Nederlandse Wielrijders Bond*). The Ministry of Transport and Public Works also has made "Road Traffic Signs and Regulations in the Netherlands" available online at *www.verkeerenwaterstaat.nl*. The main licensing bureau, *Centraal Bureau Rijvaardigheidsbewijzen*, also publishes a driving manual in English at *www.rijbewijs.nl*. Make sure that the theory book that you get covers the rules for licenses of class A (motorcycles) and/or B (cars). There are five classes of licenses in the Netherlands. You want a translation of the *Wegwijzer Verkeerstheorie AB* book. If you are going to be required to get a Dutch driver's license, you must make sure that you have the latest version of the book to properly prepare for the theory exam. If you do not wish to purchase these books, you can borrow them from your local library.

The Dutch style of driving may seem aggressive, unless you are coming from a place like Milan or Tokyo. You may benefit significantly from taking a few driving lessons from a driving school (*verkeersschool*). Even if you are not required to get a Dutch driver's license, a few hours with an instructor in your city will give you confidence and comfort on the roads.

Driving Tips

It is highly recommended that you read an official driving manual, but here are some brief driving tips:

Bicycles: Regardless of the situation, assume bicycles have the right of way. There are traffic lights which most cyclists obey. Some do not, however, and when that happens, the cyclist has the right of way EVEN IF he is not observing the rules. When there is an accident between a bicycle and a car, the car is most always considered at fault.

Right of Way and Priority Roads: This is probably the most important rule. As you drive you will see a yellow or orange diamond posted along the side of many roads. This indicates that you have the priority when you come upon a side street. When the priority ends you will see the double black lines slashed across the sign, indicating that from this point, cars coming in from the right have priority or right of way. Priority at a single intersection will be indicated by a sign with a heavy black arrow and a narrow line indicating the cross street. Another indication of priority is white triangles (known as shark teeth) painted on the road at intersections. If they are in your lane with the points facing you, you must yield. When driving on roads without any of these indications, the rule is that you must yield to cars coming in from your right—even if you are on what seems to be "the major road." Dutch drivers will assume that you are going to yield and will not even slow down as they come into an intersection. Stay alert to traffic on the right!

Traffic Circles: In most areas, priority in a traffic circle is given to those cars already in the rotary. You will have the white "shark teeth" in your lane and a sign telling you to yield (*rotondeverkeer heft voorrang*) or a standard triangular yield sign as you approach the circle. Pay attention to the traffic circle pattern as you approach.

Highway Travel: When you are on an A-road, you must stay as far to the right as you can, unless you are passing, and then move back into the right-hand lane. If you travel in the left lane when you should be in the right, you can be issued a traffic ticket. When you see a flashing electronic speed sign, it indicates that you must adapt your speed to what is posted. This change in speed may be a means of controlling traffic because of an accident ahead, construction, a detour, or simply that it is rush hour. Signs that are round, white and with a red rim give the speed limit, while square blue signs with a white figure are the recommended speeds. When passing on the highway, ALWAYS signal lane changes and pass on the left.

Pedestrians: At crossing areas with striped pavement (called zebra crossings), the pedestrian has the right of way as soon as he is about to cross the street. In general, you should yield to any bicycle, moped or pedestrian when you turn a corner.

Trams and Buses: Trams have priority over all other traffic. A bus has priority when it is pulling away from a stop. The bus driver will usually indicate with his turn signals that he is rejoining the flow of traffic. It is illegal to drive in a bus lane as indicated by the "closed in both directions" sign.

▸ Speed

In most towns and cities, the legal speed is 50 kph (kilometers per hour) or approximately 31 mph (miles per hour). It is 80 kph (approx. 50 mph) on two lane roads and 120 kph (approx. 74mph) on the A-roads unless you are near a city, and then it is reduced to 100 kph (approx. 62 mph). As you leave Schiphol Airport, there is a sign which gives you the international symbol for each of these driving situations and the posted speed for each one. You will see a similar sign at each country border in Europe that you cross as you travel. Pay attention to them to save yourself the expense of being stopped for speeding.

Speeding Tickets: The majority of speeders are captured on film by cameras which have been set up to capture traffic violations. The traffic tickets are sent to the owner of the car, who is held responsible. Be careful about who drives your car. If you receive a ticket by mail and do not believe that you are guilty, you can view the photo upon request at the police station. If you receive something from the Justice Department Collection Office *(Centraal Justitieel Incasso Bureau,)* do not ignore it. You will have eight weeks in which to pay the fine. If you do not pay the fine, it goes on your record and accrues interest, even if you move away. Someday down the road, when you come back to the Netherlands, you will be requested to pay the fine before you can clear customs. Alternatively, it could delay your exit from the country. So pay your tickets promptly to avoid unnecessary and costly inconvenience.

Driving Under the Influence: Laws against drinking and driving are strictly enforced in the Netherlands. The blood alcohol concentration limit is 0.05%, which may be lower than your home country. Depending on the seriousness of the offense, you will face a fine, possible imprisonment and revocation of your driver's license. Be smart when you're out on the town—use a "Bob" (designated driver), bicycle, taxi or public transportation (buses and trams run late into the night on weekends).

▸ Parking

The most important thing to know about parking is the international sign for "no parking." This red and blue circular sign has a slash across it indicating that parking is not allowed. If it has an X on it, you are not allowed to stop. In some areas, there are standard parking meters. In other areas, there will be parking regulated by blue painted curbs *(blauwe zones)* along the road. In such areas, you must have a parking disk, which is a blue plastic sleeve with a time dial on it (available in most newsstands, bookstores and tobacco shops). You set the dial to the time when you arrive and place it on your dashboard. Posted near the blue zone is a sign showing the maximum time allowed for parking. Usually this limit is 2 hours between the hours of 9:00 a.m. and 6:00 p.m. daily except on Sundays. In some situations, you will see a sign "*voor vergunning houders*" which means that parking is reserved for people with special permits.

- **Pre-Pay Machines in Parking Lots:** At certain lots and street parking locations, you must go to the *Betaald Parkeren* machine (usually near a blue sign with a white P) and insert coins for the amount of time you expect to be parked (the time of your departure will be shown on the LCD). In some cases, there is a limit on this amount. On each machine, there is a guide to the coins it will accept, how much time you get for each and the maximum available time that you can park. You then push the green button, and a small paper will be ejected on which is printed the time you expect to depart. Place this on your dashboard. In some cases, the parking places are numbered, and you are asked to enter the space number on the machine. In this case, you will be given no paper for the dashboard as the machine keeps a record. Some of these machines will allow you to pay with a Chipknip if you have a Dutch PIN card.
- **Post-Pay Machines in Parking Lots:** With post-pay machines at parking garages, you have two options. You may use a credit card to gain access to the lot and all outside

doors upon your return to the parking lot. Proceed to the exit in your car and insert the credit card in the card reader. Usually, a receipt is printed for you before the gate lifts, so be patient. Alternatively, you can push a button at the entrance gate and you will be given a card when you enter which is encoded with the time of your arrival. Before you can leave, you must pay for the parking at a yellow *Parkeerautomaat* or *Kassa* machine where you insert your card, the LCD tells you what you owe, and you pay that amount. Your parking card is then electronically canceled and you have 15 minutes to get the car out of the lot. If you do not leave before the 15 minute time is up, the card reader will reject your card and you must find someone to help you out, and usually have to pay again. In many cases, you may use your PIN card, Chipknip card or a credit card to pay the amount due for parking (especially useful for long-term parking at the airport).

- **Parking with Parkline:** An easier alternative that is available in most major cities around the country is to subscribe to a service called Parkline. Once you have subscribed, all you have to do is call them with your mobile phone and "sign in" when you wish to park on the street or in a garage. Each parking meter or garage has a number assigned to it. You simply punch in that number, wait for the recording to verify where you are, punch "1" to accept the charges, and you're on your way. You never need coins or small bills to pay the meters. Moreover, if there is a maximum time allowed on that meter (say, two hours), you can call from wherever you are to extend the time you wish to park. To stop the charges, simply call Parkline again and "sign out". Payment is automatically deducted from your bank account. For more information, go to *www.parkline.nl*.

Parking Tickets: If you receive a ticket (*Kennisgeving van Bekeuring*), hold onto it. You will be sent an *acceptgiro* (see the **Banking** chapter), or you can take the ticket into the main police station to pay in cash. Make sure you ask for a receipt for proof of payment. Respect the parking rules to avoid having your car adorned with a wheel clamp (wielklem).

▸ Detours

Occasionally because of road construction, you will find that the road is blocked with a sign stating "*doorgaand verkeer gestremd*" which means that it is difficult to get through, or you must detour (*omleiding*). Detour signs will be orange or yellow arrows with a number to follow to allow you to continue. It can be confusing if you cannot read Dutch and are forced to detour, so it is very important that you remember the number which is associated with the city that you are traveling to and then follow those numbers through the detour and back to the main route.

▸ Seat Belts

Seat belts are mandatory, both in the front and in the back for all ages. Children under age twelve or under 1.5 meters tall (5 feet) may not sit in the front seat. There is a fine per person for not buckling your seat belt. Children under 1.35 meters tall (4 feet 5 inches) must sit in an approved car seat.

Other Useful Laws to Know

- Unlocked cars parked on the street are illegal.
- Mobile telephones may only be used with a hands-free device while driving.
- You may not drive in the breakdown lane.
- Turns are made in front of (not behind) a policeman that is directing traffic.
- Solid white lines mean no passing.
- U-turns are allowed except across solid white lines and where posted.
- You must carry a triangular warning sign in your trunk and if you have an accident or a breakdown, it must be placed 30 meters behind your car.
- Headlights are recommended in dark, overcast, or rain, even if it is "day time".
- No one under age 18 may drive a car, even if they have a valid license from their home country.
- No one under age 16 may drive a motorized bicycle (*bromfiets*).
- If a policeman wants you to stop, he drives in front of you with a follow (*volg*) sign lit in the rear window.
- Police can stop anyone for random checks of licenses, registration, or alcohol consumption, and you must comply.

Driver's License

Residents of the Netherlands are required to have a Dutch driver's license in order to own a car and drive here. You may not drive in the Netherlands until you do, unless you fall under one of a number of exceptions to this rule:

- If you have a license from one of the member states in the European Union or the European Free Trade Association (*Europeese Vrijhandels Associatie*), the Netherlands Antilles or Aruba, you may drive using it for up to one year from when you register as a Dutch resident.
- If you have a license from a country outside of the E.U., (e.g., the U.S. or Japan), which has an agreement with the Netherlands for proficiency in driving, or if you are part of the diplomatic corps or are here with NATO, you may drive on your home country license for six months from when you register as a resident. At the conclusion of this period, you are required to acquire a Dutch driving license by "exchange."

If you do not fit into any of the above categories, once you register with the city hall (*gemeentehuis*), you may not drive until you have passed the Dutch written test and the physical driving exam. Keep in mind that once your home country license is no longer recognized as valid, you are not insured when you drive any vehicle.

There are several categories of license in the Netherlands. Driving a car is category B. An international driving license is not valid for driving in the Netherlands once you have established residency. It may, however, be useful in driving in other European countries. It can be obtained by paying a small fee and providing passport photos to your national automobile club in your home country or at the ANWB office in the Netherlands. It is only valid for one year, but you may renew it.

Exchanging Your License: If you benefit from one of the above exceptions, you need only exchange your home country license for a Dutch one. At your *gemeentehuis*, request the forms for the license exchange. The first form is a certificate of health (statement of capability) which you complete and send in. It will be returned to you within a few weeks. You then return to the *gemeentehuis* with the following:

- License application
- Two passport photos
- Your valid home country license
- The returned health form
- Copy of a letter from your employer or the tax office in Heerlen stating that you are entitled to the 30 percent ruling benefits
- Money to pay the processing fee

As soon as the processing fee is paid, the whole package is sent to the Minister of Transport. If you want to get your home country license back, you can submit at the same time, a letter requesting the return of the old license (a good reason is that it is an aid in renting a car in your home country). Your new Dutch license will come in the mail to you in four to eight weeks.

To Get a Dutch License as the Dutch Do: If you do not qualify to exchange your license, it is best to start the process of acquiring a Dutch license during the first six months you are in the country. Contact a driving school (*rijschool*) for assistance. They will be able to guide you through the long process and you will take the final driving test in one of their vehicles.

Regardless of your past driving history, you will need to take two exams which can be arranged in English. The first is a theory (rules of the road) exam given by computer and video of 50 questions. The test is designed to be very challenging. If you pass this test (45 out of 50 questions correct), you get a Certificate of Theory Proficiency which you must have to proceed. This certificate is valid for 12 months. This certificate does not permit you to drive unless you have a valid foreign license as there are no learner's permits in the Netherlands. The second test is a driving proficiency test. The proficiency test is 30 minutes of driving with a representative from the CBR. You will also need the following:

- Certificate of Theory Proficiency
- Medical health declaration
- Proof of residency
- Two passport photos

Your Old License: Keep a photocopy of your home country driving license in case you need to obtain a replacement as well as a copy of your Dutch license. U.S. citizens can renew their home country license by mail; go online to the Department of Motor Vehicles in the state where it was issued to find instructions.

If You Lose Your License: If you lose your Dutch license, report the loss to the police station in your home town. The police will give you a special report document. With the police document, two passport photos and your passport, you can then apply for a new driving license at the *gemeentehuis* (as you did initially). It will take a couple of days before you can collect it.

Importing a Car

First, you must have owned the vehicle for six months prior to importation and you cannot sell it any sooner than one year from importation. Secondly, you will want to import your auto as part of a household goods shipment to simplify the importation process. If you are coming from a European country on the continent, it is quite simple to transfer registration, but from the U.K. or U.S. there will be costs of adaptation. If you are coming from other countries, and will be here for a short period of time, it might not be worth it. The cost of transport, the import taxes (if it is relatively new), cost of adaptation to the Dutch environmental standards and safety features (different headlights, required rear fog lights, VIN stamped in the engine compartment, etc.), and the cost of taking it back with you may not be cost effective.

If you decide to import a car, there are several steps involved:

- The car must be cleared through customs through the *Invoer en Inspectie* department.
- You should have auto insurance coverage when you resume possession of your vehicle.
- You must take the vehicle to be cleared for local driving by the *Rijksdienst voor het Wegverkeer (www.rdw.nl)*. They will tell you what adaptations you need to make to the car.
- You then take the car to a dealer or a local garage for those modifications.
- Take the car to be re-inspected at the RDW and have the modifications accepted.
- File paperwork with Dutch customs (*www.douane.nl*) and they will determine if you have to pay any importation tax.
- Once the *Douane* finishes their paperwork, you will be sent registration papers. These include your Dutch license plate numbers.
- You may go to a dealership or some auto parts stores to have your plate made or ordered.
- You will also have to pay road tax (*wegenbelasting*). *Wegenblasting* is based on the weight of your vehicle and the type of fuel it uses. Generally this tax is paid quarterly and is obligatory.

▸ Buying a Car

If you purchase a car through a dealership, the dealership will take care of many of the details of registration, e.g., new license plates and tax forms. If you purchase a car from an individual, you are responsible for making certain that you and the car are legal, including registration, insurance and car inspection (*Algemene Periodieke Keuring or APK*). You can check out the local garages and auto dealers near your home for used cars. That way you can begin to build a relationship with them for when you need to service the cars. Another potential source for used cars is schools and clubs where outgoing expatriates advertise cars and used household goods.

▸ Registering a Car

As of June 1, 2008, to register a car you need to go to RDW at *www.rdw.nl* or call their office to get the forms to transfer the title of the vehicle to your name. You must have *Deel II* from the original owner, which he/she must have signed, and the copy of *Deel III*, if they have it, or the *overschrijvingbewijs* (which replaced the *Deel III*), a valid license and residence card/passport. You must also pay a road tax which is calculated on the weight of your car. When you get your registration, you will see that there are three parts to it.

- ***Deel I*** – This is the title and description of your car. You must have it with you when driving. If you live in a high theft area, don't leave it in the car, but keep it with you. If you are stopped by the police, this is one of the papers they will want to see.
- ***Deel II*** – This document has information about the owner. You must have it with you when you are driving. If stopped by the police, the *Deel II* is another paper they will want to see. *Deel II* can help prove ownership if the car is stolen. It also has an application blank for changing the car title if you sell it.
- ***Overschrijvingbewijs*** – This document has all the car information. Do not carry this with you; keep it in a safe place at home. If you sell the car you must use this in the transfer.

▸ Insuring a Car

The Netherlands has compulsory liability insurance. This means you must have Third Party Insurance, which can be arranged through an insurance agent (*verzekeringadviseur*), ANWB, bank or even the post office. Insurance is initially priced at the maximum and then discounts are available if you have a good driving record. It is recommended that you get a letter from your former insurance agent stating how long you have been accidentfree.

Types of Insurance:

- **Third Party Liability** (*WA Verzekering*) covers the damage to the other car, but not yours. This is a good choice if you own an older car.
- **All Risk** (*WA plus CASCO*) covers damages to your car as well as the other car. This type of insurance is best for a new car or car you would repair if it were in a fender bender.
- **All Risk Plus** (*WA plus mini-CASCO or WA Extra*) covers you and the other party, plus joy riding, theft, fire, storm damage, broken windows, etc.

Once you obtain insurance, you will receive a green card (known as the International Motor Insurance Card). You must always carry this card with you. It is also a good idea to notify your insurance agent when you travel. There are some eastern European countries where the insurance will not apply. When you arrange for insurance with the agent, be certain to get some accident forms in English.

Automobile Accidents

If you have an accident, Dutch insurance law requires that you and the other party agree on what happened before you leave the scene. If you cannot agree, a policeman will facilitate an agreement. Be certain that you do not leave the scene of the accident until you and the other person have agreed on what happened and have signed the accident form, which you should always carry in your automobile. You must turn this form in to your insurance agent.

Annual Inspection of Automobiles

All cars which are three years old or older must undergo an annual inspection for road worthiness called the APK *(Algemene Periodieke Keuring)*. You will be notified when it is time to visit one of the many authorized garages. The car is checked for safety, emissions and structural integrity. On passing, the garage will give you a certificate for your records.

Auto Clubs

- **ANWB (*www.anwb.nl*):** This is a membership organization. It is best known for the yellow emergency telephones along the highways. When you have a breakdown, you call and one of their traveling repair shops (*wegenwacht*) will come to help. There are many other benefits of membership. They can provide, in English, further information on importing a car from your home country or buying a new or second hand car here. They operate various safety testing facilities, so if you are thinking about buying a used car, they can inspect it and give you an opinion on needed repairs. They give lessons in driving, and have special classes on slippery roads and other driving hazards. They provide guidebooks, maps and trip planning services. They sell insurance which gives you many options—from getting a rental car (if you are in an accident) to medical coverage while traveling. The ANWB is a sister organization to the AAA in the United States. It will therefore provide 24-hour emergency assistance and other services to members of AAA.
- **KNAC (*www.knac.nl*):** Provides maps, guide books, trip planning services and insurance. They publish books in English on Dutch road signs and on the process of getting a Dutch driver's license.

Car Maintenance

Gasoline: There are lots of gas stations in the Netherlands, some familiar chains and some not so familiar. You can purchase gas with a PIN card, cash or credit card in most places, and, after hours some stations even have a machine which will give you access to the gasoline using your PIN or credit card. *Benzine* is the standard gasoline (or petrol) for most cars. Unleaded (*loodvrij* or *ongelood)* is available in standard (Euro) or premium (Superplus). Diesel is also available. When buying *benzine*, you purchase it in liters: 3.8 liters is equal to one U.S. gallon, 4.5 liters is equal to one Imperial gallon. When adding oil (*olie*) to the engine, you add it in liters or half-liters.

Service Stations: Gas stations are separate from repair stations in most cases. Most garages which repair cars specialize in a specific make and work from flat rate manuals in calculating the time needed for repairs. When you take your car in for service, you should be certain to specify exactly what you want done. Garages often will not do unauthorized repairs. Look under *Auto reparatie* in the Yellow Pages for a dealer or an independent service garage near your home. There are also special shops for tires, mufflers or shock absorbers. You can find local repair places like this in the Yellow Pages under *Uitlaat.*

▸ Safety and Police Checks (*Controle*)

Occasionally the Dutch police stop cars for spot checks:

- **Alcohol:** The penalty for driving while intoxicated is considerable and the law is rigidly enforced. If you are stopped and asked to take a breathalyzer test, you are required to cooperate.
- **Car Safety:** Police have the authority to determine on the spot if your car is unsafe, e.g., too much rust, low tire tread or other road unworthiness such as head lamps out. The police will also check to be sure that everyone is wearing seat belts. There is a stiff fine for failure to do so.
- **Registration:** You may be stopped and asked to show your registration papers. If your car does not conform to the regulations, you can be fined and the car can be impounded, regardless of the nationality of the driver.

Useful Contact Information

Amsterdam Schiphol Airport
☎ (0900) 0141 (€0,40 per minute)
www.schiphol.com

Eindhoven Airport
☎ (040) 291 98 18
www.eindhovenairport.com

Maastricht Aachen Airport
☎ (043) 358 99 99
www.maa.nl

Rotterdam Airport
☎ (010) 446 34 44
www.rotterdam-airport.nl

ANWB
☎ (088) 269 22 22
ANWB Wegenwacht road breakdown service: ☎ (088) 269 28 88
www.anwb.nl

KNAC
☎ (070) 383 16 12
www.knac.nl

Nederlandse Spoorwegen (NS) Domestic Trains
☎ (0900) 202 11 63 (€0,10 per minute)
www.ns.nl

Hispeed International Trains
☎ (0900) 92 96 (€0,35 per minute)
www.nshispeed.nl

Public Transportation Hotline
All Dutch routes on buses, trams, metros and trains
☎ (0900) 92 92 (€0,70 per minute)
www.9292ov.nl

OVChipKaarts (Dutch Transport Payment System)
www.ov-chipkaart.nl

Rijksdienst voor het Wegverkeer Bureau or Invoer en Inspectie Bureau (Import and Inspection Bureau)
☎ (0900) 07 39 (€0,10 per minute)
www.rdw.nl

Ministrie van Verkeer en Waterstaat (Ministry of Transport, Public Works and Water)
Provides "Road Traffic Signs and Regulations in the Netherlands" online
☎ (070) 351 61 71
www.verkeerenwaterstaat.nl

In cooperation with Chipdata

Chapter 9

Communication

Not only is staying connected with friends and family back home a priority, but connecting with services here in the Netherlands is also very important. In this chapter you'll learn about postal and telephone services, computer power requirements, Internet access, email, television and radio. The Netherlands has some of the highest Internet and mobile phone use in the world.

The Post Office

In the center of almost every major town you will usually find a main post office (*postkantoor*). In addition, there are several branch offices within larger residential and shopping areas of the city. There are also some shops that have small post offices where you can buy stamps and mail small packages. Most shops that sell greeting cards and postcards will also sell you postage stamps (*postzegels*) for the cards you buy. Select grocery stores, book stores and tobacco shops also sell stamps.

You may be surprised by the number and variety of services offered by the Dutch post office. You can, of course, mail letters and packages, but you can also pay your bills, transfer money, carry out car purchase and registration transactions, buy a bus or tram card (*strippenkaart*), make photocopies and send faxes. Opening times and post office locations can be found at *www.tntpost.nl*. Postal holidays are the same as banking holidays. See our **Banking** chapter for a list of these holidays.

Mailboxes

Mail is not picked up at your home mailbox. If you want to mail something, you must use one of the orange/red rectangular mailboxes (*brievenbussen*) located on many street corners and at every post office. Each mail box has two letter slots. The one on the right is for local mail and there is a list of the post codes which constitute local mail. The slot on the left, *overige postcodes*, is for all other destinations including international mail.

Mail is picked up once a day, usually around 6:00 p.m. and there will be a sign on the box showing the next day and time of pick up. No mail is picked up on Saturday, but mail is picked up again on Sunday evening.

Mail is delivered Monday through Saturday, excluding holidays. Domestic service is very fast, usually taking only one day for delivery. After settling in to your new abode, you may be deluged with unwanted advertisements and free local newspapers. If you'd like to control if you receive junk mail, go to the town hall (*gemeentehuis*) and ask for a mailbox sticker. *Ja/Nee* stickers allow free newspapers to be delivered, but not advertisements. *Nee/Nee* stickers stop all unaddressed mail.

Addressing Mail

To address a letter sent to another Netherlands address, follow this example:

Familie B. van der Laan	(Name)
Enveloppestraat 1	(Street then house number)
1234 AB PAKKETSTAD	(Postcode then town name)

Always write your own address, using the above format, on letters and packages so they can be returned if there is a problem. Return addresses should be on the front top left-hand corner of an envelope or a package, or on the back side of an envelope.

To address a letter or package to an address outside the Netherlands, be sure to write the country of destination, in capital letters, on the last line of the address.

Business Reply Mail

You don't need to pay any postage when the address contains an *antwoordnummer*. An envelope or postcard may have a little box in the upper right hand corner in which something like *postzegel is niet nodig* or *mag ongefrankeerd verzonden worden* is written. These can be mailed in the Netherlands without a stamp.

Postal Services

Letters

When sending letters outside Europe, you have two choices: Priority or Standard. Priority offers the fastest service. You get a Priority sticker when you buy stamps for outside the Netherlands. Within Europe, all letters go Priority except for printed matter that can be sent Standard.

Allow two to three working days for Priority letters to be delivered in Western Europe. For letters to the U.S., allow four to six working days, Canada five to six working days, Japan four to five working days and Australia six to eight working days. For information on delivery times to other countries, check the post office website at *www.tntpost.nl*.

Registered Mail: It is also possible to send a letter by registered mail. For an additional fee, you can also request a signed return receipt (*bericht van ontvangst*).

Packages

Packages (*pakjes/pakketten*) are any pieces of mail that do not fit into a standard letter box. Packages for destinations outside the Netherlands can be sent by one of these two services: Priority or Standard.

All packages mailed in the Netherlands are registered with a bar code sticker placed upon them. You get a copy of the number of the package and the bar code in case the package is lost. If it is lost, in most cases, there is some kind of remuneration. For priority packages, you also have the option of requesting insurance (*verzekerd vervoer*). You also have a choice of sending your printed matter (*drukwerk*) by standard mail, but it makes very little difference in the cost.

Customs Value: Check carefully for the customs value limit in the country where the package is being sent. To avoid charging duty and tax to the recipient, the package should be marked "Unsolicited Gift—Value Less Than_____." List the value in local currency.

The reverse is also true. Be careful when ordering something for yourself by mail. Also, notify friends and family back home to carefully and accurately fill out customs forms when mailing packages to you or you will not get the package until you pay the tax due.

Mailing Boxes: The post office sells sturdy cardboard mailing boxes of various sizes that come with enough tape and string for a perfect seal. All you supply is the carefully wrapped contents. Prices are quite reasonable and they are perfect for mailing those wonderful Dutch treasures to family and friends back home. Remember that pressure-sensitive filament or reinforced paper tapes must be used to seal packages. Cellophane and masking tapes are not acceptable because they break easily.

Package Delivery: If you happen to be out on the day a package is delivered to your home, the mail carrier will try to leave the package with a neighbor. If your neighbor is not home, you will receive a note advising you that the mail carrier tried to deliver the package and they will check one of two options: Delivery service (*Bezorgservice*) or Pick-up service (*Afhaalservice*). If *Bezorgservice* is indicated, they will try again to redeliver the next day (excluding Sunday). If they cannot deliver it the second time, you will receive an *Afhaalservice* notice instructing you to pick up the package at a specified post office (usually the one nearest you) after a certain hour. If you do not want your package left with a neighbor, tell the sender to write *alleen huisadres* on the package. When you pick up a package, take along the notice plus an identification card.

December Stamps

Every December the postal service sells December stamps (*decemberzegels*) in sheets of 20 stamps for normal-sized greeting cards. These entitle you to send unsealed envelopes or postcards within the Netherlands for less than the normal price of a stamp. These stamps are only valid for such usage during December of the year in which they are issued. After that December they are still usable, but only for the printed face value (purchase price) of the stamps.

Children Stamps

Every year starting in November and before Christmas, children all over Holland knock on doors and take orders for children's stamps (*kinderzegels*). Part of the money you pay goes to the post office and the rest goes to children's charities. The allocations are stated on the stamps and they will be delivered to you in time to use on Christmas cards.

Change of Address

Check online at *www.tntpost.nl* or get a brochure at the post office for the *verhuisservice*, a packet that contains the forms you will need to change your mailing address. Apply at least one month in advance. The post office will forward your mail within the Netherlands free for one month. There is a fee for international forwarding. In addition, they will also contact businesses such as newspapers, the ANWB and charitable organizations advising them of your address change. There is a multi-part list in the packet. For a fee, you also have the option of having them make postcards for you to send to people announcing the change, and having them forward your mail for longer than the standard period. Once you file the form with them, they will send you a letter confirming everything you specified.

Holding Mail

If you plan to be out of town for a week or more, you can have your mail held for you until you get back. You can choose between picking your mail up at the post office or having it all delivered after you return. You must apply for the *Bewaarservice* at least seven days before you want the service to begin. To sign up go online to *www.tntpost.nl/voorhuis/*. There is a charge for this service.

The Telephone

Land Line Phone Service

KPN (*www.kpn.com*) is the major provider of in-home land line phone service, however, there are other companies to choose from as shown on *http://telecom.pagina.nl*. The Netherlands is overflowing with phone stores, and many of them can help you decide whom to choose for your phone services including mobile phones. The KPN store is called Primafoon and is usually located on the major shopping street in town. It may be easier to go into one of these stores to set up your account than attempting to handle the transaction over the phone. You will need to bring your passport and proof of residency. You may be required to pay a deposit, but it is fully refundable in one year if there are no problems with the account. You can arrange to have your bill deducted automatically from your bank account or pay by *acceptgiro*.

There are a variety of calling plans available with rates that vary depending on how many calls you make. Which one is best for you will depend on how much calling you will do in your local area and further afield in the Netherlands. You may consider bundling your phone, Internet and cable TV together as one package. There are many models and styles of phones from which to choose. Equipment can be purchased at the telephone store or at other electronics dealers. Phone stores also rent phones and answering machines, but make sure that the rental period meets your needs. Services such as voice mail and call waiting are also available.

Keep in mind that you can also shop around for long distance companies, some of which offer very competitive rates to the U.S., U.K. and other countries. Many companies now offer incredibly low rates utilizing Voice-Over-Internet-Protocol (VOIP). One such company is *www.bel1649.nl*. You can register online in English; to make calls you dial 1649 before the phone number to access their system. You are emailed a monthly statement and payment is automatically deducted from your bank account. Other companies include: *www.budget-phone.nl*, *www.tele2.nl* and *www.telediscount.nl*.

Another VOIP service that offers a wide range of calling options is **Skype** at *www.skype.com*. Skype also offers free computer-to-computer video calling. With a webcam for your computer and Skype's free software, you can make video calls to friends and family with a similar set-up. What a great way to stay connected!

▸ Cellular Phone Service

Cellular phones are incredibly popular in the Netherlands. If you already have an older cell phone from your home country, it probably will not work here unless it is a GSM phone, dual band, with 900/1800 frequency. If you have a U.S.-issued GSM mobile phone, it operates at 1900 MHz and is incompatible with the European GSM services. CDMA-based mobile phones won't work either. Many international travelers choose an unlocked, tri-band cell phone. This lets you use SIM (Subscriber Identity Module) cards from just about any country and offers the simplicity of only having to deal with one phone.

The mobile options are plentiful: prepaid, SIM-card-only contract, and phone plus contract to name just a few. To purchase a service contract, you will need your passport, proof of residence and a bank account in your name. Spend a few minutes at the local phone store to scope out the offerings to see what is right for you. In addition, whichever phone you buy, most sales people can set it to use the English language option if desired.

Major Cellular Phone Companies

Hi Society	*www.hi.nl*	**Tele2**	*www.tele2.nl*
KPN	*www.kpn.com*	**Telfort**	*www.telfort.nl*
T-Mobile	*www.t-mobile.nl*	**Vodafone**	*www.vodafone.nl*

▸ Directory Assistance

If you get completely frustrated when trying to use Dutch phone books, you can call directory assistance and ask the operator to look up a number for you. Operators are multilingual and very helpful. There is a cost for this service. Operators checking for national numbers will want to know the city and possibly the street address of the person or business you are calling.

- Directory assistance within the Netherlands: ☎ (0900) 80 08
- Directory assistance for international numbers: ☎ (0900) 84 18

▸ Online Directory Assistance

Online versions of both white and yellow page phone books are available. When you access *www.telefoongids.nl*, you have three options: *De Telefoongids* (for an individual), *De Bedrijvengids* (for a business), or a web search. You can also use *www.goudengids.nl*, which offers similar search capabilities. Here is a translation of the search fields:

De Telefoongids		*De Bedrijvengids*	
Wie	Who	*Wat*	Company, keyword or name
Plaats	Where	*Regio*	City/Town
Zoek	Search	*Zoek*	Search

▸ Telephone Recordings

Frequently when dialing an information number the first thing you hear will be the following recordings:

Dit nummer kost # cents per minuut...	This number costs # cents per minute.
U bent verbonden met....	You have reached... .
Een ogenblik, alstublieft...	One moment, please.
Er zijn nog acht wachtenden voor u...	You are ninth in line.
In gesprek...	The line is busy.

Calling Within the Netherlands

All phone numbers in the Netherlands are ten digits made up of two parts: the city code number (*netnummer*) and the individual house or business number (*abonneenummer*). For example, a phone number is: (070) 665 55 55. The *netnummer*, 070 (either three or four digits) indicates the city, in this case, The Hague area. If you are calling a number that has the same *netnummer* as the phone you are calling from, say within The Hague, you only need to dial the subscriber number (*abonneenummer*), 665 55 55. A complete list of area codes (*netnummers*) can be found in the white pages.

Dial 112 For Health, Fire And Police Emergencies

112 is the single European emergency phone number:

- To contact any emergency service
- In any EU country (except certain regions in Bulgaria)
- From fixed phones, including payphones, or mobile phones
- Free of charge

When can you call 112?

Dial 112 in any emergency requiring an ambulance, the fire brigade or the police:

- You have been involved in or have witnessed a serious road accident
- You notice a building on fire
- You spot a house being broken into

Do not call 112 for the following:

- Traffic reports
- Weather reports
- General information and queries

What happens when you call 112?

- A specially trained operator will answer your call. The operator will either deal with the request directly or transfer you to the most appropriate emergency service.
- Operators are increasingly able to answer 112 calls in more than one language.
- **Give your name, address, telephone number.** It is necessary to identify callers to avoid confusion—the same incident may already have been reported by a number of people.
- **Do not hang up if you (or your child) call 112 by mistake!** Tell the operator that everything is OK. Otherwise, emergency assistance may have to be sent out to check there is no problem.

Calling Internationally

You can dial direct to any country from the Netherlands. Here's how:

- Dial 00 for an international line.
- Dial the country code and area/city code.
- Dial the individual telephone number. Example: If you would like to call your Grandma Alice in Peninsula, Ohio, U.S., you must dial: 00 1 (216) 555 0000.

- To call within Europe, be sure to drop the zero before the city code. It will sometimes be written as (0) as in +44 (0)20 5555 5000. Example: To call London, you would dial 00 44 20 5555 5000.

You can find a very complete listing of country codes, selected city codes and time differences in the back section of the white pages under *Netnummers Buitenland*.

Operator Assisted Calls

To place an operator assisted call dial: ☎ (0800) 04 10. There will be an extra charge for person-to-person and collect calls, and a higher per-minute rate will be charged for utilizing operator assistance. Note, too, that if you receive a collect call, the charge is higher than if the call was made by dialing direct.

International Calls to the Netherlands

If you expect your family and friends from home to keep in touch by phone, be sure to pass on the following information:

International dialing is accomplished by dialing first the international access number for the country you are in, then the country code for the Netherlands (31), then the city code (*netnummer*) without the zero, and the individual number (*abonneenummer*).

To dial direct to the Netherlands from the United States, dial 011 to get an international line, then 31 (country code), then the city code (drop the first zero) and the individual number. For example, if your phone number in Delft is (015) 262 5555, your family would dial: 011 31 15 262 5555.

Pay Phones

As more people carry cell phones, pay phones are becoming harder to find. Most pay phones no longer accept coins, but require phone cards that can be purchased at the post office, VVV, Primafoon, major train stations, some grocery stores or wherever you see a *telefoonkaarten* sign. Card-operated phones may also accept Chipknip (see the chapter on **Banking**) or credit cards. Some phones allow you to select English instructions by pushing the appropriate button.

Dutch-English Letter Pronunciation Alphabet

Knowledge of this alphabet can come in very handy, especially when spelling over the phone. In particular, it is recommended that you learn *Anna* for A, *Eduard* for E, *Izaak* for I and *Victor* for V as these letters carry the greatest potential for confusion. We recommend that you keep a photocopy of this alphabet near your phone.

	Dutch	English		Dutch	English
A	*Anna*	Alpha	N	*Nico*	November
B	*Bernard*	Bravo	O	*Otto*	Oscar
C	*Cornelis*	Charlie	P	*Pieter*	Papa
D	*Dirk*	Delta	Q	*Quotiënt*	Quebec
E	*Eduard*	Echo	R	*Rudolf*	Romeo
F	*Ferdinand*	Foxtrot	S	*Simon*	Sierra
G	*Gerard*	Golf	T	*Theodor*	Tango
H	*Hendrik*	Hotel	U	*Utrecht*	Uniform
I	*Izaak*	India	V	*Victor*	Victor
J	*Jan*	Juliet	W	*Willem*	Whisky
K	*Karel*	Kilo	X	*Xantippe*	X-ray
L	*Leonard*	Lima	IJ	*Ijmuiden*	Eye
M	*Marie*	Mike	Y	*Ypsilon*	Yankee
			Z	*Zaandam*	Zulu

▸ Special Telephone Numbers

There are three kinds of telephone prefixes:

- ☎ 0800 is for toll-free numbers.
- ☎ 0900 is for toll numbers with charges applicable. Access to 0900 numbers can be blocked from your account, however, remember that would mean you couldn't call the phone company or the bank.
- ☎ 06 is the prefix for mobile phones.

▸ Phone Books

New telephone books are available yearly. If yours is not delivered to you, call ☎ (020) 408 64 00 for the Telephone Book (*Telefoongids* or *www.detelefoongids.nl*), and ☎ (020) 567 67 67 for the Yellow Pages (*Gouden Gids* or *www.goudengids.nl*). Books for your area are free, but for a fee you may get others. Once on the list of subscribers, these books will automatically be delivered each year.

Tips for Using Dutch Phone Books: First, make sure you are looking in the right city, as most phone books cover several communities. Dutch phone books are arranged—for the most part—alphabetically. However, keep in mind: Dutch "ij" is equivalent to "y" and is listed alphabetically with "y." i.e., "*Kontrast*" comes before "*Konijnenburg*" in the White Pages.

When a name begins with prefixes such as *van*, *de*, *der*, and *ter*, the prefix is treated as an initial. For instance, Jan van der Molen is written as Molen, j. vd in the phone book, and listed under "M" for Molen.

When more than one telephone subscriber has the same surname, they are listed alphabetically by street name. For example, using the surname de Jong:

- Jong, h. de, v almondestr 62
- Jong, a. de, v almondestr 62/1
- Jong, prof dr d. de, botaniestr 40
- Jong, j j c. de, zomerdykhof 1
- Jong-bennewitz, p. de, papenstr 20/k10
- Jong-van oosten, j. de, a jacobsstr 136
- Jong-thoolen, y e l. de, a v scheltemapln 12

Abbreviations Used in Dutch Phone Books:

Abbreviation	Dutch term	English translation
afd.	*afdeling*	department
b.g.g.	*bij geen gehoor*	if no answer, call...
boekh.	*boekhouding*	accounting
eig.	*eigenaar*	owner
ink.	*inkoop*	purchasing
kant.	*Kantoor*	office
mag.	*Magazijn*	warehouse/store
spr.u.	*spreekuur*	time to call or visit without an appointment
volg. afspr.	*volgens afspraak*	hours by appointment
werkpl.	*werkplaats*	workshop
woonh.	*woonhuis*	residence

Computers

▸ 220V versus 110V

The power supply in the Netherlands is 220V and 50hz. This can be a problem for older computers purchased in the U.S., so be sure to check your laptop, CPU and all peripherals to see if they self-adapt to 220V. If not, you will need a transformer to adapt the power from 220V to 110V. This should be a heavy duty transformer, not one used for shavers and small appliances. Failure to supply the correct power to your computer and peripherals will cause a blown power supply in your home, not to mention a nonfunctioning computer. If your computer equipment can handle 220V, you should only need plug adaptors, which can be bought in specialty electronics stores.

Internet Access

There are reputedly more than 100 Internet Service Providers (ISPs) in the Netherlands. Some major ISPs are:

- **KPN** (*www.kpn.com*)
- **XS4ALL** (*www.xs4all.nl*)
- **Ziggo** (*www.ziggo.nl*)

A visit to the Primafoon store can help you sort through some of the options. High speed broadband services are available or you can choose service delivered via cable modem. Depending on which service you decide upon, you will pay the phone company, an ISP or the cable company. You can arrange to have your bill deducted automatically from your bank account or pay by *acceptgiro*. It can be a slow process to have your Internet connection activated at your new home, so in the meantime you might want to access a computer at a friend's, the library or an Internet café.

Email

After settling in, you will no doubt want to email everyone at home. A quick option is to set up a free email account with Yahoo, Google or another web-based email provider before you move. These accounts are accessible from any computer with Internet access and will assure that you are not without email as you make the transition to living in the Netherlands.

Computer Stores

Each town has at least one computer store. Some of the larger chains to be found in the larger cities include Media Markt (*www.mediamarkt.nl*) and Computerland (*www.computer-land.nl*). To find your local computer store, service center or a place to purchase software, look in the Yellow Pages under *Computer*.

Television and Radio

You will be able to watch many English-language programs and movies from the U.S., U.K. and Australia while living in the Netherlands. Films are broadcast in their original language with Dutch subtitles. Reruns and special programs of worldwide interest are also shown.

TV Compatibility

The Dutch television and video format is PAL, and is not compatible with NTSC (U.S. and Japanese system). There is also a compatibility issue with DVDs from a region outside of Europe. You might want to consider purchasing a multi-system television set, DVD and/or video player to play movies from your home country as well as the Netherlands. You will also want to investigate compatibility of any video gaming systems you might wish to bring.

Cable TV

Cable TV is available throughout the Netherlands. Without it, you can receive some broadcasts, but the quality will not be very good. Look under *Kabeltelevisie* in the pink pages of your telephone book. Some major cable or digital TV providers are:

- **KPN** (*www.kpn.com*)
- **UPC** (*www.upc.nl*)
- **Ziggo** (*www.ziggo.nl*)

Each city decides what channels to offer the people of their jurisdiction. About 30 channels are available. If you want more channels, you can get satellite TV. Depending on where you live, you may receive the following channels:

Dutch Stations: Films and documentaries broadcast in original version with Dutch subtitles.

- *Nederland* 1, 2, 3
- Net 5
- RTL 4, 5
- SBS 6
- Veronica

Belgian Stations:

- Belgie 1, 2
- Ketnet/Canvas in original version with Dutch subtitles; main language: French

British Stations:

- BBC 1, 2,
- BBC World, Prime

Other Stations:

• Animal Planet	English
• CNN International	American news channel
• Discovery Channel	English
• EuroSport	Dutch and English
• MTV Music Television	English
• National Geographic	Dutch and English
• Nickelodeon	Children's channel, Dutch and English

Subscriber-Only Channels

There are also are subscriber-only channels that broadcast films and special programs. For more information, call your cable provider or look in the Yellow Pages.

Radio

With the advent of broadband, many radio stations offer live streams online 24 hours a day. You might even be able to listen to your favorite radio station from your home country via the Internet. Radio broadcasts in English are dominated by the BBC.

TV and Radio Guides

Dutch-language weekly TV and radio guides are easily understood, and can be bought at newsstands, bookstores, and supermarkets, and are also available by subscription. Newspapers also carry daily TV listings. Each Dutch broadcasting corporation makes its own guide which lists all programs on all channels. You can check the TV or radio stations' websites for schedules. Also, there is an online guide at *www.tvgids.nl*.

Useful Websites

www.tntpost.nl	National postal service
http://telecom.startpagina.nl/	Lists major telecom companies in the Netherlands
www.bel1649.nl	Discounted long distance phone service
www.telediscount.nl	Discounted long distance phone service
www.budgetphone.nl	Discounted long distance phone service
www.tele2.nl	Land line and mobile phone, Internet, Cable TV
www.kpn.com	Land line and mobile phone, Internet, Cable TV
www.upc.nl	Land line and mobile phone, Internet, Cable TV
www.ziggo.nl	Land line phone, Internet, Cable TV
www.t-mobile.nl	Mobile phone service
www.vodafone.nl	Mobile phone service
www.telfort.nl	Mobile phone, Internet
www.xs4all.nl	Internet Service Provider

Chapter 10

Children

Bringing a child to the Netherlands or having a baby here can add a level of concern that you might not otherwise have. There are a lot of ways to find what you need. In the chapter on **Health Care**, you'll find specifics about children's care and pregnancy. Talk to the people at ACCESS about their childbirth and recovery classes. Join the Moms, Pops and Tots program through your local American Women's Club or in another club listed in our **International Education** or **Church and Community** chapters. Most of all, remember that you are not alone; there are lots of other mothers and dads feeling a little overwhelmed by the unfamiliarity of it all. Below you will find information about the available support systems of bringing up a child in a foreign country and how to have some fun, too.

Babysitting

There is a range in the types of help that you might decide you need, from occasional nights out, to after school care, to full-time housekeeper. Below are some ideas on how to find what you need.

Keep in mind that the very best way to obtain reliable help is by asking friends and colleagues for recommendations. Many international schools have a list of student babysitters as does ACCESS and many of the women's clubs listed in our **Church and Community** chapter. If you live around an academic community, you can place an ad in the student paper. You or your employed partner can ask in the workplace for young people looking to earn a few extra euros. Part-time child care can usually be found in your neighborhood. Many foreign teenagers will babysit. Nearly all Dutch teenagers speak English and are delighted to earn their own spending money. As with any caregiver, take particular care to be explicit in your instructions since they may not have a lot of experience with children.

One professional child care option is to use a "guest parent" (*gastouder*). They usually watch several children in their home and the fees are very reasonable and sometimes tax deductible depending on your job situation. Contact your local child care center (*Stichting Kinderopvang*) or City Hall (*Gemeente*) for a list of registered *Gastouders*. If you have some knowledge of Dutch, you may also search for *Gastouders* in your area at *www.gastouderopvang.nl* or *www.flexmoeders.nl*.

Day Nurseries, Play Groups and After School Care

Your local City Hall (*Gemeente*) will have a list of registered child day care centers for children from ages 0 to 12 known as *Kinderdagopvang* (0 to 4 years old), *Peuterspeelzalen* (2½ to 4 years old) and *Naschoolse* or *Buitenschoolse opvang* (4 to 12 years old). Usually these city lists or registers will be accessible via the Internet. Search for child care on *www.google.nl* using the word *kinderopvang* and your city's name. Alternatively, search your *Gemeente's* website. These should give you the addresses and contact information for you to start your search. Many of the day care facilities have their own websites that are in both Dutch and English, so surf the web a little to narrow down your list. If you prefer to use the Yellow Pages (*Gouden Gids*), look under *Kinderopvang* and/or *Kinderdagverblijven* to find a licensed and accredited organization.

Commercial day care centers have multiple branches with care for some or all age groups. Once you have found an organization with a branch location of your liking, you should arrange a tour. The tours usually last about half an hour and give you all the information you need. It is advisable to visit several organizations and branches since they do vary somewhat. Each branch only takes a limited number of children and depending on the city that you are in, there may be long waiting list for open positions. Call the main office of the day care center and they can inform you how their waiting list stands. Nevertheless, most day care branches will give a tour regardless of whether or not they have open positions.

Most organizations work on a first come, first serve basis. Once you are registered with a facility they will give you an open position at a branch or place you on a waiting list. There are busy and calm days during the week, so if you do not need full-time day care, you may be able to clear a waiting list sooner.

The American Women's Club of The Hague offers a crèche for club-sponsored events for its members and has an active Kid's Club (kidsclub@awcthehague.org / *www.awcthehague.org*). The same is true for the Amsterdam chapter. There are also many English-speaking playgroups and preschools associated with the American and international social clubs (see our **Church and Community** chapter for listings). Keep in mind that the ability of young children to learn multiple languages is well documented. You can immerse your child in Dutch at school without worry. Your children can still have English as their "home" language. The one language at home and another at school will allow them to go back and forth between two languages. You can find a lot of advice on this on the Internet or from your favorite bookstore and decide what is best for your family situation during your stay in the Netherlands.

Day Care Centers/Crèches

The Activity Shop
Hallenkstraat 28A, Wassenaar
☎ (070) 514 67 38
www.tasid.nl
Day care, out of school care and after school care for children from 0 thru 12 years old.

The Clown Club
Johan de Wittstraat 33, 2242 LA Wassenaar
☎ (070) 514 09 81
www.theclownclub.com
International day care for ages 0 to 4. Four English groups and two Dutch groups.

Comme à la Maison
Duinweg 1, Den Haag
☎ (070) 404 97 50
www.commealamaison.nl
Ages 0 to 6; a small-scale childcare center for children of full-time working parents with demanding work schedules.

The Lorax International Day Care
Wijndaelerduin 1, 2554 BX Den Haag
☎ (070) 325 58 00
www.triodus.nl
The Lorax, part of Triodus Day Care, is a small day care center for ages 0 to 4 at the International School of The Hague.

Triodus Day Care
Zoutmanstraat 44, 2518 GS Den Haag
☎ (070) 312 00 10
www.triodus.nl
Day care, out-of-school care and holiday care for ages 0 thru 13 in multiple locations throughout The Hague.

Playgroups/After School Care

Daisy Chain Playgroup
Anglican Church Hall, Riouwstraat 2C, Den Haag
☎ (070) 888 03 67
http://admindaisychain.googlepages.com/home
Ages 2½ to 4 years; well established playgroup for 25 years.

The English Speaking Playgroup
Boschfluiters, Sixlaan 4, Voorschoten
☎ (071) 576 56 64
www.english-playgroup-voorschoten.nl
Ages 2 to 4 years; meetings on Monday, Tuesday, Thursday and Friday afternoons.

Robbeburg International Playgroup
Jekerstraat 84, Amsterdam
☎ (020) 640 56 47
www.robbeburg.com
Ages 0 to 4; established in 1974, this group offers play sessions in English, Germany, Japanese, & Spanish.

Red Fish Blue Fish
Schelpkade 43-45, Den Haag
☎ (070) 354 65 02
www.rfbf.nl
Morning sessions for ages 2½ to 4 years.

Robbie's Place After School Club
Vlamenburg 38, Den Haag
☎ (070) 326 82 63
www.afterschoolclub.nl
Offers after school care for ages 4 to12 in association with the British School.

Storks After School Club
Schapenatjesduin 1, Den Haag
☎ (070) 326 82 63
www.afterschoolclub.nl
Offers after school care for ages 4 to 12 in association with the International School.

The Rijswijk English Speaking Playgroup
Labouchèrelaan 1, Rijswijk
☎ (070) 394 79 55
www.rijswijkplaygroup.nl
Morning and afternoon sessions for ages 2 to 4 years.

Willows English Language Playschool
Oostdorperweg 54-54a, Wassenaar
☎ (065) 123 16 04 Ginny
Morning and afternoon sessions for ages 18 months to 4 years.

The Windmill
Therasiastraat 310, Den Haag or
Elzendreef 6, Voorburg
☎ (070) 327 20 88
www.thewindmill.nl
Ages 0 to 4 years for toddler groups and ages 2 to 5 years for preschool.

Mother and Toddler Groups

Baby Signing Classes
Statenlaan 58, 2582 GP, Den Haag
Therapist, Fiona Curtis
☎ (070) 354 75 42
Email: *kandfcurtis@planet.nl*
Communicate with your baby before your baby can talk, classes taught by qualified speech and language therapist.

Bumps & Babies Group
Ary van der Spuyweg 1, 2585 JA, Den Haag
☎ (065) 063 44 34 Tina Keogh
www.greatexpectations.nl
English speaking group for pregnant mums and parents of newborns and babies not yet walking.

In Touch
Hazelaarweg 40, Rotterdam
www.InTouchNL.com
Mother and toddler group with meetings every Tuesday morning.

Mother and Toddler Group
Deijlercentrum Hofkampweg 3, Wassenaar
☎ (070) 517 60 10 Susan Ranebo or
☎ (070) 514 43 42 Nina Busch
Meets every Thursday morning.

American Women's Club of Amsterdam
www.awca.nl
Mom & Tot groups meet in Amsterdam, Haarlem, Amstelveen, and the t'Gooi areas.

Daisy Chain Playgroup
St. John & St. Philip Anglican Church Hall
Ary van der Spuyweg 1, Den Haag
Email: daisy_chain_playgroup@yahoo.com
www.stjohn-stphilip.org
Morning and afternoon meetings catering to the needs of the international community.

Mother and Toddler Group Parish Hall
Bezuidenhoutseweg 157, Den Haag
☎ (070) 382 53 77 Eileen Heaney
Meets every Tuesday morning.

Mothers and Others
Amsterdam/Amstelveen
☎ (020) 441 45 25
This is the babies/toddlers group from the British Society. All nationalities are welcome. The mums take turns to host.

Mothers of Preschoolers (MOPS)
Gruttolaan 23, Leidschendam
☎ (070) 517 80 24
www.mopsinholland.org
Ages 0 to 5 years. Meets 1st and 3rd Thursday mornings. Church-based organization to talk about parenting and other issues related to moms.

Parent and Toddler Group
Church Hall, Koningskerk
Bruijnings Ingenhoeslaan 2/4, Voorburg
Meets on Wednesday mornings.

Special Needs

If you have a child with special needs, there are English support groups here for you. Contact one of the following:

Autism Association for Overseas Families in the Netherlands (AAOF)
Amsterdam, The Hague and Rotterdam
www.aaof.info

Children with Special Needs
An organization which assists children and parents with special needs and organizes Contact Days for special educational needs departments in both international and Dutch schools in the Netherlands.
☎ (071) 362 58 35 Jim and Norma or Email: *j_taylor@versatel.nl*

English Language Speech Centre
Their mission is to serve those in the English-language community in need of speech and language therapy in a warm and caring manner.
☎ (070) 369 38 48 or Email: *speech@euronet.nl*

The Escape
English-speaking activity center providing respite and day care for children, adults and families with special needs located in Rijswijk. Provides a variety of activities that are fun, stimulating and which foster a sense of achievement and independence.
☎ (070) 380 93 45 or (062) 237 95 84 or Email: *the-escape@planet.nl*

Hague Support Group

A group of parents of children with various special needs (medical, behavioral, educational) who meet regularly for coffee to offer mutual support, exchange information and pool resources.

☎ (070) 317 51 01 Cathy or ☎ (070) 319 38 08 Nathalie or Email: *panat@orange.nl*

Dyslexia Parent Support Group — The Hague

This group's principle aim is to put parents of dyslexic children in touch with one another, meeting monthly for a coffee morning or a chance to listen to a guest speaker.

☎ (071) 889 15 52 Debra or Email: *debra.lambert@uku.co.uk*

Live-in Help

Live-in help can be a professional nanny who is trained to care for your children or an au pair (a student/young adult who will provide child care in exchange for room, board and a small salary). There are English-speaking services that can provide either type of help. You can find these by looking in the English-language magazines and newspapers or by contacting local English-speaking organizations such as ACCESS.

When you hire live-in professional help, it is advisable to prepare a contract covering issues such as working hours, salary, taxes, general duties, time off each week and vacation time. Look in our **Housekeeping and Maintenance** chapter for further information on the responsibilities of an employer in the Netherlands.

Dutch Child Care Allowance

It is important to note that up to 80% of child care costs may be tax deductible under the Dutch government child care allowances for families. Two reputable English web pages with more on the subject are *www.expatica.com/nl/woman/kids* and *www.blueumbrella.nl*. Blue Umbrella specializes in selection of child care and education in the Netherlands and offers assistance in claiming your Dutch day care allowances.

Infant Formulas *(Zuigelingenvoeding)*

Infant formula (*volledige zuigelingen-voeding*) for normal healthy babies is available at supermarkets. The major brands are available with baby food hotlines:

- Nutrilon made by Nutricia (*www.nutriciakindervoeding.nl*) ☎ (0800) 022 26 26
- Friso made by Hero Nederland BV (*www.frisokindervoeding.nl*) ☎ (0800) 022 74 34
- Similac made by Abbott BV (*www.similac.nl*) ☎ (0900) 746 45 22 (€0,25/minute)

Infant formulas are available primarily in powdered form, although some liquid formulas are available. The major brands all have standard cow's milk and hypo-allergenic formulas for healthy babies. Foods for babies that require extra care or have special food requirements (*speciale voedingsbehoefte*) are available from drugstores and pharmacies. It is recommended that you consult your doctor before using them.

Helpful Vocabulary

Bijspugen, obstipatie en krampjes	For babies that spit up, are constipated or have cramps
Ermstige lactose-intolerantie	For babies with serious lactose intolerance
Ermstige veterings en absorptiestoornissen vanaf geboorte	For babies with serious digestive or absorption problems from birth
Ermstige voedsel allergie	For babies with serious allergies from birth
Hongerige	For hungry babies
Koemelk allergie	For babies with allergies to cow's milk
Krampjes	For babies with cramps
Milde lactoseintolerantie	For babies with mild lactose intolerance
Speentjes	Pacifiers
Spenen	Nipples
Spugen	For babies that spit up
Tot 6 maanden	From birth to 6 months
Vanaf 6 maanden	From 6 months
Visolie voor zwangervrouwen	Fish oil for pregnant women
Vloeibaar	Liquid formula
Zuigelingenmelk voor prematuur en dymatuur geboren kinderen	For premature or underdeveloped babies, weighing 3500 grams or less
Zuigflessen	Baby bottles

Other Products

- Oral rehydration formula (Dioralyte) is available at the pharmacist. It is the same as Pedialyte in the U.S. It is made with sucrose in place of glucose and has an orange flavor: Frisomed ORS.
- Baby bottles and nipples can be purchased at the supermarket, pharmacist and drugstore. There are 125 ml (½ cup) and 250 ml (1 cup) bottles with a beginner's nipple (*startspeen*), which has three small holes and with a follow-up nipple which has three larger holes. You may wish to use bottled water as Dutch tap water is very hard and leaves residue in bottles even after boiling. Disposable systems are also available.
- Pacifiers are widely available in supermarkets and drug stores like Etos and Kruidvat.

Solid Foods for Infants

Jars

Jars of baby foods and junior foods (*baby voeding* or *baby maaltijd*) can be purchased in supermarkets, pharmacies and drugstores. There is a wide selection to choose from. The most widely available is Olvarit (Nutricia at *www.nutriciakindervoeding.nl*). Organic baby food brands are Olvarit Bio and Zonnatura. There are pictures on the jar to identify the ingredients. The labels also specify the age appropriateness:

- Baby: *Baby (vanaf 4 maanden)*
- Toddler: *Peuter (vanaf 8 maanden)*
- Tiny Tot: *Kleuter (vanaf 15 maanden)*

Cereals

There are several types of cereals (*kindermeel*) available in ready-to-eat (just add liquid) form. Bambix and Nutrix are the major brand names available and both are made by Nutricia.

Cookies and Biscuits *(Kinderbiscuits)*

Snacks (*kindervoeding tussendorortjes*) for babies and toddlers include Liga (*www.liga.nl*) and Bambix (*www.nutriciakindervoeding.nl*) brands.

Child Illness

In the event of an urgent, but not life-threatening emergency, contact your family physician (*huisarts*) first. If your child requires more specialized care, your *huisarts* will refer you. They will make house calls if your child is ill and the situation warrants it.

When your child is ill, yet it is not an emergency, contact your *huisarts* during regular appointment hours. If you must see a doctor outside regular office hours, your *huisarts* may still accommodate you, but normally you will be referred to one of several central medical practices that operate throughout the night.

A doctor's prescription can be filled at a pharmacy (*apotheek*). Your local *apotheek* should be open during normal working hours. Most towns have a rotating schedule of pharmacies so that at least one is open 24 hours a day and on Sundays. It is published in the weekly paper and will be posted on the door of any closed pharmacy.

You may find that some medical practices differ slightly from what you are accustomed to at home. For example, antibiotics are not prescribed as freely and nose drops are often given to children with colds to prevent ear infections. Suppositories are often prescribed for nausea and vomiting (be sure to check the dose). An oral rehydration solution (Pedialyte in the U.S.), may be obtained over the counter at the pharmacy; however, supervision by a doctor is advisable. For the Body Temperature Conversion Chart and more information about what to do regarding child illnesses, see the chapter on **Health Care**.

10 Children

Emergency — Dial 112 for life-threatening emergencies

Clothing and Basics

It is always safest to let your child try on children's garments to be sure of a proper fit. In Europe, clothing is very sensibly sized according to a child's height. Here is a chart to help you get started:

▸ Children's Clothing Size Chart

Please note that the metric clothing sizes actually available are measured in six-centimeter increments, i.e. the sizes available are: 56, 62, 68, 74, 80, 86, 92, 98, 104, 110, 116, 122, 128, 134, 140, 146, 152, 158, and 164.

American size	Weight		Height	
	pounds	kilograms	inches	centimeters
3–6 months	11–14	5–6.3	22–24	55.8–60.9
6–9 months	14½–18	6.6–8.2	25–27	64–69
12 months	18½–23	8.4–10.5	27½–30½	70–77
18 months	23½–26	10.7–11.8	31–33	79–84
24 months	26½–28	12–12.7	33½–35½	85–90
2T	26½–28	12–12.7	33½–35½	85–90
3T	28–32	12.7–14½	36–38½	91–98
4T	32½–37	14.8–16.8	39–41½	99–105
4	32½–37	14.8–16.8	39–41½	99–105
5	37½–42	17–19	42–44½	107–113
6	42½–47	19.3–21.4	45–46½	114–118
6X/7	47½–54	21.6–24½	47–48½	119–123

▸ Shoes

You can use the chart on the next page, which provides American and Netherlands (Continental Europe) sizes for reference. U.K. sizes are similar to American sizes, but are not always exactly the same.

Babies:

U.S.	NL	U.S.	NL
1	16	8	24
2	17	8½	25
3½	18	9	26
4	19	10	27
5	20	10½	28
5½	21	11½	29
6½	22	12	30
7	23	13	31

Children:

U.S.	NL	U.S.	NL
1	32	4	36
1½	33	5	37
2	34	6	38
3	35		

Where to Shop for Children's Clothing and Furniture

Most major department stores have children's clothing departments, and there are many smaller specialty shops with fine items and good end-of-season sales. Some of the places to shop for clothing and furniture are listed below. Also check in the Yellow Pages for children's clothing under *Kinderkleding*, for children's furniture under *Kindermeubelen* and baby carriages under *Kinderwagens*.

- **Bijenkorf** *(www.bijenkorf.nl)*: upscale children's clothes.
- **HEMA** *(www.hema.nl)*: good selection for basic clothing needs and necessities (as close to Target as you will get).
- **H&M** (*www.hm.com/nl*): children's outfits, basics.
- **IKEA** *(www.ikea.nl)*: cribs, toys and accessories.
- **Peek and Cloppenburg (P&C)** *(www.peek-cloppenburg.nl)*: medium-priced clothing.
- **PreNatal** *(www.prenatal.nl)*: children's outfits, maternity wear, strollers, highchairs and all baby and children's necessities.
- **Vroom and Dreesman (V&D)** *(www.vd.nl)*: maternity wear and reasonably priced baby and children's necessities.

Toys

There are plenty of toys for kids of all ages. Department stores have toy departments and most towns have a specialty toy store. Look under *Speelgoed* in the Yellow Pages. For children's bicycles, see *Fietsen*. Larger chain toy stores include:

- **Toys 'R Us** (*www.toysrus.nl*)
- **Bart Smit** (*www.bartsmit.com*)
- **Intertoys** (*www.intertoys.nl*).

Places to Go with Your Kids

While some parents are hesitant to take their children to museums, there are many museums in the Netherlands that are very child friendly. Check out the local VVV and ANWB offices for unique museum opportunities in your area or wherever you are visiting. Most VVV's are open Monday through Saturday and some are also open in the summer on Sunday. For complete listings of the over 1,000 museums in the country, visit *www.museum.nl*. This website has an English option and tells you in advance whether your museum card (see our chapter on **Sightseeing** for a further explanation of the *Museumkaart*) will be accepted, the admission prices, opening hours, etc.

There are many day trip opportunities in the Netherlands. The website *www.eropuit.nl* is run by the Dutch train service suggesting itineraries for day trips and weekends away. It's full of adventures that are accessible from the train for you and your children of all ages. A good reference book is the *Kids Gids* (Kids Guide), which is available in English in most VVV's and English-language book stores. In addition, two good "What to Do with Kids" websites are *www.daysout.nl* and *www.uitmetkinderen.nl*.

Amsterdam Area

Artis Zoo: The country's oldest zoo, planetarium and geologic museum.
Plantage Kerklaan 38-40, Amsterdam
☎ (020) 523 34 00
www.artis.nl

NEMO: This interactive science museum has exhibits in four languages.
Oosterdok 2, Amsterdam
☎ (020) 531 32 33
www.e-nemo.nl

Scheepvaart Museum: Step back into the history of sailing at this maritime museum. This museum closed in 2007 for renovation and is expected to reopen in 2009.
Kettenburgerplein 1, Amsterdam
☎ (020) 523 22 22
www.scheepvaartmuseum.nl

The Hague Area

Bubble Jungle: Indoor playground with separate play area for ages 0–2.
Vlasbaan 7, Leiderdorp
☎ (071) 589 97 77
www.bubblejungle.nl

Corpus: a "journey through the human body" during which the visitors can see, feel and hear how the human body works. Minimum age is 8. Reservations are required.
Willem Einthovenstraat 1,
2342 BH Oegstgeest
☎ (071) 751 02 00) 75 10 200
www.corpusexperience.nl

Drievliet: Small amusement park.
Jan Thijssenweg 16, Rijswijk
☎ (070) 399 93 05
www.drievliet.nl

Duinrell: Small amusement park with large indoor water slide park.
Duinrell 1, Wassenaar
☎ (070) 515 52 55
www.duinrell.nl

Kids Playground: Indoor playground with separate play area for ages 0–4.
Kleveringweg 35, Delft.
☎ (015) 219 06 73
www.kidsplayground.nl

Kinderboerderij: Many towns have children's petting barnyards open to the public several days a week.
Essepad 8, Voorburg
☎ (070) 387 68 22

Madurodam: Very detailed models of the Netherland's most famous landmarks in miniature.
George Maduroplein, Den Haag
☎ (070) 416 24 00
www.madurodam.nl

Molen "De Valk": A windmill museum with 7 floors to visit and a great view of Leiden.
2e Binnenvestgracht 1, Leiden
☎ (071) 516 53 53
www.molenmuseumdevalk.nl

Museon: An interactive museum featuring temporary exhibits from around the world and permanent exhibits on science and natural history.
Stadhouderslaan 37, Den Haag
☎ (070) 338 13 38
www.museon.nl

Naturalis: National Museum of Natural History.
Darwinweg 2, Leiden
☎ (071) 568 76 00
www.naturalis.nl

Sealife Center: Learn about the sea at this aquarium.
Strandweg 13, Scheveningen
☎ (070) 355 87 81
www.sealifeeurope.com

Zwembaden Den Haag: The Hague has 5 recreational swimming centers that offer many swim programs and open swim times.
www.denhaag.nl/zwemmen

't Gooi Area

Amersfoort Zoo: Small and manageable zoo, great play area and picnic tables.
Barchman Wuytierslaan 224, Amserfoort
☎ (033) 422 71 00
www.amersfoort-zoo.nl

Hilvert's Hofje Poppentheater (Puppet Theater): This theater can do pre-arranged English performances.
Hilversum Hilvertshof Shopping Center
Groest 86, Hilversum
☎ (035) 526 41 94
www.gooisch-poppentheater.nl

Militair Luchvaart Museum (Military Aviation): This free aviation museum features an extensive collection of planes and helicopters which will delight all ages.
Kampweg 120, Soesterburg
☎ (034) 635 60 00
www.militaireluchtvaartmuseum.nl

Speelpark Oud Valkeveen: A fun park geared for children up to age 12, Open March through October with access to a beach on Gooimeer Lake. Activities include bumper cars, trampolines, mini-cars, row boats, snack bar and a playground.
Oud Huizerweg 2, Naarden
☎ (035) 694 42 23
www.oudvalkeveen.nl

Rotterdam Area

Blijdorp Zoo: This zoo features a large aquarium and wonderful playground in addition to many traditional land animal habitats.
Blijdorplaan 8, Rotterdam
☎ (010) 443 14 31
www.diergaardeblijdorp.nl

Plaswijck Park: Includes a small zoo, playground, merry-go-round, paddle boats, snack bar and more.
Ringdijk 20, Rotterdam
☎ (010) 418 18 36
www.plaswijckpark.nl

Arnhem Area

Apenheul: Enjoy walking through the park and observing gorillas and monkeys in their habitats. In some areas, the monkeys roam freely among the visitors. Open mid-March to early November.
Park for Park Berg en Bos, J.C. Wilslaan 21-31, Apeldoorn
☎ (055) 357 57 57
www.apenheul.com

Burgers Zoo: A zoo that features animals in their natural habitats.
Antoon van Hooffplein 1, Arnhem
☎ (026) 442 45 34
www.burgerszoo.nl

Hoge Veluwe National Park: One of the Netherlands oldest and largest national parks, it features the Kröller Müller Museum (*www.kmm.nl*) and Museonder (world's first underground museum), a hunting lodge to tour, loads of free bikes to ride and acres of nature trails to explore. Picnic or eat at one of the restaurants. Open all year. Campsites available.
Houtkampweg 9, Otterlo
☎ (0900) 464 38 35 (€0,20/minute)
www.hogeveluwe.nl

Open Lucht Museum (Open Air): This museum focuses on the everyday lives of ordinary people. Visit each of the Dutch provinces and learn about its architecture, agriculture and commerce by going into historical buildings that have been moved here from around the country. There are several good restaurants. Open from late March to late October.
Schelmseweg 89, Arnhem
☎ (026) 357 61 11
www.openluchtmuseum.nl

Further Afield

Batavia Shipyard: In this shipyard, full-size replicas are built by hand of the VOC (Dutch East India Company) ships of the golden era of Dutch trading. Visit the Batavia, the first replica ship built in the yard and launched in 1995, and learn about living on such a ship.

Oostvaardersdijk 01-09, Lelystad
☎ (032) 026 14 09
www.bataviawerf.nl

Deltapark Neeltje Jans: You can visit the Delta Works and walk through the inside of the storm surge barrier. There is a water playground, a water museum, a seal show and a 3-D movie.
Eiland Neeltje Jans, Faelweg 5, Vrouwenpolder
☎ (011) 165 56 55
www.neeltjejans.nl

Dierenpark Emmen: A zoo with an indoor play area.
Hoofdstraat 18, Emmen
☎ (059) 185 08 55
www.dierenpark-emmen.nl

Dolfinarium: Aquarium with a variety of shows featuring dolphins, walruses and seals.
Strandboulevard Oost 1, Harderwijk
☎ (034) 146 74 67
www.dolfinarium.nl

Efteling: Amusement park based on fairy tales. Fun for all ages. Open late March to late October.
Europalaan 1, Kaatsheuvel
☎ (041) 628 81 11
www.efteling.nl

Linnaeushof: Europe's largest playground. Open late March to late September.
Glipperweg 4c, Heemstede
☎ (023) 584 76 24
www.linnaeushof.nl

Luchtvaart Museum: Learn about 100 years of aviation. Reservations are needed for sightseeing flights.
Pelikaanweg 50, Lelystad Airport
☎ (900) 284 63 76 (€0,25/minute)
www.aviodome.nl

Olmenhorst Orchard: Go apple and pear picking (seasonal).
Lisserweg 481, Lisserbroek
☎ (025) 241 31 65
www.olmenhorst.nl

Safaripark Beekse Bergen: Go on safari through Africa on foot, boat, bus or your own car.
Beekse Bergen 31, Hilvarenbeek
☎ (0900) 233 57 32 (€0,15/minute)
www.safaripark.nl

Walibi World: Large amusement park. Open late March to late October.
Spijkweg 30, Biddinghuizen
☎ (032) 132 99 99
www.walibi.nl

There are many other parks and museums around Holland. Check at the VVV for more information. Always verify opening days and times as they may vary season to season.

Children's Parties

For those very special days, look up *Kinderactiviteiten* in the Yellow Pages for party clowns, venues, etc. Most of the places listed above in the *Places to Go with Your Kids* section can help you host a party and many have information in English on their websites. Local swimming pools (*zwembad*) often have special arrangements for children's parties. Indoor play places specialize in parties for young children. For other suggestions, check with the VVV in your city for local ideas.

Extracurricular Activities

International schools host a variety of after-school activities for their students including sports, art, dance, drama, and language classes. Some of these activities are free while others have instruction fees. For younger children, there are also a variety of activities offered including those below. Many of the locations listed in the chapter on **Hobbies and Recreation** also offer courses for children.

ABF International Sports Club: Various team sport activities: basketball — ages 6 and up; baseball — ages 8 and up; soccer (called football) ages 4 and up; teeball — ages 5–8.
Ammonslaantje 1, Wassenaar
☎ (070) 514 65 15
www.abfsport.nl

Kindermusik: Mother and toddler music and movement program for ages 18 months to 3 years.
Juliana Van Stolberglaan 154, The Hague or
Bermweg 332, Capelle A/d Ijssel/ Rotterdam
☎ (010) 442 79 64 Raquel Teitler-Lopez
www.kindermusik.com

Swimming lessons: Group lessons start at age 4, but private lessons can start at 3. Check with your local swimming pool (*zwembad*) for details. Usually the information is also on each city's (*Gemeente*) website. Registering early is recommended, because waiting lists aren't uncommon.

Swim Kids: Small group swimming lessons taught in English.
Holiday Inn Leiden, Haagse Schouwweg 10, Leiden
☎ (062) 127 57 67
www.swimkids.eu

Chapter 11

Church and Community

The Netherlands is a former colonial and shipping power which had interests as far east as Indonesia, as far south as South Africa and as far west as the Caribbean. Many residents of these colonies settled in the Netherlands. They have been joined by guest workers from all over the world, international business people and their families, and religious and political refugees from many countries. This has resulted in an interesting tapestry of citizens in the Netherlands today. These non-native residents have formed a number of homeland-oriented communities within the major cities of the Netherlands. Community, in this context, is not geographical but rather emotional.

You will become part of an international community where you can pursue Christian, Jewish, Buddhist, Islamic, Hindu or other beliefs, in churches, synagogues, temples and mosques with services conducted in many languages. You can find an organization and activity group oriented to your interests, with the added benefit of greatly enriching your life through friendships with people from all over the world including, of course, the Dutch.

Places of Worship

As you would expect, there are as many denominations of worship as there are cultures in the country. All you need to do is look and find the option which feels right for you. Read the listings in local English language newspapers, club and school newsletters or just "Google" English-speaking churches in the Netherlands. Ask new friends if you can't find the affiliation you desire. We have included a partial listing below.

Amsterdam Area

Baptist Community - Lighthouse Baptist Church
Benny Goodmanstraat 32, Almere
☎ (036) 533 4176
www.lbc.nl

Christ Church – Church of England & Episcopal
Groenburgwal 42, 1011 HW Amsterdam
☎ (020) 624 88 77
www.christchurch.nl

The Church of Jesus Christ of Latter-Day Saints
Zaaiersweg 17, 1097 SM Amsterdam
☎ (020) 663 69 84
www.kerkvanjezuschristus.nl

Crossroads International Church
Amstelveen College, Startbaan 12, Amstelveen
☎ (020) 545 14 44
www.xrds.nl

English Reformed Church
Begijnhof 48, 1012 WV Amsterdam
☎ (020) 624 96 65
www.ercadam.nl

First Church of Christ Scientist
R. Wagnerstraat 32, 1077 VW Amsterdam
☎ (020) 662 74 38

Friends Center – Quakers
Vossiusstraat 20, 1071 AD Amsterdam
☎ (020) 679 42 38
www.quakers.nu

House Church (Christian Evangelical)
Spinnekop 47, Amsterdam North
☎ (020) 631 49 08
www.housechurch.nl

Jewish Community
van den Boechhorststraat 26, 1081 BT Amsterdam
☎ (020) 646 00 46
www.nihs.nl

Liberal Jewish Community
Jacob Soetendorpstraat 8, 1079 RM Amsterdam
☎ (020) 642 35 62

Roman Catholic Church – Parish of the Blessed Trinity
Zaaiersweg 180, 1097 ST Amsterdam
☎ (020) 465 27 11
www.blessedtrinity.nl

Netherlands Unitarian Universalist Fellowship
Keizersgracht 566, Amsterdam
☎ (015) 369 26 14
www.nuuf.nl

The Hague Area

American Protestant Church of The Hague
Esther de Boer van Rijklaan 20, 2597 TJ Den Haag
☎ (070) 324 44 90
www.apch.nl

Buddhist – Karma Trinley Ling Buddhist Group
Goeverneurlaan 115, 2523 BC Den Haag
☎ (065) 210 13 36
www.karma-trinley-ling.nl

Church of Christ
De Gaarde 61, 2542 CB Den Haag
☎ (070) 329 73 80
www.gemeentevanchristus.nl/denhaag

The Church of Jesus Christ of Latter-day Saints
Leersumstraat 11, 2546 TE Den Haag
☎ (070) 329 69 17
www.kerkvanjezuschristus.nl

Church of Our Saviour – Roman Catholic
Ruyrocklaan 126, 2597 ES Den Haag
☎ (070) 328 08 16
www.parish.nl

Church of St. James
Church services held at the British Senior School:
Jan van Hooflaan 3, 2252 BG, Voorschoten
☎ (071) 561 15 28
www.stjames.nl

Church of St. John & St. Philip – Anglican & Episcopal
Ary van der Spuyweg 1, 2585 JA Den Haag
☎ (070) 355 53 59
www.stjohn-stphilip.org

Crossroads International Church
Bezuidenhoutsweg 249, 2594 AM Den Haag
☎ (070) 322 24 85
www.crossroadschurch.nl

First Church of Christ, Scientist
Andries Bickerweg 1B, 2517 JP Den Haag
☎ (070) 363 66 52

Hindu Ram Mandir
Mijtenstraat 183, 2522 VC Den Haag
☎ (070) 389 98 23

Liberal Jewish Community
Prinsessegracht 26, 2514 AP Den Haag
☎ (070) 365 68 93
www.ljgdenhaag.nl

Muslim Information Center
Beeklaan 207, 2562 AE Den Haag
☎ (070) 361 44 63

Orthodox Jewish Synagogue
Cornelius Houtmanstraat 11,
2593 RD Den Haag
☎ (070) 347 32 01
Scheveningen Synagogue
Doorniksestraat 152, 2587 AZ Den Haag,
☎ (070) 358 63 63

Society of Friends – Quaker
Stadhouderslaan 8, 2517 HW Den Haag
☎ (071) 561 74 61
E-mail: willem@furnee.nl

Trinity Baptist International Church
Gruttolaan 23, 2261 ET Leidschendan
☎ (070) 517 80 24
www.trinitychurch.nl

Rotterdam Area

Church of English-Speaking Catholics – Church of the Sacred Heart
Rijnstraat 1, 3114 SP Schiedam
☎ (010) 202 39 00

The Church of Jesus Christ of Latter-day Saints
Oosteinde 73, 3061 SN Rotterdam
☎ (010) 214 22 00
www.kerkvanjezuschristus.nl

Hope International Baptist Church of Rotterdam
Schiedamse Vest 121, 3012 BH Rotterdam
☎ (010) 447 25 51
www.hope-baptist-church.com

Progressive Jewish Community
Mozartlaan 99, 3055 KJ Rotterdam
☎ (010) 461 26 06
http://home.planet.nl/~rdam0002/

The Scots International Church
Schiedamse Vest 121, 3012 BH Rotterdam
☎ (010) 412 47 79
www.scotsintchurch.com

St. Mary's Church – Anglican & Episcopal
Pieter de Hoochweg 133, 3024 BG
Rotterdam
☎ (010) 476 40 43
www.stmarys.nl

Synagogue N.I.G. – Orthodox
A.B.N. Davidsplein 4, 3039 KA Rotterdam
☎ (010) 466 97 65

Community

As you get yourself settled in your new country, you will discover that you have many places to turn to find friendship and community. The most critical part of that sentence is YOU. Nothing happens if you sit at home. You have to discover how to make friends and to put the energy into making things happen that allow you to feel like you belong here. The options are endless. Perhaps it is playing rugby, cricket, baseball, tennis or rock climbing. Maybe you want to start your own business. Maybe you are going to start or complete a graduate university degree. Perhaps it is in finding a group of other mothers and fathers with small children for playgroups.

▸ Volunteering to Help the Community

You may also want to find ways to volunteer your time to help the community. Volunteering in your local community is an excellent way to help you accelerate your understanding of the Dutch, and in turn, more quickly overcome culture shock. It will also help to increase your comfort level and sense of being in control in this "foreign" environment. And, of course, it's a good thing to do. It can even be a route to landing a paying job, help you polish some skills or give you something interesting to put on a resumé to cover the time that you are here. There are literally thousands of opportunities to volunteer in the Netherlands, even if you don't yet have command of the Dutch language.

The first step is to think about:

- What you want to do
- Whom you want to help
- How much time you want to donate
- Just what your motives are (e.g., fill up free time, utilize education/job expertise, expand knowledge base, gain practical experience or help others)

Once you have answered the above questions, there are several options for identifying organizations that need volunteers. Think about the obvious: schools, churches, hospitals, sport clubs, the Red Cross (Het Rode Kruis at *www.rodekruis.nl*), the Salvation Army (Het Leger des Heils at *www.legerdesheils.nl*) and all the causes you knew back home, such as cancer, Aids, MS, seeing-eye dogs, and the environment. Check the White Pages of your local phone directory or "Google" the organizations. Contact the Chamber of Commerce (Kamer van Koophande at *www.kvk.nl*) for addresses and phone numbers since all reputable charities are listed with them.

Another resource is the Vrijwilligerscentrales (VWC at *www.vrijwilligerscentrales.nl*) or "Volunteer Centers." These store-front offices can be found throughout the Netherlands. They are job centers for volunteer work. They are subsidized by the local government and through donations, and are staffed by paid and volunteer personnel.

Finally, a helpful hint: the more your volunteer efforts focus on visual or helping activities—and less on verbal skills—the easier it is to get by in English. (There are also refugee centers called Asielzoekers Centers where the asylum seekers don't speak Dutch, but use English as the universal language.) Whatever you need to feel like you belong in this place, your new "home," the Netherlands has it. It is a wonderful country for just about everything you might want to do. There are plenty of available resources; you just need to find them. We have listed some preliminary places to find other people from similar backgrounds. Many of the social groups publish a monthly newsletter from which you can glean a wealth of information. You can also contact ACCESS for subjects that no one else seems to know about.

Index of Social Resources

Amsterdam Area

ACCESS
Prinses Irenestraat 59, 1077 WV
Amsterdam
☎ (020) 423 32 17
www.access-nl.org

American Women's Club of Amsterdam
Postbus 70133, 1007 KC Amsterdam
☎ (020) 644 35 31
www.awca.nl

The British Society of Amsterdam
Postbus 7429, 1007 JK Amsterdam
☎ (065) 170 08 81
www.britishsocietyofamsterdam.org

International Women's Contact, Amsterdam
Postbus 3722, 1001 AM Amsterdam
www.euronet.nl/users/iwc_amst

The Hague Area

ACCESS
Stadhuis, Spui 70 Atrium
Den Haag
☎ (070) 346 25 25
www.access-nl.org

American Women's Club of The Hague
Nieuwe Duinweg 25, 2587 AB Den Haag
☎ (070) 350 60 07
www.awcthehague.org

Australian and New Zealand Women's Club
Postbus 25, 2501 CA, The Hague
www.anzwc.nl

British Club of The Hague
Nieuwe Duinweg 25, 2587 AB Den Haag
☎ (070) 346 19 73
www.bwclubthehague.demon.nl

Canadian Women's Club
www.canadianclubnetherlands.com

Connecting Women
Christus Triumfatorkerk
Juliana van Stolberglaan 154, Den Haag
www.connectingwomen.nl

Decorative and Fine Arts Society (DFAS The Hague)
Schoolstraat 23, 2271 BZ Voorburg
☎ (070) 387 2606 Jane Choy
www.dfas.nl

International Women's Contact, The Hague
Vierloper 10, 2586 KV Den Haag
☎ (070) 355 88 63
www.iwcthehague.nl

The Irish Club - Netherlands
www.irishclub.nl

Petroleum Wives Club
Postbus 655, 2240 AP Wassenaar
www.pwc-thehague.com

The St Andew's Society of the Netherlands
www.standrews.nl

South African Women's Club
www.sawcnl.com

Rotterdam Area

The American Netherlands Club of Rotterdam, ANCOR
P.O. Box 25036, 3001 HA Rotterdam
www.ancorotterdam.com

Pickwick Women's Club of Rotterdam
☎ (087) 190 21 29
www.welcome.to/pickwick

Other Areas

Amersfoort British Women's Club
☎ (034) 344 33 59

British Women's Club Utrecht
Nedereindseweg 435, 3437 PL Nieuwegein
☎ (030) 604 08 05

International Women's Contact, Utrecht (IWCU)
☎ (033) 494 14 15
www.iwcu..nl

Stichting Nederland- Verenigde Staten (Holland-USA Foundation)
Wolweverdlaan 27, 3454 GK De Meern
☎ (030) 666 26 31
www.nl-vs.nl

Index of Business Resources

The Netherlands offers a variety of business resources to make your transition easier if you are looking for employment. There are many employment agencies servicing even those without knowledge of the Dutch language. Office centers are also available to help businesses get started in the Netherlands and can provide everything from a legitimate mailing address to an office with shared secretarial services. Rates are highly competitive.

Job Search

Octagon
www.octagon.nl
Employment agency in The Hague concentrating on international professionals.

Blue Lynx Employment
www.bluelynx.nl
Employment agency with locations in Amsterdam, The Hague and Rotterdam.

English Language Jobs
www.englishlanguagejobs.com
An online employment agency.

Expatica
www.expatica.com
An online employment agency.

Undutchables
www.undutchables.nl
Employment agency with locations in Amsterdam, Amstelveen, Eindhoven, Rotterdam and Utrecht.

Office Centers

Euro Business Centre
Keizersgracht 62–64, 1015 CS Amsterdam
☎ (020) 520 75 00
www.eurobc.nl

International Office Centre
Molenstraat 15, 2513 BH Den Haag
☎ (070) 361 17 11
www.ioc-denhaag.nl

New Offices – Park Centre
Parkweg 2, 2585 JJ Den Haag
☎ (070) 416 60 60
www.parkcentre.nl

Regus Business Centres
www.regus.com

Business Organizations

The American Chamber of Commerce in the Netherlands
WTC D-Tower, 6th fl, Schiphol Blvd. 171, 1118 BG Schiphol Airport
☎ (020) 795 18 40
www.amcham.nl

Amsterdam American Business Club
Keizersgracht 62–64, 1015 CS Amsterdam
☎ (020) 520 75 34
www.aabc.nl

Commercial Anglo-Dutch Society
http://cads-amsterdam.org/

Democrats Abroad
www.democratsabroad.nl

Foundation of Interservice
☎ (034) 840 21 53 Niko Boer

Republicans Abroad
www.republicansabroad.nl

Rotary Clubs in Holland
☎ (020) 623 24 05
www.rotary.com

Rotterdam American Business Club
☎ (010) 786 03 13
www.rabc.nl

Society of Technical Communication, Netherlands Chapter
www.stc-nl.org

Chapter 12

Links to Non-English Communities

In the diverse international community that exists in the Netherlands, there is the possibility that English is not your first language. You may want to conserve the traditions of your home country and prepare your family to return there smoothly. As such, you might make different choices than your English-speaking fellow newcomers. These choices might be determined by your mother tongue. Unfortunately, it would be impossible to address all of the different languages throughout the expatriate community, so we'll concentrate on the French-, German-, Indonesian-, Italian- and Spanish-speaking communities.

French Community

There is an active French-speaking community in the Netherlands. If you live in the vicinity of The Hague, the easiest way to access this information is to consult the city's international web pages at *www.denhaag.com*. From there you can access the French web pages that list helpful resources. Here are some essentials from around the Netherlands to help you make your way into the community:

Ambassade de France a La Haye
Smidsplein 1, 2514 BT Den Haag
☎ (070) 312 58 00
www.ambafrance.nl

Consulat Général
Vijzelgracht 2, Amsterdam
☎ (020) 530 69 69
www.consulfrance-amsterdam.org

Lycee Francais Vincent van Gogh
Scheveningseweg 237, 2584 AA Den Haag
☎ (070) 306 69 20
www.lyceevangogh.nl

Alliance Francaise
Kettingstraat 2, 2511 AN Den Haag
☎ (070) 362 15 23
www.aflahaye.nl

Centre Medical Francophone
Laan van Middenburg 2, 2275 CC Voorburg
☎ (070) 386 21 91
www.cmfonline.nl

Centre Culturel Français Groningen
Oude Kijk in 't Jatstraat 26, Kamer 1909,
9712 EK Groningen
☎ (050) 363 61 06
Email: *ccfrance@let.rug.nl*

Institut Francaise Maison Descartes
Vijzelgracht 2A, 1017 HR Amsterdam
☎ (020) 531 95 01
www.maisondescartes.nl

Eglise Evangelique de La Haye
Zoutkeetsingel 113, 2512 HR Den Haag
☎ (070) 399 74 19

Eglise Wallonne de La Haye
Noordeinde 25, 2514 GB Den Haag
☎ (070) 365 75 86

Accueil Francophones de La Haye
Postbus 17156, 2502 CD Den Haag
www.accueillahaye.com

German Community

The German-speaking community is the second largest group of internationals in the Netherlands. Due to the easy adjustment to the Dutch language, they tend to blend in more easily than others. In an effort to maintain a connection to their culture, there are many social clubs covering various interests:

Deutsche Botschaft
Groot Hertoginnenlaan 18-20, 2517 EG Den Haag
☎ (070) 342 06 00
www.den-haag.diplo.de

Deutsches Generalkonsulat
Consulaat-generaal van de Bondsrepubliek Duitsland
Honthorststraat 36-38, 1071 DG Amsterdam
☎ (020) 574 77 00
www.den-haag.diplo.de

Goethe-Institut Niederlande
Herengracht 470, 1017 CA Amsterdam
☎ (020) 531 29 00
Westersingel 9, 3014 GM Rotterdam
☎ (010) 209 20 90
www.goethe.de/ins/nl/ams/

Deutsche Internationale Schule Den Haag
van Bleiswijkstraat 125, 2582 LB Den Haag
☎ (070) 354 94 54
www.disdh.nl

Deutsche Bibliothek Den Haag
Witte de Withstraat 31-33, 2518 CP Den Haag
☎ (070) 355 97 62
www.deutschebib.de

Deutscher Klub
Frau Drs. B.U. Couwenbergh-Rapke (Vorsitzende)
Postbus 85 678, 2508 CJ Den Haag
☎ (070) 333 38 97
Email: *bucouwenbergh@zonnet.nl*

Deutschsprachige Katholische Gemeinde in den Niederlanden – Rafaelshaus
Badhuisweg 35, 2587 CB Den Haag
☎ (070) 355 42 40

Deutsche Evangelische Kirchengemeinde Amsterdam
J.J.Viottastraat 44, 1071 JT Amsterdam
☎ 020 673 25 22
Email: *devkiam@xs4all.nl*

Deutsche Evangelische Gemeinde
Bleijenburg 3b, 2511 VC Den Haag
☎ (070) 346 57 27
Email: *deg.haag@tiscali.nl*

Kirche und Gemeindebüro: Deutsche Evangelische Gemeinde Rotterdam
's-Gravendijkwal 65, 3021 EE Rotterdam
☎ (010) 477 20 70

Indonesian Community

The single largest international community living in the Netherlands is the Indonesians. They number about 387,000 people with deep roots in a long historical connection between the Netherlands and Indonesia. The best way to get into contact with the Indonesian community is through the Embassy in The Hague, which is the largest embassy in the country, and also a very helpful resource in the transition process.

Embassy of the Republic of Indonesia
Tobias Asserlaan 8, 2517 KC Den Haag
☎ (070) 310 81 00
www.indonesia.nl

Attaché of Education and Culture Embassy of the Republic of Indonesia
Tobias Asserlaan 8,
2517 KC, Den Haag,
☎ (070) 310 81 68
www.indonesia.nl

Indonesian School in the Netherlands
Rijkstraatweg 679, 2245 CB Wassenaar
☎ (070) 517 88 75
www.sekolahindonesia.nl

Halin Relief Foundation
Zoutmanstraat 23-II, 2518 GL Den Haag
☎ (070) 346 12 85
www.stichtinghalin.nl

Indonesian Scientific Institute
Waldeck Pyrmontkade 906
2518 JV Den Haag
☎ (070) 363 20 87
Email: *Iwi.denhaag@planet.nl*

Italian Community

In addition to connecting with the Italian community through international schools, the following contacts might prove helpful:

Italian Embassy
Alexanderstraat 12, 2514 Jl Den Haag
☎ (070) 302 10 30
www.amblaja.esteri.it

Consulaat-Generaal Van Italië Te Amsterdam
Vijzelstraat 79,1017 Hg Amsterdam
☎ (020) 550 20 50
www.consamsterdam.esteri.it

Ufficio Scolastico
☎ (020) 550 20 68
Email: *ufficioscolasticonl@yahoo.it*

Italiaans Instituut Voor Buitenlandse Handel (Ice)
Westermarkt 2, IV, 1001 EW Amsterdam
☎ (020) 540 88 00
Email : *amsterdam@amsterdam.ice.it*
www.ice.gov.it

Italiaanse Kamer Van Koophandel Voor Nederland
De Ruyterkade 5, 1013 AA Amsterdam
☎ (020) 751 33 63
www.italianchamber.nl

Spanish Community

The Spanish-speaking community from Latin America tends to be very active in charity organizations. Below you will find many resources regarding immigration and social clubs:

Embajada de España
Lange Voorhout 50, 2514 EG Den Haag
☎ (070) 302 49 99
www.claboral.nl

Consulado General de España
Frederiksplein 34, 1017 XN Amsterdam
☎ (020) 620 38 11
www.claboral.nl

Sociedad Cultural Recreativa "O Lar Galego"
Hoornbrekerstraat 10B, 3011 CL Rotterdam
☎ (010) 433 41 41
www.largalegorotterdam.galiciaaberta.com

Asociación Iberoameriana Eindhoven
Hugo de Grootplein 47 A, 5652 LL Eindhoven
☎ (040) 252 17 08
www.aie-eindhoven.nl

Sociedad Española, Casa del Emigrante
Laaresstraat 25–27, 7514 ZA Enschede
☎ (020) 620 71 26

Centro Recreativo, Deportivo y Cultural Español
Pontanusstraat 26, 6524 HG Nijmegen
☎ (024) 324 24 90

Sociedad Espanola, La Iberica El Hogar Español
Gerad Doustraat 21, 7412 TD Deventer

Mutualidad de Espanoles de la RDM
Gerad Goustraat 1, 2981 CE Ridderkerk

Federacion de Asociaciones de Emigrantes Espanoles en Holanda
Mijdrechtstraat 49, 3522 HT Utrecht

Instituto Cervantes
Domplein 3, 3512 JC Utrecht
☎ (030) 242 84 77
www.institutocervantes.nl

Radio Nederland Español
☎ (035) 672 43 06
www.informarn.nl

Chapter 13

Customs and Etiquette

One of the most important aspects of living in and traveling throughout Europe is getting to know the people and their customs. You will quickly learn that what you might consider to be customary and polite may differ substantially from what is expected in some countries. Do not be misled by the sometimes seemingly brusque Dutch manner as behind it lies a friendly good humor and an old-fashioned dependability. What some may take for unfriendliness may also stem from the fact that although many Dutch speak English quite well, it is not their mother tongue. Without a native speaker's command of the language, it is easy to sound curt. Remember to smile liberally so that you will come across as friendly.

The best way to develop insight into a new culture and to begin to understand why things are done as they are is to do your homework in advance. In this chapter we hope to help you by anticipating what you might expect of the Dutch and what they might expect of you. Guidelines covering most social situations you will encounter in the Netherlands are included.

Greetings

Throughout Europe everyone, including small children, will extend a hand when introduced. While you are shaking hands you should repeat the person's name if you know it. Whether it is a small and casual or a large and formal gathering, you will be expected to introduce yourself to each person individually when you arrive. Avoid using first names until your new Dutch acquaintance suggests it. First names are rarely used except with relatives, intimate friends and children. When a Dutchman asks you to use his first name, it indicates that he regards you in a special way. Use *Meneer* (Mr.) or *Mevrouw* (Mrs.) with an older person, a person in a position of authority or anyone you dont't know well.

When you are accepted into the inner circle of Dutch friends, you will be greeted by a kiss on each cheek, and often one extra kiss on the cheek for good measure. It is also customary when leaving a gathering to shake hands and say goodbye to each person on your way out.

On the Telephone

Making or receiving phone calls also has its own set of rules. When placing a call to a friend or place of business, it is polite to first mention your name and then state the reason for your call. For example: "Good morning, this is...calling. May I please speak to...?"

"Goedemorgen, u spreekt met... Mag ik met...spreken, alstublieft?"

When answering the telephone, it is polite to greet the caller and state your name. For example: "Good morning, this is..."

"Goedemorgen, u spreekt met..." or simply, **"Met..."**

Dutch has a familiar "you" (**je** or **jij**) and a formal "you" (**u**). When in any doubt, use the formal version. The familiar one is for acquaintances, relatives or those significantly younger than you.

Dutch Courtesy

Please: *Alstublieft* is often seen abbreviated "*a.u.b.*" To a Dutch person, a simple please has more than one meaning. In response to a question, it implies "yes" or "yes, please." It is commonly heard when someone hands you something, meaning "Please take it, it is yours." If it is said after you say thank you, it means "you're welcome."

Thank you: *Dank u* (formal), *Dank je* or *Bedankt* (familiar). *Dank u* is used to thank someone for a gift or favor. However, in response to a question it implies "no" or "no, thank you." *Dank u wel* means "thank you very much." At first, avoid using informal forms.

I am sorry: *Het spijt mij.* This is somewhat formal and used to express regret, such as for spilling red wine on someone's white carpet.

Excuse me: *Pardon, Sorry.* Say *pardon* (with the accent on the second syllable) when you would like someone to move aside for you. Say *sorry* (pronounced "sew-ree") when you have bumped into someone.

I beg your pardon: *Neem me niet kwalijk.* A more formal way of saying you are sorry, it can also be translated as "Please do not take offense."

Hello and Goodbye: *Dag, Goeiedag, Tot ziens, Tot straks.* You will hear *dag* many times each day as you enter and exit shops. It means either hello or goodbye. *Goeiedag* is an extension of this colloquialism and frequently heard. *Goedendag* would be the really proper way to say it, but much too stiff, like enunciating every word in "How-are-you-doing?" After all, people really do say "How ya doin'?" *Tot ziens* means "Bye, see you later," and *Tot straks*, "See you soon."

As a New Neighbor

The tradition of welcoming a new family to the neighborhood practiced in the U.S. since frontier days is reversed here. Unless your neighbors are well-traveled or have known other expatriates, they will respect your privacy and wait for you to take the first step in signifying that you wish to become acquainted. We would like to encourage you to invite your Dutch neighbors for coffee or cocktails when you are ready and willing to meet them.

Morning Coffee, Afternoon Tea

You might like to invite your Dutch neighbor for coffee in the morning or tea in the afternoon. The 10:30 a.m. coffee break and 3:00 p.m. tea break are generally observed both at home and at work. Of course, you may serve either coffee or tea during these occasions. Note, however, that the casual offer of a cup of coffee may mean more than that to the Dutch. You may be asked to indicate a specified time and you may be certain that your Dutch guests will be punctual. You are opening your home to convey personal warmth and genuine interest and this invitation will not be taken lightly.

Your home should be presentable and you should take care to arrange an attractive table. Plan for those little details which show you really care for your guests' comfort, but avoid being pretentious. Above all, don't try to be Dutch! Your style of entertaining is expected to be different. In fact, they may be disappointed if it is not. The Dutch are fascinated by foods and customs from other countries and are eager to try new dishes.

Most of the same rules apply when you are the guest. Although your hostess may seem very contemporary and may have worded her invitation "come for a cup of coffee," you should not interpret this as being casual. Even if you are the only guest, she will have taken the time to arrange for a pleasant occasion and you should not appear in a track suit or sweats.

It is always appropriate to bring a modest bouquet of flowers or a small plant for the hostess. After morning coffee or afternoon tea, a hostess may offer her guests a glass of sherry to indicate the conclusion of the occasion.

Come for Dinner

When extending an invitation, tell your guests if you are celebrating a special event or just inviting some friends for drinks or dinner and would like to include them as well. It is wise to make the invitation for a day other than Sunday since that is a family day for many Dutch. Please note that potluck dinners are not a Dutch tradition.

Stick to familiar dishes when choosing a menu and prepare them with confidence. Many dishes of what you consider to be old favorites will be new to your guests. If you serve a family favorite, your Dutch guests will be honored that you cared enough to prepare it for them.

Have several empty vases on hand for the flowers your guests will likely bring. As soon as possible, put each bouquet into a vase and bring them into the room where the guests are. All gifts received should be opened in the presence of the giver. Some dinner guests may bring bottles of wine or boxes of chocolates. You may want to serve the chocolates with the coffee, but generally a gift of wine is not served. It is set aside for a future occasion.

Shortly after guests arrive you may want to serve an appetizer and beverage. Keep in mind: the Dutch generally consider it poor manners to help oneself to anything unless specifically invited to do so, and perhaps not even then! Be prepared to make the drinks and refills, and to pass the snacks to your guests several times.

The buffet is an uncommon way of serving dinner in Dutch homes and it will work only as long as your guests know what to expect. Be sure to make an announcement inviting everyone to the food table. You may also want to guide the first few people through the line. If you have elderly Dutch people at your party, you may want to ease the way by offering to fill a plate for them. They are generally accustomed to more formal dinner arrangements.

▸ But First — the Ceremony of the "First Sip"

This is a tradition you will recognize as a guest in a Dutch home. It can be elaborate or simple, but Dutch guests will expect it. The host lifts his glass of wine or cocktail, exchanges a glance with each of the guests, simply says "Welcome to our home," and takes a sip. Only after this has happened should guests take a first sip. You may encourage your guests to help themselves, but remember that the Dutch will find it quite awkward.

As a Guest

Being invited into a Dutch home is somewhat of an honor. A Dutchman's home is his castle, and when he extends an invitation, you may be sure that he isn't making an impulsive gesture. Your response should be in the same thoughtful spirit. Don't offer to help prepare the meal (or to bring a dessert) unless you know the hostess very well. She will expect, and usually prefer, to do everything for you herself.

▸ Be on Time

First and foremost, it is important to be on time. If your host says 8:00 p.m., you should arrive at 8:00 p.m. Punctuality shows consideration for the host as well as for other guests.

▸ Bring a Hostess Gift

A bouquet of flowers is always appreciated. You may take either cut flowers or a potted plant. The florist's wrapping should be left on and a card is not necessary. The flowers should be handed to your hostess when she greets you at the door. You may consider having flowers delivered earlier in the day, thus saving your hostess the trouble of having to arrange them while others are arriving. In this case, do include a card; the hostess will leave it attached to the gift. When visiting a family with children under age 10, remember to take some candy, a small toy or other inexpensive gifts for the kids.

When You Arrive

Both your host and hostess will greet you at the door and shake your hand. After you have given your gift of flowers or wine and have thanked them for the invitation to their home, you will be shown into the living room to meet the other guests. If for some reason you aren't formally introduced at a gathering, go around and briefly introduce yourself and shake hands with each person.

You will find that a Dutch host will make a great effort to assure that you and the others enjoy a pleasant visit. You will be served a drink, possibly Dutch *jenever* (gin), and offered hors d'oeuvres. Light conversation will follow.

Dutch Manners

- **Do not** help yourself to the crackers and nuts placed on the cocktail table in front of you. Wait until they are passed to you or until the hostess asks you to help yourself.
- **Respect** the privacy of the Dutch and do not appear too inquisitive about their family or profession.
- Be aware that the Dutch consider it polite to be a bit self-effacing. Because of this, they tend to downplay their virtues, importance and accomplishments. For example, if someone says, "I don't speak English very well," certainly don't agree with him or suggest a good language course. Accentuate the positive and don't boast about yourself.
- **Never** make jokes about the Royal Family.
- **Do not** "talk shop"—do not talk about work at social events.
- **Avoid** political discussions—unless you are prepared to hear some strong views about what is happening in your country. The Dutch are well informed and may even put you to shame with their knowledge of world events. However, at the same time, they will expect you to present an opposite point of view if you have one and will respect you for it.
- **Do** talk about sports and travel, and be sure to compliment your host's taste in artwork and home furnishings.

Seating Arrangements

If you are invited for a meal, your hostess will probably indicate where she wishes you to sit. This doesn't mean she likes to be excessively formal, but that she has thought out in advance which seating arrangement might make for the most comfortable and relaxed conversation.

At a Dutch sit-down dinner, the hostess may serve herself first. How ungracious? Not at all—she is showing how the food is to be served—a big help to her guests! When you and all other guests have been seated at the table and served wine, your host will lift his glass, exchange glances with each of his guests (and they with each other), and welcome you all with a simple toast such as "*Proost*" or "Welcome to our home."

After the first sip, the glasses may be raised again and the exchange of glances repeated. By raising your glass and returning the glance to your host and other guests, you are expressing your gratitude. Remember, taking a sip before this observance is considered a breach of good manners. Don't start eating until your hostess has taken the first bite. Taste a little of everything and expect the hostess to offer seconds.

The Dutch believe that it is rude to leave a hand under the table (on your lap) during a meal. Keep both wrists lightly on the table surface. You will, in fact, need both of your hands to eat if you do it the European way; hold your fork in your left hand and your knife in your right. Sandwiches and pizza are eaten with a knife and a fork. Pay close attention to your host's table manners, just to be safe.

Coffee isn't typically served with dessert, but afterwards. Your hostess will generally ask your preferences regarding sugar and cream and then will add them to your cup for you. Don't help yourself unless your hostess specifically requests you do so. After dessert and coffee it is customary to offer liqueurs, sherry or a light mixed drink. This is a graceful signal that the evening is entering its last phase, and your guests will also expect it.

When leaving any social gathering, unless the group is very large, you should shake hands and say goodbye to your hosts and attempt to do the same with each guest. A brief thank-you note or phone call to your hosts after a party or dinner will always be appreciated.

Dress Code

Major fashion trends sweep Europe and many other countries almost simultaneously. The younger Dutch are quite fashion conscious, but the older people here tend to dress conservatively, with more emphasis on propriety than on high fashion.

Like most places, style of dress in the Netherlands is dependent on the situation. Due to the wet weather, it is almost always necessary to dress practically. Raincoats are essential throughout the year.

▸ Informal

"Informal" dress will generally equate to what we may term "business casual," such as nice pants and shirt for a man or nice slacks/skirt and sweater for a woman. Once you've made your decision about what clothes to wear, get dressed and don't worry. The larger Dutch cities have long been sophisticated, cross-cultural melting pots. It won't be a disaster if you don't appear as a carbon copy of everyone else at the party.

Formal

Formal events may be more perplexing, and the whims of fashion can quickly render rules out of date. Boutique windows and European fashion magazines can keep you informed of current trends, but when in doubt, it is a good idea to ask your hostess or others on the guest list. If this is impossible, a full length dress is almost always a safe bet. Long skirts and dresses are always appropriate for a dinner party in a private home, but are seldom worn to restaurants.

Formal wear may be rented (*verhuurd*). Agencies are listed under *Gelegenheidskleding* in the Yellow Pages (*Gouden Gids*). Below is a list to help you decipher invitations which specify appropriate dress:

Avondkleding, avondtoilet	Evening dress
Jacquet	Morning coat, long dress
Rok	Tails, long dress coat
Smoking	Tuxedo, cocktail or long dress
Pak/Kostuum	Business suit

Lifetime Events Dutch Style

13 Customs and Etiquette

Births

A birth (*geboorte*) is announced in the newspaper, but Dutch parents also take great pride in sending birth announcements. They also might display a wooden stork outside the door with a baby (doll) hanging from its beak. When the father returns to work, he will distribute the traditional *beschuit met muisjes*, which are Dutch rusks spread with butter and topped with pink or blue and white sugar-coated anise seeds.

After receipt of a birth announcement, send a note, some flowers or a gift for the baby. If you know the parents well, phone and ask when you can visit to admire the baby. Keep your visit brief. Take along flowers or a gift for the baby. The custom of baby showers isn't common.

Birthdays

If there is one day that's important to every Dutch man, woman and child, it's a birthday (*verjaardag*). The entire family comes to call to celebrate this important event. When your Dutch friend tells you his birthday is approaching and invites you to his home, you will know that you've made it to the inner circle of friendship. Once your relationship has become this close, you must never forget a friend's birthday. It is always appropriate to congratulate someone on his or her birthday with: "*Gefeliciteerd met je verjaardag!*" You can also congratulate family members, mutual friends and even neighbors at the gathering!

There are a few milestones which are especially important: 40 years, at which point one generally holds a large party, and 50 years. For this birthday, family and friends really outdo themselves. Their enthusiasm is predominantly expressed in extravagant decoration of the yard, doors and windows of the lucky 50-year-old in question. Signs go up requesting passing motorists to honk their horns. A life-size stuffed "Abraham" or "Sarah" doll, humorously clothed, may adorn the front yard and toilet-paper may be strung in trees and bushes.

Be careful about overspending on a present. An appropriate amount would be €5–8, for a child, €6–12 for an adult acquaintance and €10–15 or more for a close friend. If you spend too much, you may create an uncomfortable situation. Chocolates, a nice bouquet of flowers or a plant make good presents for an acquaintance.

If your child attends school, you should treat everyone on his or her birthday. Set a date and time with the teacher and bring a small treat for everyone including the teacher. Cupcakes, mandarin oranges or boxes of raisins work well, or possibly a special treat from your home country. The teacher's birthday will also be celebrated and a small gift is appropriate. It is also thoughtful to give your child's teacher a present before you move away from the school.

Birthday calendars: A birthday calendar *(verjaardagkalender)* hangs as a reminder in most Dutch family's bathroom. This is a perpetual calendar especially for recording birthdays and anniversaries. Although you may be tempted, never write your own name on another family's birthday calendar.

▸ Engagements

An engagement *(verloving)* is announced to friends by sending the individual cards of the couple in one envelope. If you are invited to a reception, you may send flowers to arrive on that day. If you are well acquainted, you may send a gift in advance. It isn't necessary to send regrets if you can't attend, but an RSVP is always appreciated.

▸ Marriages

An invitation to a wedding *(huwelijk)* is printed on a folded card. Traditionally, one side contains a formal announcement by the bride's parents; the other side an announcement by the groom's parents. It will state the time and location of the required civil ceremony at the Town Hall, the optional church wedding which may follow and the reception. Again, the invitation doesn't require a reply, though replies are appreciated. Congratulatory flowers may be sent in lieu of a gift to the wedding reception of a casual friend or a business acquaintance. It is proper to call the parents to ask if the bride has a list of gift preferences or if her choices have been listed at a local shop. Wedding presents start at about €15 and go up. Bridal showers are not customary in the Netherlands.

Anniversaries

The Dutch celebrate their anniversary (*huwelijksfeest* or *bruiloft*) each year, but there are three anniversaries that are especially important: 12½, 25 and 50 years. A twelve-and-a-half year anniversary of marriage (copper anniversary or *koperen bruiloft*) is referred to as "halfway." You will find appropriate greeting cards in stationery stores, and gifts and flowers are always appreciated, especially if you're invited to the celebration by the couple.

Deaths

Notices of death (*overlijden*) are placed in the newspaper by relatives or business associates. The families also send out announcements or letters edged in black or gray to family and friends. Respect the request for no flowers (*geen bloemen*) or no visitors (*geen bezoek*), if mentioned. It is customary for the family to assemble in the chapel after the burial service and receive condolences from friends. Afterwards, guests are served a cup of coffee and a piece of cake. Only a few brief words and a handshake are expected, and you should send a sympathy card even if you attend the service.

Out and About

In a Shop

Always greet the shopkeeper with "good morning" (*goedemorgen*), "good afternoon" (*goedemiddag*) or simply by saying "*dag*." The shopkeeper will wait on only one customer at a time and may even escort each one to the door. Never interrupt. Your turn will come and you, too, will be extended that same personal treatment. A "thank you" (*dank u wel*) and a "goodbye" (*dag*) should be repeated when you are leaving. You might indicate you will be back with "see you later" (*tot ziens*).

In a Restaurant

Unless it is an exclusive restaurant, you will probably seat yourself. Of course, you will see dogs in cafes and in the smaller bistros, but don't be alarmed. They are welcomed by the owners and are usually very well behaved. You will rarely be rushed or hurried—even if you would rather have it that way. Be prepared to spend some time at the table.

Helpful Vocabulary

Appetizers	*Voorgerechten*
Available (e.g., a table)	*Vrij*
Bill	*Rekening*
Complaints	*Klachten*
Desserts	*Nagerechten*
Entrées, main courses	*Hoofdgerechten*
Included (in the price)	*Inbegrepen/inclusief*
Occupied (e.g., a chair)	*Bezet*

Reserved	*Gereserveerd*
Service	*Bediening*

▸ Tipping

Hairdressers: Hairdressers should get a small tip of €3–5 depending upon the extent and type of service received.

Hotels: Porters should receive about €1–2 for each piece of luggage. Cloakroom attendants get the same amount for each coat.

Household help: At New Year's, it is customary to tip your household help, garbage men, newspaper boy and regular delivery men (about €1–3 for the latter three; more for your in-house help). Often you will be handed a card as a reminder. On their birthdays, household help will expect a cash bonus.

Restaurants: Tipping in restaurants is often a concern for those who are accustomed to leaving a percentage of the bill for the waiter. In the Netherlands, however, restaurants include a 15% service charge when totaling your bill. This kind of bill is called *inclusief*. If you have asked for special attention or have received exceptional service, you MAY leave an additional amount, but it should never exceed half of the included tip. About a third of that amount or 5% of the total bill is typical. Tips are not expected, but generally leaving a few euro coins is appreciated.

Taxis: Taxi drivers may add 15% to the amount clocked on the meter and tell you the amount to pay. If in doubt, ask if the metered amount is *inclusief*. If it is *exclusief*, then €3–5 is a reasonable tip for an average ride.

Observing Special Days

One of the best ways to really ground yourself in the culture and feel as if you belong here is to fully participate in the days which are special to the Dutch. You will find that some of these holidays may be unfamiliar to you. Your country's traditional holiday calendar is not honored here. If you are American, there will be no Thanksgiving Day celebration and if you are French, your calendar will have no Bastille Day. However, you will have a chance to celebrate Queen's Day, watch the arrival of *Sinterklaas* and hear the church bells in the air during the two minutes of silence on *Dodenherdenking*. Below is a list of the special days from the Dutch Calendar.

▸ Carnival — *Carnaval*

Traditionally this holiday was celebrated in the predominantly Catholic southern provinces although it is now being celebrated in some Protestant areas as well. The bigger parades and street parties are held in Brabant and Limburg. The Dutch also like to take this opportunity to make political and social statements. Sometimes, whole communities act on a particular theme. This all happens in the week preceding Ash Wednesday.

▸ Easter — *Pasen*

The Dutch also have Easter egg hunts, sometimes with a practical, peculiarly Dutch twist. In Delft, for example, an annual hunt is held at the local "Water Playground," where balsa blocks are buried in the sandy beach. Children come with their own buckets and pails and dig for this buried treasure. Later, the wooden blocks may be exchanged for real eggs.

▸ April 30 — *Koninginnedag*

Traditionally, the Dutch celebrate Queen's Day on April 30th which is in fact the Queen Mother's birthday. When Queen Juliana abdicated in favor of her daughter, Beatrix, the new queen kept the celebration on her mother's birthday since April weather is indeed better for a holiday than that in January.

Most communities plan a big celebration with bands and clowns, etc. On this day, it is legal for private individuals to conduct tax-free commerce (similar to a flea market or yard sale). You will see a lot of people selling the products of their spring cleaning, and every kid who has ever taken a music lesson will be on the street, serenading for cash. This is generally held in a designated area such as a main street.

Amsterdam is the unofficial center of Queen's Day. Beginning the evening of the 29th, the downtown becomes an endless, throbbing flea market and side show. People actually camp out (and party heavily) on a piece of sidewalk all night in order to reserve a prime commercial site for the following day. It is an amazing experience; just be prepared for the crowds. Vondel Park is a bit less hectic than the narrow downtown streets—and no less interesting.

▸ May 4 — *Dodenherdenking*

The eve of Liberation Day is the official Dutch Memorial Day. It's not a holiday, but rather a day of remembrance for those who lost their lives during World War II. From 6:00 a.m. until sunset, flags fly at half-mast. At approximately 8:00 p.m., all activity stops while the nation observes two minutes of silence. A moving ceremony is held. Families silently lay wreaths upon memorials to the Dutch war prisoners who died.

▸ May 5 — *Bevrijdingsdag*

Liberation Day is a time of rejoicing. Organized sport competitions for the community are held, Dutch schools are closed, and the nation remembers and celebrates this important moment in its recent history.

▸ September — *Prinsjesdag*

The Opening of Parliament is celebrated on the third Tuesday in September in The Hague. Queen Beatrix rides to the *Binnenhof* in the famous Golden Coach (*Gouden Koets*) to open Parliament and read the State of the Union message. Schools and government offices are closed, flags fly and people from all over line up to catch a glimpse of the Queen.

▸ November 11 — *Sint Maarten's Dag*

This holiday, Saint Martin's Day, manifests itself as a cross between trick-or-treating and Christmas caroling. If children sing at your door, give them a little treat.

▸ December 5 — *Sinterklaas*

Around the middle of November, *Sinterklaas* sails to the Netherlands from his summer home in Spain. Every year his arrival into a different Dutch city is televised. He also makes pilgrimages to other localities, also by boat, and subsequently upon a white steed. (Watch your local newspaper for details.) With *Sint* travel his Moorish companions, Black Petes (*Zwarte Pieten*). According to legend, *Zwarte Pieten* represent the Moorish servants of the Spanish courts in the days of Saint Nicholas. In the pre-Christian era, a similar figure was the controller of the moon cycle; he would capture the moon, steal it away in his bag and scatter the stars. Today, *Zwarte Piet* tosses *pepernoten* (tiny ginger cookies) and other small treats to children.

From the time *Sinterklaas* and his cohorts arrive until December 5th, parents allow children to put out their shoes at night – preferably by the chimney. They hope that *Zwarte Piet* will leave some treats (*pepernoten*, marzipan figures, fruit, chocolate letters, small toys). Sometimes children put out carrots, hay and water for *Sint's* horse.

December 5th marks the main *Sinterklaas* event—the eve of the birthday of St. Nicholas, the patron saint of children. Families, and sometimes close friends, exchange small, cleverly-wrapped and/or disguised presents (one example: a necklace hidden in a cucumber), accompanied by a thoughtful, funny, teasing poem.

Some Dutch exchange gifts on this day instead of or in addition to December 25th. The St. Nicholas festival day has traditionally been one of the Netherlands' most popular holidays. The trend towards celebrating on December 25th has diminished interest in this beautiful festival and often only the traditionally-minded Dutch and those with small children continue the custom. Christmas trees and outdoor lighting begin to go up as of the first Saturday after December 5th.

▸ December 25–26 — *Kerstmis*

Once *Sinterklaas* is past, the zaniness of the season is over. The quiet serious side of the religious holiday comes to the fore. Christmas music fills the churches; towns decorate their trees with thousands of white lights. You can purchase a tree with roots for planting later, or one which has been cut to fit in your Christmas tree stand. Garden centers are filled with unique ornaments. There are holiday markets in many cities with special gifts available.

This holiday is celebrated over two days. Christmas Day (*Eerste Kerstdag*) is a family holiday. The day after Christmas, Boxing Day (*Tweede Kerstdag*) is a day for seeing friends and exchanging small gifts. On both of these days, dining out is very popular. If you are planning to do the same, be sure you make your reservations early.

December 31 — *Oudejaarsavond*

New Year's Eve is traditionally celebrated with family and close friends. Many people also attend church services. Traditional fried and fruit-filled Dutch doughnuts called *oliebollen* are eaten. When the clock strikes twelve, hold your ears! The American 4th of July celebration is tame in comparison to Dutch fireworks on New Year's Eve. Factories and ships blow their whistles, churches ring their bells and fireworks and bonfires light up the skies. Fireworks are available in shops at the end of December. Most restaurants are closed on this evening. The Dutch generally don't celebrate with hotel parties on New Year's Eve.

Since this is a rather rowdy holiday, it might be wise to keep your pets inside, have a fire extinguisher handy and park your car well out of harm's way. Some insurance companies don't cover damages incurred on *Oudejaarsavond*.

January 6 — *Driekoningendag*

Known in English as the Feast of the Epiphany, or literally translated as "Three Kings' Day," this holiday marks the end of the Christmas season. Decorations come down and Christmas trees are burned (assuming your tree has not been set afire on New Year's Eve!) Often, local fire departments organize bonfires. At this time, someone brings to school a round pound cake into which is baked one lone almond. The child who is lucky enough to get the slice containing the nut gets to be King for a day, with all the attendant privileges of royalty.

Flag-Flying Days

There are many special days when the red, white and blue flag of the Netherlands and the orange banner of the House of Orange-Nassau, the Dutch royal family, will be flying. Included among these days are the anniversaries, birthdays and graduations of Dutch royal family members, Queen's Day and Liberation Day. You will also see gaily decorated flagpoles throughout the Netherlands to indicate a family celebration of a special birthday or anniversary. You may even see an old school bag hanging from the flagpole when a Dutch child graduates from high school.

References

Try to read as much as possible about the Netherlands and its people before leaving home. Once you have arrived, you can still learn more about the Dutch by reading the selections on our **References** list at the back of this book.

Chapter 14

Speaking Dutch

"Do I really have to learn to speak Dutch?" This is the question most frequently asked by newcomers to the Netherlands, especially by those who might not be natural linguists.

The answer is, "No, you don't have to learn to speak Dutch." Due to a strong emphasis on languages in the Dutch educational system, supplemented by heavy English-language television programming, almost everyone speaks at least a little English.

However, there are definite rewards in knowing at least some of the language of your host country. Your sense of isolation from the community at large will be relieved once you can recognize key words on billboards, in newspapers and on TV. In addition, it seems friendlier and much more polite when you make the effort to greet your neighbors in their own language.

Unless you make a determined effort, it is unrealistic to think that you will become fluent in Dutch in a short period of time. However, with a few hours of study each week for several weeks, almost anyone can acquire a basic vocabulary.

Getting Started

If you have the opportunity to begin studying Dutch before you arrive, by all means go ahead and start. Create simple word games with the entire family. Consider it an adventure and a challenge, and encourage each other to repeat those unfamiliar sounds without fear of being embarrassed.

Once you are in the Netherlands and before you become too busy, choose the best approach for continuing your studies: private instruction, group classes, intensive training, etc. If you plan to be here for only a short time, you probably won't want to spend the entire time studying a language you may never use again. It may be more practical to select a specified period of time—perhaps three months—and try to concentrate on learning as much as possible to acquire a basic foundation. If you are willing to invest your time and money learning to speak Dutch, try to obtain the best instruction. If you need help in finding a class, seek recommendations from fellow expatriates and read the advertisements in club publications.

▸ Teachers

If you want to learn as rapidly as possible, private lessons or very small group lessons are strongly recommended. They may be more expensive, but if the instructor is competent, the result should be that you will learn more per hour spent in class.

You may decide to register for intensive training of six-to-eight hours each day over a short period of time or a slower-paced once or twice per week format. Before enrolling for classes, discuss with the teacher the method used and the text followed. A good teacher will work out a study plan to fit the needs of each student.

▸ Language Schools

There are many language schools in the Netherlands. Look in the Yellow Pages under *Talenonderwijs*. Teaching methods vary, so weigh the differences. If you find yourself unhappy with your learning situation, try to change it rather than giving up entirely.

Other places to check for language courses are in the White Pages under: Schools-Continuing Education *(Scholen, Voortgezet Onderwijs)*, Open University *(Vrije Akademie)*, and People's University *(Volksuniversiteit)*. Also try Adult Education *(Volwassenen Onderwijs)* in the Yellow Pages. Such places usually offer the least expensive courses. (Remember that *Vrije Akademie* will be found alphabetically under *Vrye*—see the **Communications** chapter for hints on using the Dutch phone book.)

If you plan to stay for several years or wish to pursue a job that requires some fluency in Dutch, one option is a program called NT2 *(Nederlandse Tweede Taal)* or *Dutch as a Second Language*. At the end of five semesters of study (ten hours of class per week), students may enroll for the *Staatsexamen*, a national proficiency exam. Students passing this exam are given a diploma that certifies a reasonable command of the Dutch language and they can show this to potential employers. Check the telephone books for a NT2 program in your area. You can also check with colleges or universities in your area as they frequently have programs for foreign students who study at their institutions. Sometimes a course may be closed to non-students, but you may be able to use a language laboratory.

▸ Texts

When you enroll in a class, the teacher will indicate which text or study materials to buy. If you want to study a bit before you arrive, the website *www.learndutch.org* is an excellent source for learning Dutch. It is a set of 60 lessons based on the process of opening a cafe in the city. You can hear the words spoken in correct Dutch as well as read them. Short tests are included with each lesson. You can also try the websites *www.dictionaries.travlang.com* to help find reference words and phrases or *www.translate.google.com* to help with basic translations.

Language Learning Tips

Your Dutch will improve if you:

- Keep your ears and eyes open.
- Listen to Dutch conversations.
- Pay attention to how the Dutch say things in English. Their errors often illustrate the grammatical differences between Dutch and English.
- Watch English television programs with an eye on the Dutch subtitles.
- Be alert for words that are similar to English words.
- Scan Dutch periodicals to see if you grasp any ideas.
- Make out shopping lists in Dutch.
- Look up words you might need in a given situation.
- Practice speaking as much as possible, even if you have to talk to yourself. Research shows that doing so dramatically improves language skills, especially the ability to remember new words.

A Few Basics

The Dutch Alphabet

Learn to say the alphabet in Dutch so that you can spell your unusual-sounding foreign name to a Dutch person, and they can spell their long, complicated name to you.

The Dutch alphabet consists of the same letters as the English, but the letters Q, X and Y are used only in foreign words.

A	B	C	D	E	F	G	H	I
ah	bay	say	day	ay	eff	HGay*	hah	ee
J	K	L	M	N	O	P	Q	R
yay	kah	ell	emm	enn	oh	pay	koo	air
S	T	U	V	W	X	IJ	Y	Z
ess	tay	oo	vay	way	iks	aye	eeHGrek*	zett

*HG is our way of approximating the Dutch "G," and is similar to the sound made when you clearing your throat. See below.

Special Sounds

One of the most important sounds to learn is the Dutch "G." It is pronounced with a soft guttural sound that is never heard in English. You can approximate it by pronouncing a harsh "H" sound deep in the back of your throat. A reasonable approximation of this sound is better than a hard English "G." While trying to master this, you will come to realize why the Dutch good-humoredly say theirs is "not a language, but a throat disease."

Other special, difficult sounds include the "sch" or "sg" sound as in Schiphol and Scheveningen, and "ui" sound as in the word for onion, *uien*, and the formal you, *uw*. It is worthwhile to practice these sounds and keep in mind that confusion may result when you use words with these sounds.

Time and Dates

The Dutch tell time differently from the way some people expect. If it is 8:30, some say eight-thirty or half past eight, but the Dutch say half nine (*half negen*). Nine forty would be said as ten past half ten (*tien over half tien*). In such cases it is best to repeat the time in your own system. Moreover, the use of 24-hour "military" time is more prevalent when written than the 2 x 12-hour system. Thus, 6 a.m. will be 6.00 (*zes uur*), but 6 p.m. will be written as 18.00 (*achttien uur*). Six o'clock in the evening (*zes uur's avonds*) is the norm in conversational use.

The Dutch express numerically written dates in the sequence: day-month-year. For example, May 16, 2008 reads 16-05-08.

This can be a major source of confusion, so when making appointments in Dutch, it is wise to rephrase the meeting date and time to be sure that you understand each other.

Morning	*morgen, ochtend*
This morning	*vanmorgen*
Afternoon	*middag*
This afternoon	*vanmiddag*
Evening	*avond*
This evening	*vanavond*
Yesterday	*gisteren*
The day before yesterday	*eergisteren*
Last night	*gisterenavond*
Today	*vandaag*
Tomorrow	*morgen*
Tomorrow night	*morgenavond*
The day after tomorrow	*overmorgen*

Days of the Week

Monday	*maandag*
Tuesday	*dinsdag*
Wednesday	*woensdag*
Thursday	*donderdag*
Friday	*vrijdag*
Saturday	*zaterdag*
Sunday	*zondag*

Days of the week and months of the year are NOT capitalized in Dutch.

- Push the button marked "*bon.*" A sticker with the name of the item, its weight and its price will print out.
- Place the sticker onto your bag.

Waiting in Line: In general, the Dutch don't form lines. If there are several customers ahead of you at the meat, bread or cheese counter who are waiting to be helped, keep a sharp eye on those who are before and after you so that you can be served. It is up to you to speak up quickly when it is your turn or you will be passed by. Listen for the clerk to ask who is next in line, "*Wie is aan de beurt?*" Some specialty shops have a number system where you pull a number and wait until it is ticked off on a strategically placed clock.

Ordering the Right Amount: While at first, the metric system might seem baffling, it won't take long for you to be ordering a "*half kilo.*" It is common to use exact measurements in grams, but there are some other standard measurements:

een ons	100 grams
half pond	250 grams
een pond/half kilo	500 grams
anderhalf pond	750 grams
een kilo	1000 grams
anderhalve kilo	1500 grams

You might also hear the local shoppers ask for *anderhalf ons* (150 grams), but that usually applies only to cold cuts.

Shopping Bags: No one will help pack your grocery bags or take them to your car. It is customary to bring your own tote bags for groceries and pack everything yourself. Plastic or cloth bags are usually available, but at an extra cost. There is no charge for the cardboard boxes stacked near supermarket exits, but the supply is variable. Always have a bag or two on hand.

Self Check-Out: Some of the newer supermarkets have put in special self check-out lanes. Sometimes this means that you scan the grocery items yourself at the cash register and other times you use a hand-held scanner as you walk around the store, which can be very entertaining if you have kids along. Don't be afraid to try these new methods. If the system at your store doesn't have an English option, ask an employee or other customer for help.

Savings Stamps: Some supermarkets offer savings stamps (*spaarzegels* or *zegels*) at the check-out counter. Completed books are usually redeemable for full cash value plus a token bonus. If they are not free, it is probably not worth the trouble.

Glass: Return for a Deposit or Recycle?: You will be required to pay a deposit on most soda, beer and mineral water bottles, even plastic ones. These bottles have the word *statiegeld* printed on the label or on the bottle itself. Most stores have an automatic return center for refundable bottles:

- Insert your bottles one at a time or place a crate of bottles on the conveyor belt.
- After you have placed all your bottles in the machine, push the "*bon*" button. The machine will print a receipt for you.
- When you check out, give the receipt to the cashier, who will deduct the total from your grocery bill.

All non-returnable glass items should go into the large recyling containers marked "*glasbak*" located at shopping centers. If possible, remove all metal from bottle necks and lids before recycling. For additional details, please see the chapter on **The Environment**.

Food Shopping Options

There are many other food shopping possibilities in addition to supermarkets. Soon after your arrival, you will probably be tempted by the display windows of specialty cheese, meat, poultry, bread, pastry, greengrocer and fish shops. Since Dutch housewives often shop for fresh items on a daily basis, these shops can be rather crowded. However, lines move quickly since purchases tend to be small.

You should also try the colorful street markets, usually held in or near the center of town. They have the whole gambit of fresh flowers, herbs, produce, poultry, fish and cheese—all at competitive prices. These are held weekly, always on the same day of the week, with each town in the immediate vicinity using a different day. See the chapter on **Shopping** for a list of markets in the larger cities or visit *www.hollandsemarkten.nl* to search for markets in your area.

Keep an eye out for "for sale" (*te koop*) signs as you tour the countryside. You might also see a sign for a cheese farm (*kaasboerderij*) where you can buy cheese and sometimes butter, eggs, milk, yogurt, buttermilk and produce directly from the farmer. You may also see signs indicating the sale of produce such as potatoes: "*Aardappelen te koop.*" If you are bold enough to stop by a greenhouse some morning, you will likely be able to buy small quantities of produce or a house plant directly from the producer.

Basic Baking and Cooking Ingredients

Today's Dutch cooking is changing very quickly to encompass ethnic foods from all over the world. Thus, everything you need to stock your basic pantry is available here although the ingredients might look different to you. It is just a matter of knowing what to ask for and then learning how to use the products.

Baking Soda (*maagzout*): Also known as bicarbonate of soda, baking soda is sometimes sold in Asian supermarkets and stores that cater to American and British tastes. You may also find it at the pharmacy (*apotheek*).

Baking Powder (*bakpoeder*): The basic difference between double acting and single acting baking powder is that the leavening agents in double acting work twice, once when liquid is added and again when it comes into contact with heat. Baking powder in North America is usually double acting and the container is clearly marked. The baking powder sold here comes in packets and doesn't stipulate whether it is single or double acting. Thus, we recommend that for the purpose of cooking that you treat it as double acting. You can also buy double-acting baking powder at import stores.

Cream of Tartar: You can buy it at any of the stores that cater to American and British tastes. Some Asian stores also carry it.

Flour (*tarwebloem*): Dutch flour may cause you a bit of frustration. The Dutch all-purpose flour (*patentbloem*) has 11 grams of gluten per cup, while GoldMedal and Pillsbury have 10 to 12 grams per cup. Thus, there should be no reason why the flours can't be used interchangeably. However, some chefs complain that the local flour becomes too liquid when overbeaten. Test a cookie before you pop them all in the oven and check your quick breads before taking them out. Just to be on the safe side, add one extra tablespoon of flour per cup required for cookies and quick breads. Use *patentbloem* for all things except breads and try the Kristal brand flour in particular for American recipes.

Bread flour (*broodmeel*): Look for bread flour in a natural foods store (*reformhuis*). Bread flour is made with a high percentage of American spring wheat. Another possibility is to ask at your local bakery for some wheat gluten (*eiwitpoeder*, protein powder). You can add this to regular Dutch flour in any bread recipe; use ½ cup for 8 cups of flour.

Cake Flour (*cakemeel*): What you see in the shops as cake flour is not what you may be expecting. It already has some ingredients added and it makes a loaf similar to pound cake. If your recipe calls for regular cake flour, substitute: 1 cup less 2 tablespoons all-purpose flour for 1 cup cake flour.

Self-rising flour (*zelfrijzendbakmeel*): The local self-rising flour is available in most supermarkets or you can make your own by mixing 2¼ pounds (one kilogram) of all-purpose flour with 4 tablespoons cream of tartar and 2 tablespoons baking soda.

Fats, solid: There are three basic types of solid fats available: animals fats which include butter (*boter*), lard (*reuzel*) and beef suet (*rundvet* or *rundniervet*); deep-frying fats (which are a combination of animal and vegetable fats), and margarine. There is no real Dutch equivalent of Crisco shortening, but the Dutch have some adequate substitutes. *Frituurvet* and *Ossewit* are basically deep-frying fats, but can be combined with butter to make good pie crusts and biscuits. Also try *Bakgraag* by Bona for baking. For pan frying, try *Braderije Braadboter voor Bakken en Braden* or *Croma*.

Sugar (*suiker*): While most Dutch sugar is made from sugar beets and differs very little from cane sugar, there are some special sugars that are not available in many other countries. *Basterd suiker* is soft and moist and still has some molasses clinging to it. It dissolves quickly and is excellent for use in yogurts, cereals and baking. It comes in three types: white, light brown and dark brown. Granulated sugar is also available in a fine granulated form (*fijn kristal suiker*) or a more coarse granulated form (*kristal suiker*). Dark, strong molasses made from cane sugar can be found at a health food store (*reformhuis*).

Yeast (*gist*): If you still insist on baking your own bread after visiting the local baker, you will need to know that fresh yeast is not sold in compact cakes in supermarkets. You will have to get it from the same baker that sold you that wonderful bread. One American cake of yeast usually weighs ¼ ounce or 7.5 grams. Seven grams of active dry yeast equals 25 grams fresh yeast. Active-dry yeast is also available in the baking section of supermarkets.

Condiments: You will find an ample supply of catsup/ketchup, mustards, pickles, relishes and Worcestershire sauces in the Netherlands. Although some products and brand names will look familiar to you, there may be subtle differences in flavor if they are manufactured outside of the U.S. Try the curry catsup that is often served in restaurants along with French fries (*friets*). You may enjoy experimenting with some of the varieties of soy sauce (*soya saus*), including light, dark, Indonesian sweet (*ketjap manis*) and Indonesian salty (*ketjap asin*).

The Butcher Shop

Supermarkets carry beef, veal, pork, lamb, poultry and cold cuts. Some of their meats are pre-packaged and appear in coolers next to the meat department, but the butcher is always there for special requests. You may also enjoy trying the independent butcher shops (*slagerijen*) found in almost every city and village. Many of these butchers have bigger selections than the supermarkets and may have a special meat supplier. They are very innovative and offer prepared Dutch meat dishes, salads with meat in them and sauces for fondues. They will also prepare special party platters for fondue, table grill or barbeque.

Keep in mind that European butchers may cut meats differently than your home country butchers do, and you may not see cuts that are familiar to you. If you have a picture of the special cuts, a friendly butcher generally will try to accommodate you. Give plenty of advance notice for special orders. The butcher gets his wholesale cuts and carves them up on selected days. Some butchers who are familiar with American and English cuts and carry imported beef are listed in the "World Foods and Flavors" section in this chapter. For a listing of meat terms, see our vocabulary list at the back of this chapter. For your convenience, we have listed the best cuts for different methods of preparation.

▸ Beef *(Rundvlees)*

You will be amazed at the freshness and the variety of beef cuts that are available in the Netherlands. The local beef is low in fat and has no preservatives or hormones. While it may be better for your health, it does create a challenge to cooks who are accustomed to tender, corn-fed beef. Unless cooked for a very short time or with liquids for prolonged periods of time, it can get dry and tough. Some butchers carry imported marbled beef that produces tender cuts. However, there is no reason why Dutch beef can't be used for specific recipes and popular cooking methods. The Dutch usually eat about 100 grams (3 ounces) per person per meal and this is reflected in pre-cut meats. The butcher will be happy to cut any size you like.

Beef cuts for pan-frying/sautéing or grilling: These steaks *(biefstukken)* are the most tender and expensive cuts of local beef. They are usually pan-fried, but can be broiled, grilled or barbecued. Brush them with oil before putting them on the grill. Good cuts of beef include:

- loin steak *(lendebiefstuk)*
- filet mignon *(biefstuk van de haas)*
- chateaubriand *(chateaubriand)*
- eye of the round*(kogelbiefstuk)*
- filet or tenderloin *(ossehaas)*
- top loin similar to New York steak *(entrecote)*
- medallions *(tournedos)*
- For grilled kebabs, try loin rolled roast*(lenderollade)* and rib *(rosbief van de dikke lende)*
- For hamburgers, meatballs and kofta, try ground beef *(rundergehakt)* or half ground beef and half ground pork *(halfom half)*
- *Tartaar* is a very lean ground beef, quite often eaten without cooking.

Beef cuts for roasting and braising:

- If you can eat your roasts very rare, buy rib roast with bones *(rosbief* or *riblap met been)*.
- For braising, use a rolled roast *(rollade)* or a chuckroast *(braadstuk)*.
- The most tender *rosbief* comes from the rib and is called *rosbief van de dikke lende*. Others are from the short loin and sirloin *(slip van de lende)* and fore shank *(van het schouderstuk)*.
- The most tender *rollade* is a top loin rolled roast *(lenderollade)*. Others are from the rump or round *(van de bovenbil)*, a streaky roast from the brisket or short plate *(doorregenrollade)* and flank *(vang)*.
- Also for braising, try the beef ribs from the rib section *(losgesneden ribben)*. Cook slowly in beef broth until tender.

Beef cuts for stewing: You will see various cuts on sale called *lap*, *lappen* or *lapjes* which simply means slice(s). They come from various parts of the beef and are good for stewing. Some *lappen* you will see are:

- breast slices *(borstlappen)*
- loin slices *(lendelappen)*

- ribslices *(riblappen)*
- fore shank or chuck slices *(sukadelappen)*
- collective term for all other slices *(runderlappen)*.

Veal *(Kalfsvlees)*

Dutch veal is very good and easy to prepare.

Veal cuts for pan-frying/sautéing and grilling:

- breaded veal cutlets *(schnitzels)*
- veal chops *(kalfskoteletten)*
- veal steak*(kalfsbiefstuk)*
- veal tenderloin *(kalfshaas)*
- veal medallions*(kalfsoesters)*

Veal cuts for roasting and braising:

- For a wonderful oven roast, try *kalfsfricandeau*. It is cut from several parts of the calf. That from the *dikke lende* is the most tender.
- Also try the rolled roast from the loin *(lenderollade)* and the roasting piece *(braadstuk)* from the shoulder *(bovenhals)* and breast *(borst)*.
- For braising, use the breast of veal *(kalfsborst)* which is commonly filled with a stuffing of ground meat and vegetables or the veal shank *(ossobucco)* in the wonderful Italian-style.

Veal cuts for stewing: For your recipe for Blanquette de Veau or Veal Goulash, try any of the *kalfslappen*, the most tender being the slices from the loin *(lendelappen)*.

Lamb *(Lamsvlees)*

As you drive along the dikes and *polders* of the Netherlands, you can't help but notice the abundance of sheep. Thus lamb meat is available in most butcher shops and shops that cater to residents from the Middle East. The meat is of good quality, particularly that which comes from Texel. It is considered a *pré salé* or pre-salted lamb because it has been fattened close to the sea. You generally need to add only pepper to compliment its unusual flavor.

Lamb cuts for pan-frying/sautéing:

- lamb chops *(karbonaden)*
- cutlets *(koteletten)* cut from rib *(rib)*, back *(rug)* and neck *(hals)*

Lamb cuts for grilling:

- kebabs: try slices from the leg, shoulder, breast and neck *(lamslappen)*; leg of lamb *(lamsbout)* and ground lamb *(lamsgehakt)*.
- leg of lamb *(lamsbout)*

Lamb cuts for roasting and braising:

- leg of lamb (*lamsbout*)
- saddle or rack of lamb(*zadel* or *rug lamribstuk*)
- rolled lamb roast (*lamsrollade*)

Lamb cuts for stewing:

- rolled roast (*rollade*)
- slices from the leg, shoulder, breast and neck (*lamslappen van de bout,schouder, borst, nek*)

Pork (*Varkensvlees*)

Dutch pork, the other white meat, is of superior quality. It is lean, and like beef, must be cooked until a little pink inside or just done.

Pork cuts for pan-frying/sautéing and grilling: These pork cuts also happen to be the most tender cuts:

- pork filet (*varkenshaas*)
- tenderloin chop (*haaskarbonade*)
- rib chop (*ribkarbonade*)
- porkcutlets which may be breaded (*schnitzels*)
- small cuts from the rear leg and tenderloin (*varkensbiefstuk* and *varkensoester*)
- chops from the shoulder (*schouderkarbonaden*)
- For kebabs, try the pork slices (*varkenslappen*), ground or minced pork (*varkensgehakt*) and ground half beef and half pork (*half om half*).
- For spare ribs, use the "spare ribs" which have more meat on them and are better for grilling.
- *Krabbetjes*, another type of spare rib are traditionally used for making soups.
- For stir-fry dishes, use the *varkenslappen*, *hamlappen* or*doorregen verse lappen* which are all slices from various parts.
- *Doorregen spek lappen* are streaky belly cuts of pork.

Pork cuts for roasting and braising: Of the roasting pieces, the *varkensfricandeau*, a piece from the leg or shoulder, is probably the tastiest. It should have a layer of fat on the outside to keep it from drying out. Also try to roast or braise any of the rolled roasts, but remember that they are usually pre-seasoned by the butcher. You may special order an unseasoned roast. These rolled roasts are listed in order of tenderness:

- rolled loin roast (*lenderollade*)
- blade rolled roast(*schouderfiletrollade*)
- streaky rolled roast (*doorregenvarkensrollade*).
- shoulder piece (*schouderstuk*) has some fat in it and is thus also suitable for roasting or braising

Pork cuts for stewing: Try the fresh ham cuts (*hamlappen*).

▸ Sausages & Cold Cuts

Like many Europeans, the Dutch may only eat one hot meal a day. Thus, they eat a lot of cold cuts and sausages (*worst en vleeswaren*), of which the quality is superior. You will find a good selection in supermarkets, delicatessens and butcher shops. They are most often made from beef and pork, but may also be prepared with chicken (*kip*), turkey (kalkoen) or horse meat (*paardevlees*). The Dutch usually eat their bacon (*spek*) or ham (*ham*) as a cold cut. If you are cooking bacon and eggs for breakfast, you might like to try breakfast bacon (*ontbijtspek* or *katenspek*). The *katenspek* is more like American or British bacon.

Poultry, Game Birds and Game

Poultry and poultry-related products are sold in most supermarkets and butcher shops, but for a greater variety try a shop that specializes in poultry (*poelier*). They carry various types of chicken and chicken parts, eggs, turkey and turkey parts, and game birds (*wild engevogelte*) in addition to various cuts of game (especially during the holidays). For a list of types of poultry offered, please refer to the vocabulary list at the end of this chapter.

Fish

The Dutch have always enjoyed the fruits of the waters around them. Most of the fish (*vis*) sold here has recently been swimming in the cold North Sea and in fish farms in the area, though you may also find fish here from the Mediterranean or the Nile.

While the larger supermarkets may carry fresh seafood and frozen seafood products, the best place to buy seafood is at the local fish shop (*vishandel*). You might also want to try the fish stalls at the farmer's market and the mobile fish vendors that are strategically stationed at shopping centers, most often on Thursdays or Fridays. Fish vendors all serve the Dutch favorite, raw herring (*nieuwe haring*), and you have a choice of eating it with or without raw onions. You can also buy freshly fried haddock (*lekkerbekjes*—*lekker* means delicious, *bekje* means mouth) and deep-fried cod pieces (*gebakken kibbeling*). The Dutch and Belgians are very fond of mussels (*mosselen*) and they most often appear in the shops during the months with an "r" in them. They are cooked in a variety of ways, but the most popular is simply steamed in white wine with vegetables (leeks and carrots) and served with a mayonnaise-base sauce. Clams are much more difficult to come across.

You will find sole (*tong*), cod (*kabeljauw*), flounder (*bot*), herring (*haring*), mackerel (*makreel*), eel (*paling*), salmon (*zalm*) and various kinds of shrimp (*garnalen*) throughout the year. In addition to fresh fish, you can buy frozen fish and canned tuna, sardines, shrimp and salmon in all supermarkets. For a complete list of types of fish in the Netherlands, please refer to the vocabulary list at the end of this chapter.

Dairy Products

Milk and Milk Products

Prominent on the Dutch landscape is the lovely black and white Holstein cow that produces some of the world's finest milk (*melk*) and milk products (*zuivel producten*). These varied and delicious milk products are usually sold in supermarkets, but may also be delivered to your door.

Fresh milk and whipping cream are pasteurized and sold in cartons, single use plastic bottles or returnable glass bottles. The last date on which the milk should be sold is stamped on each container. Sterilized or canned milk and coffee cream are also available. Milk is sold whole fat (*volle*), low-fat (*half volle*) and skim (*magere*). For evaporated or condensed milk, use coffee milk (*koffiemelk*). Sweetened condensed milk (*gecondenseerde melk met suiker*) is also available. If you don't find it in your supermarket, check the Asian stores (*toko*). Butter is very popular and, unless otherwise specified, is always unsalted. For a non-dairy whipping cream substitute, you can try lightly sweetened Klop Klop, which you are likely to find near the coffee and coffee creamers at the supermarket.

While there are various types of yogurt available, do try the Dutch yogurt (*yoghurt*). It is thick and creamy, but still liquid enough to pour. *Biogarde* is a type of yogurt that has different bacteria in it and is less sour. There are two basic types: *roer* and *stand*. The difference is mainly texture. Both *yoghurt* and *biogarde* come plain (*naturel*) and flavored with fruit. Various flavors of custard/pudding (*vla*) are also available. Their packaging is similar to milk and yogurt, so check your cartons carefully. Ice cream is sold by the carton or individual bars at the supermarket and in a wonderful array of flavors in ice cream parlors. Soft ice cream is sold at ice cream parlors and also by some street vendors.

Some cheeses are found in the milk products aisle at the supermarket, but they are mostly fresh cheeses like *kwark*, cottage cheese (*hüttenkäse*), cream cheese (*roomkaas*) and spreading cheese (*smeerkaas*). *Kwark* is a skim-milk dairy product which is a soft, smooth, fresh curd cheese. It is wonderful when combined with fruit for a delicious dessert or spread on a raisin roll. Try using it to make a type of cheese cake similar to those served in New York delis. For cream cheese, Philadelphia brand is sold in many stores, but the local Mon Chou also works well in cheese cakes. For more types of dairy products, please refer to the vocabulary list at the end of this chapter.

Eggs

Eggs (*eieren*) are generally sold in cartons of 6 or 10 and are classified according to size: S-small (*klein*), M-medium (*middel groot*), L-large (*groot*) and XL-extra large (*extra groot*). You may find that the eggshells are dirty. Eggs are not washed before they are packaged because washing removes the natural protective coating which keeps eggs fresh.

Some people consider it inhumane to keep hens cooped up in laying boxes, and so there is a demand for eggs laid by chickens which live more comfortably. As a result, you now have a choice between free range (*scharrel*), less free ranging (*voliere*) and laying battery (*legbatterij*) eggs. Also available are eggs from hens which eat a more varied diet, for example four grain eggs (*vier-graneneieren*).

Dutch Cheese

Dutch cheese (*kaas*) is made from pasteurized and unpasteurized (raw) milk. The unpasteurized is known as farmer's cheese (*boerenkaas*). Since raw milk cheese can't be sold in some countries, the Dutch must keep their best cheeses for local consumption. The Dutch love *boerenkaas*, because pasteurizing kills the bacteria that give the cheese special flavors while it ages.

Supermarkets and delicatessens all carry a wonderful selection of Dutch cheese and cheese from all over Europe. However, the connoisseurs shop at their local cheese specialist (*kaasspecialist*) or the cheese farm (*kaasboerderij*). They not only have the largest selection, but they age the cheese naturally. They also know precisely the age of each globe or ball. Cheese is made of 60% solids and 40% liquid. Dutch cheese is labeled with fat content (percentage of fat in the solids):

- Full-fat — *Volvet, vv.* or 48+
- Medium-fat — 40+
- Low-fat — *Mager* or 20+

When buying some Dutch cheese, such as Gouda, you will have the following selections:

- Young — *Jonge*
- Slightly ripe — *Jong belegen*
- Ripe — *Belegen*
- Extra-ripe — *Extra belegen*
- Old — *Oud*
- Year-old — *Overjarig*

You can buy cheeses by weight and in many different forms:

- Sliced — *Gesneden*
- Grated — *Geraspt or gemalen*
- Wedge — *Punt stuk*
- Flat Chunk — *Plat stuk*

Visit your cheese specialist in a quiet period and tell him what kind of cheese you like in terms of taste and texture and what you plan to do with it, and he can suggest something special. You will also be able to taste the cheese before you buy. Some Dutch cheese has cumin seeds (*komijn zaadjes*), whole cloves (*kruidnagelen*), mustard seeds (*mosterd zaadjes*) or nettles (*netels*).

Various types of Dutch cow's milk cheeses include:

- *Leidsekaas* 20+
- *Edammer* 40+
- *Gouda* 48+
- *Friese nagelkaas* 40+
- *Old Amsterdam* 48+ (the only Dutch cheese to be awarded the title Premier Grand Cru Classé)
- *Maasdammer* 45+ (also known as *Leerdammer* or *Hollandse gaten kaas* for it resembles the Swiss cheese, *Emmenthaler*)
- *Trenta* 48+(a vegetarian cheese from synthetic rennet)
- *Maaslander* 48+
- *Pardano* 45+ (has an Italian character and is good for pizzas and pastas)
- *Milner* 30+
- *Altena* 48+ (for salt reduced diets)

Dutch goat's milk (*geitenkaas*) and sheep's milk (*schapenkaas*) cheeses are also becoming very popular. The cheese shop **De Kaas Specialist** (*www.dekaasspecialist.nl*) has its own in-house brands.

Soft fresh cheese (*verse kaas*): There are several kinds of soft fresh cheeses. They are sometimes used interchangeably in cooking, but their textures vary.

- Cream cheese: Mon Chou, Philadelphia, La Cuisine
- Cottage Cheese: Danon *Hüttenkäse*
- Curd cheeses: fromage blanc, fromage frais, ricotta
- *Kwark*: Danon, Mona, Milram
- *Biogarde*: Jockey Leger
- *Mascarpone* is a sweetened whipping cream cheese

Fruits and Vegetables

If you ask a Dutch lady what she is serving for dinner, she is likely to mention the vegetables first and only then the meat and dessert (which is often fruit). Thus, many of the world's popular vegetables and fruits are available here, grown in the Netherlands' greenhouses and in the Betuwe region around Tiel.

Supermarkets have their own fruit and vegetable departments, but you might also try the greengrocer (*groenteman* or *groenteboer*). Produce is often sold by weight, but sometimes by the piece (*per stuk*). In some supermarkets you may have to select and weigh your own. The greengrocers will generally select and weigh them for you. There are also vegetables that are already pre-cleaned and pre-cut, and some are pre-mixed for soups and stir fries. Frozen and canned vegetables are also available. Some types of fruits and vegetables are discussed below with many others listed in the vocabulary list in the end of the chapter.

Fruits *(Vruchten)*

Apples (appels): Some of the apples will be familiar to you, because countries share much of the information on new developments.

• Alkmene	Eat fresh or baked
• Elstar	Tart apple for baking
• Fuji	Eat fresh
• Granny Smith	All purpose, tart
• Golden Delicious	Eat fresh or baked
• Goudreinet	Cooking apple
• Jonathans/Jona Gold	Eat fresh or as applesauce
• Pink Lady	Eat fresh or as applesauce

Pears (*peren*): Regular eating pears (*handperen*) and stewing pears (*stoofperen*) are popular here during the winter season.

Eating pears:

- Conference
- Doyenne de Comice
- Triomphe de Vienne
- Beurre Hardy

Stewing pears: Saint Remy

Vegetables *(Groenten)*

While most vegetables may be known to you, these are readily available and some varieties might be new to you.

Asparagus (*asperges*): Until recently the Dutch ate only the white asparagus, which are buried in mounds until they mature. The result is a mouthwatering, buttery white asparagus with very light pink tips. It has a fibrous outer skin and must be peeled very carefully. Green asparagus is now seasonably available.

Beans (*bonen*):

- *Tuinbonen* are broad or fava beans that look like lima beans, but have a different taste. They must be shelled and cooked.
- *Sperziebonen* are snap beans consisting of two types: *princessebonen* and *slabonen*.
- *Snijbonen* are sliced runner beans and are what some would call French green beans.
- The thin dwarf French green beans (*haricots vert*) are wonderful.

- Canned white beans in tomato sauce (*witte bonen*) area a good substitute for baked beans once you doctor them up.

Belgian or French endive (*witlof*): This is a gourmet vegetable that is a member of the chicory family. Endive heads are grown in darkened greenhouses to preserve their white color. They can be served raw in a salad or chopped and boiled or cooked. If cooking, remove about ½ inch of the core with the sharp point of a knife. Escarole (*andijvie* or *frisée*) and curly endive (*krulandijvie*) are also members of this family. Chopped escarole is often added to mashed potatoes and bacon to make *andijvie stamppot*. Curly endive is usually a salad green as is the red leafed *raddicchio*.

Cabbage (kool): The white cabbage (*witte kool*) sold here is a bit too solid to be used in coleslaw and is generally used to make sauerkraut. Use *spitskool* for recipes that call for green cabbage.

Celery (bleekselderij): For stalk celery, ask for *bleekselderij*. What the Dutch call *selderij* is an herb used mainly in pea soup along with root celery (*knolselderij*).

Kale (*boerenkool*): It is generally cooked with potatoes and smoked sausage then mashed (after the sausage is removed) to create what the Dutch call a *stamppot* dish.

Leeks (*prei*): Leeks are extremely popular in the Netherlands. They are a necessary ingredient in many of the Dutch soups such as pea soup (*erwtensoep*). They look like giant spring or green onions, but their flavor is much more subtle.

Potatoes (*aardappelen*): Potatoes can be bought at the greengrocers, supermarkets and farmer's markets. If you want potatoes for home fries or French fries (*patates frites*), for baking (*poffen*) or mashing (*pureren*), tell your greengrocer you want *aardappelen om to poffen* or *om tepureren* and he will recommend the potatoes for you. There are many different types of potatoes in the Netherlands, the most popular of which are called *Bintjes*.

Bread & Pastries *(Brood en Banket)*

Dutch bakeries (*bakkerijen*) are a delight to the senses. If you go early in the morning, the bread and rolls will still be warm from the oven. A *warme bakker* or *brood en banket* shop usually specializes in fresh daily baked bread, rolls and cookies. A *banketbakkerij* specializes in pastries such as cakes, tarts and candies or bonbons. In addition to the small bread and pastry shops, larger supermarkets have a bakery department with either fresh or factory-made products. *Kouwebakker* means it is a factory bread and has a longer shelf life. Bread can be purchased by the whole (*heel*) or half (*half*) loaf and you may also ask to have it sliced (*gesneden*) or not sliced (*niet gesneden*).

Festive Breads and Pastries

During the holidays be sure to try *speculaas* cookies made with cinnamon, cloves and nutmeg, and sometimes topped with sliced almonds, which come in different sizes and shapes. When *speculaas* pastries are filled with almond paste, they are called *gevulde speculaas*. Another pre-Christmas treat is the *roomboter amandelstaafje*, a buttery flake pastry roll filled with almond paste. Tiny ginger cookies (*kruidnoten*) sometimes covered in chocolate appear before the *Sinterklaas* holiday on December 5th.

Oliebollen and *appelbollen* are a New Year's Eve specialty. *Oliebollen*, literally "oil balls", are deep-fried breads with currants and raisins dipped in powdered sugar, and *appelbollen* are similar to apple fritters.

Herbs and Spices *(Kruiden)*

A large variety of herbs and spices are available. They are usually sold fresh in small quantities, dried in bottles or dried in small refill packets at supermarkets. The biggest selection is sold in plastic tubs at the Asian markets. In addition, some fresh herbs like chives, thyme, bay leaf, coriander, dill, oregano and rosemary can be purchased by the pot at many supermarkets, greengrocers and garden centers. For a further list of herbs and spices available, see the vocabulary list later in the chapter.

Beverages

There are plenty of beverages for everyone here: fruit juices, soft drinks like Pepsi and Coca Cola, teas, coffees, beers, wines and mineral waters.

Coffee *(Koffie)*

The Dutch are very fond of coffee. Many initially find the Dutch coffee a bit strong, but grow to love it within a short time. The secret is in the different roasting system. You can buy regular coffee or caffeine-free (*caffeinevrije*). All ground coffee is drip grind, but you can also buy the whole beans (*bonen*) and grind them yourself. There are a large variety of coffee pads available for Senseos and other coffee makers using a single cup pad system. Instant, freeze dried (*vriesdroog*) coffee is also available in regular, expresso and cappucino.

Liquor, Wine & Beer *(Sterke Drank, Wijn & Bier)*

The supermarket sells beer and wine. However, to purchase hard liquor, you will need to visit the liquor store (*slijterij*). You will find a huge assortment of liquors, excellent wines from around the world, and mixes and syrups for mixed drinks.

If you would like a real Dutch treat, try *Jenever*, the mother of all gins. It was invented by a 17th-century medical professor at the University of Leiden. In those days, juniper berry oil was used as a diuretic, and the professor added a little alcohol to make it more palatable. Not surprisingly, it made his patients feel better. Keep a bottle in the freezer for guests, and serve it very, very cold without ice before—not after—dinner. *Advocaat* is another traditional Dutch concoction you may want to try. This thick egg liqueur is yellowish in color and creamy in texture, and is eaten with a small dessert spoon. It is delicious on ice cream and pancakes.

Heineken and Amstel are world-famous beers which are brewed right here in the Netherlands. Beer is rarely sold in cans, but rather in bottles individually, in 6-packs or in convenient recyclable crates that hold 24. Excellent Belgian beers are readily available and specialty beer stores sell beers from around the world.

Glühwijn is popular around the Christmas holidays. It is wine spiced with cloves, cinnamon and sugar served hot for a warming winter drink. You can buy it pre-mulled by the bottle or experiment by making your own.

Health Foods *(Natuurvoeding)*

Many shopping streets now have at least one good health food store that caters to health food enthusiasts and vegetarians. In addition, many of the greengrocers carry organically grown (*biologische* or *eko*) produce. Supermarkets have also expanded their vegetarian and organic offerings over the years—look for the V and/or Eko logo. To find a health food shop near you, look in the Yellow Pages under *Natuurvoeding en Reformartikelen.*

Eko Plaza
Grote Marktstraat 115, 2511 BJ Den Haag
☎ (070) 328 13 78
Also in Alkmaar
www.ekoplaza.nl

Natuurwinkel
Theresiastraat 113, 2593 AD Den Haag
☎ (070) 335 2670
Also in Amsterdam, Haarlem, Eindhoven and others
www.denatuurwinkel.com

Gaia Natuurvoeding
Lange Groenendaal 80-82, 2801 LV Gouda
☎ (018) 251 32 60
www.gaianatuurvoeding.nl

Wassenaars Reformhuis
Johan de Wittstraat 6/A, 2242 LB Wassenaar
☎ (070) 511 18 20

World Foods and Flavors

If after all of this you are still homesick for familiar food products, you will find several shops which cater to your needs. Most of them are located in or around the cities where most of the foreigners live. In the shops which cater to North Americans, you will find American cake mixes and other baking ingredients, cereals, Mexican foods, pickles, marshmallows and sauces. Naturally, these items are more expensive than at home, but sometimes there is just nothing that can replace the taste of a favorite food.

At last count there were over 900 Asian food stores in the Netherlands. You can find them listed under *Oosterse producten* in the Yellow Pages. The supermarkets carry products from all parts of Asia. The Indonesian shops *(toko)* specialize in Indonesian foods but also carry food products from other Asian countries. Some have prepared Indonesian foods for take-out. Foods from many other countries are also available throughout the Netherlands. India, Italy, Turkey and some Balkan countries are well represented in separate shops or farmer's markets in larger cities. Some of the international shops are listed below.

American and British Foods:

Arkwright's British Food Emporium
Rozengracht 13, 1016 LP Amsterdam
☎ (020) 320 07 10
www.arkwrights.nl

C1000 Supermarket
Luifelbaan 1, 2242 KL Wassenaar
☎ (070) 5123310
www.c1000.nl

Van Dijk Supermarket
Ursulaland 80, 2591 HA Den Haag
☎ (070) 385 64 65

Gransjean Wijnen & Delicatessen
Bankastraat 12, 2585 EN Den Haag
☎ (070) 350 39 80
www.gransjean.nl

Kelly's Expat Shop
Piet Heinstraat 105, 2518 GT Den Haag
☎ (070) 346 97 53
www.kellys-expat-shopping.nl

Kingsalmarkt Delicatessen
Rembrandtweg 621, 1181 GV Amstelveen
☎ (020) 643 37 51
www.kingsalmarkt.nl

Woodleaf & Furn
Bermweg 250b, 2906 LG Capelle aan den Ijssel
☎ (065) 208 46 76
www.woodleaf.nl

Thomas Green's
Frederick Hendriklaan 71, 2582 BT Den Haag
☎ (070) 358 75 86
Sarphatipark 114, 1073 ED Amsterdam
☎ (020) 673 60 61
www.thomasgreen.nl

Tucker Box
Botermarkt 23, 2311 EN Leiden
☎ (071) 512 47 77
www.tuckerbox.nl

Butchers carrying imported meat products:

Chateaubriand
Binneweg 163, 2101 JH Heemstede
☎ (023) 528 26 55
www.chateaubriand.nl

Slagerij Marcel Horneman
Grote Krocht 7, 2042 LT Zandvoort
☎ (023) 571 90 67
www.slagerijhorneman.nl

Groeneveld Slagerij
Luifelbaan 26, 2242 KV Wassenaar
☎ (070) 511 24 81
www.groeneveld.keurslager.nl

Wholesalers (Membership Required)

HANOS Internationale
www.hanos.nl
Locations in Amsterdam, Eindhoven, Groningen, Haarlem and others. AWC members are entitled to access.

Makro
www.makro.nl
Locations in Amsterdam, Best, Breda, Delft and others. Makro membership can be obtained with a KvK number.

Sligro
www.sligro.nl
Locations in Den Haag, Gouda, Leiden, Rotterdam and others. AWC members are entitled to access.

Asian Supermarkets

Amazing Oriental
Grote Marktstraat 113, 2511 BJ - Den Haag
☎ (070) 363 15 52

Wah Nam Hong
Geldersekade 90-92, 1012 BM Amsterdam
☎ (020) 627 03 03
Westkruiskade 4-6, 3014 AP Rotterdam
☎ (010) 241 73 55
Gedempte Burgwal 8, 2512 BT Den Haag
☎ (070) 360 19 77

Using the Metric System

Metric measurements are used in buying and preparing foods, and most Dutch cooks use a scale to weigh ingredients. Scales are available here in both grams and ounces. Also available here are measuring cups which show volume in ounces and milliliters.

▸ Metric Conversion Charts

Key:	C = cup	T = tablespoon	t = teaspoon
	oz = ounce	ml = milliliter	dl = deciliter (100 ml)

Dry Measures

American/British	**Metric**
1 ounce	30 grams
½ pound	225 grams
1 pound	450 grams
2.2 pounds	1 kilogram

Liquid Measures (Measurements are rounded off. See key above.)

American	British	Metric
½ t	¾ t	2½ ml
1 t	1½ t	5 ml
1 T	1 T	15 ml
¼ C	2 fl oz	0.6 dl (60 ml)
½ C	4 fl oz	1.2 dl (120 ml)
1 C	8¼ fl oz	2.4 dl (240 ml)

Dutch Measures	American Measures	Dutch Measures	American Measures
1 *ons* = 100 gram	3½ ounces	1 *liter*	1 quart + 3 T
5 *ons* = 500 grams = 1 pond	1.1 pounds	½ *deciliter* (dl)	3 T+ 1 t
1 *kopje*	½ C + 1 T	1 *deciliter* = 1/10 liter	6 T +1 t
1 *eetlepel* (el) =15 ml	1 T	1½ *deciliters*	½ C + 1½ T
1 *theelepel* (tl) = een lepeltje	½ t	2 *deciliters*	¾ C + 2 t
		2½ *deciliter*	1 C
		3 *deciliter*	1 1/3 C

▸ At Home on the Range

Did you ever wonder why that heavy round pan was called a Dutch oven? In the past, kitchens in the Netherlands didn't have ovens and Dutch housewives cooked meals in a large pan (*braadpan*) on top of the stove, in what some call a Dutch oven. Even today, the Dutch do most of their cooking on the stove top. Dutch butchers are aware of this and, therefore, cut and portion most of their meats so they taste best when so prepared. So, if you have a Dutch oven, by all means, bring it—you will use it.

For more suggestions about which kitchen pans and appliances to pack, see our **Housekeeping and Maintenance** and **Essentials to Bring** chapters.

An ideal stove would be a gas top and electric oven with the temperatures confirmed by an independent oven thermometer in both Fahrenheit and Celsius. Many of the new ovens in Dutch homes are convection ovens. These are equipped with fans to circulate the air thereby cooking the food more evenly. They are supposed to take 25% less time and for most foods you can plan on using 25% less heat. There are also convection/microwave ovens in which the benefit of the circulating air shortens the microwave cooking process.

Oven and meat thermometers are available in the household section of large department stores and in smaller household goods stores. These are an absolute must if you are using a gas oven because there are variances in oven temperature markings.

Below, a chart compares approximate oven temperatures and markings. In this temperature range, to approximate you can divide °F by two to get °C.

°F	°C	8-Mark	10-Mark	Description
300	150	1-2	2	Slow
325	165	2-3	3	
350	180	3-4	4	Medium
375	190	4-5	5	Medium Hot
400	205	4-5	6	
425	220	5-6	7	Hot
450	230	6-7	8	
475	245	6-7	9	Very Hot
500	260	7-8	10	

Basic Baking and Cooking Ingredients

Baking powder	*Bakpoeder*
Baking soda	*Maagzout*
Bread crumbs	*Paneermeel*
Chocolate	*Chocolade*
• Cocoa	*Cacao*
• Milk	*Melk*
• Semi-sweet pure	*Puur*
Coconut	*Kokos/kokosnoten*
Crumb crust	*Kruimel bodem*
Fats, solid	
• Animal fat	*Dierlijk vet*
• Butter	*Boter*
• Butter for frying	*Boter voor bakken en braden*
• Deep frying	*Frituurvet*
• Lard	*Reuzel*
• Margarine	*Margarine*
• Vegetable fat	*Plantaardig, Diamant*
Flour, wheat	
• All-purpose	*Patentbloem*
• Bread	*Broodmeel*
• Rye	*Roggemeel*
• Self-rising	*Zelfrijzend bakmeel*
• Whole-wheat	*Volkoren meel*
• Brown	*Tarwemeel*
• White	*Tarwebloem*
Flour, non wheat	
• Arrowroot	*Arrowroot*
• Corn starch	*Maizena*
• Potato	*Aardappelmeel*
• Rice	*Rijstbloem*
Gelatin	*Gelatine*
Grains	*Granen*
• Barley	*Gerst*
• Buckwheat	*Boekweit*
• Corn	*Mais*
• Cornmeal	*Maïsmeel*
• Oats	*Haver*
• Oatmeal	*Havermout*
• Rice	*Rijst*
• Quick cooking	*Snelkookrijst*
• Brown	*Zilvervlies*
• Rye	*Rogge*
• Wheat	*Tarwe*
• Wheat germ	*Tarwekiemen*
• Bran	*Tarwezemelen*
• Cream of wheat	*Tarwe greismeel*
Gravy *Jus*	
Nuts	*Noten*

- Almonds *Amandelen*
- Cashews *Cashew noten*
- Chestnuts *Kastanjes*
- Coconuts *Kokosnoten*
- Hazel nuts *Hazelnoten*
- Peanuts *Pindas*
- Pecans *Pecannoten*
- Pine nuts *Pijnboompitten*
- Walnuts *Walnoten*

Oil *Olie*

- Corn *Maïsolie*
- Olive *Olijfolie*
- Sunflower *Zonnebloemolie*
- Sesame *Sesam olie*
- Soya *Sojaolie*

Peanut butter *Pindakaas*

Pectine *Pectine*

Sugar *Suiker*

- Granulated or crystal *Kristal*
- Fine crystal or castor *Zeer fijne tafelsuiker*
- Molasses *Melasse*
- Cane *Rietsuiker*
- Powdered/confectioner's *Poedersuiker*
- Raw *Ruwe netsuiker*
- Soft, white *Witte basterdsuiker*
- Soft, light-brown *Lichtbruine basterdsuiker*
- Soft, dark-brown *Donkerbruine basterdsuiker*
- Sugar cubes *Suikerklontjes*
- Sugar for preserves *Geleisuiker*

Syrup *Siroop*

- Heavy *Stroop*
- Heavy but pourable *Schenkstroop*
- Light but pourable *Siroop*

Tea *Thee*

Vanilla *Vanille*

- Extract *Essence*
- Bean *Stokje*

Vinegar *Azijn*

Yeast *Gist*

Meats

Beef *Rund*

Veal *Kalf*

Pork *Varken*

Lamb *Lam*

Beef steak *Biefstuk*

- New York *Entrecot*
- Ribeye *Rib eye*
- Filet Mignon *Biefstuk van de haas*
- Eye of round *Kogelbiefstuk*
- Filet Slice *Oester/Tournedo*

Bone Bot *Been*

Brisket *Klapstuk*

Chop *Karbonade*

Cutlet *Kotelet, schnitzel*

Filet or tenderloin *Haas*

Ground/minced meat *Gehakt*

- Ground sirloin *Tartaar*
- Half beef/half pork *Half om half*

Lean *Mager*

Loin *Lende*

Rolled roast *Rollade*

Shin *Schenkel*

Short ribs *Borstlappen met been*

Slices *Lappen*

Ham *Ham*

- Raw ham, salted, smoked *Rauwe ham*
- Cooked *Gekookte ham*

Liverwurst *Leverworst*

Salami *Salami*

Sausage *Worst*

• Fresh	*Vers*
• Cocktail sausages	*Borrelworstjes*
• Smoked	*Rookworst*
• Smoked (very fine)	*Gelderse rookworst*
Hot dogs	*Frankfurter, knakworstjes* or *Amerikaanse hot dogs*

▸ Poultry and Game Birds

Chicken	*Kip*
• Broiler	*Jong haantje*
• Corn-fed	*Maïskip*
• Free range	*Scharrel*
• Roasting or stewing	*Poularde*
• Small fryer	*Braadkuiken*
• Soup chicken	*Soepkip*
• Spring chicken	*Piepkuiken*
Chicken Pieces	
• Breast, deboned	*Kipfilet*
• Cutlet, breaded	*Kipschnitzel*
• Drumstick	*Kippepootje, Drumstick*
• Drumstick & thigh	*Kippebout*
• Rolled roast/ spiced	*Rollade*
• Wing	*Vleugel*
• Gizzard	*Kippemaag*
• Liver	*Kippelever*
Duck	*Eend*
Goose	*Gans*
Pheasant	*Fazant*
Quail	*Kwartel*
Turkey	*Kalkoen*
Boar, wild	*Wild zwijn*
Deer	*Ree* or *hert*
Frog's legs	*Kikkerbilletjes*
Rabbit	*Konijn*

▸ Eggs

Chicken eggs	*Kippen eieren*
• Free ranging	*Scharrel eieren*
• Less free ranging	*Volière eieren*
• Battery	*Legbatterij eieren*
• Four grain	*Viergranen*
• Organically raised	*Eko-eieren*
Duck eggs	*Eenden eieren*
Quail	*Kwarteleieren*

▸ Fish and Seafood

Anchovy	*Ansjovis*
Angler (monkfish, goosefish)	*Zeeduivel*
Catfish	*Meerval*
Cod	*Kabeljauw*
• Small pieces of cod	*Kibbeling*
Crab	*Krab*
Eel, fresh	*Paling*
• Smoked	*Gerookte paling*
• Sea water	*Zeepaling*
Flounder	*Schol*
Haddock	*Schelvis*
Halibut	*Heilbot*
Herring	*Haring*
• New herring	*Nieuwe haring*
Lobster	*Kreeft*
Mackerel	*Makreel*
• Smoked *mackerel*	
Mussels	*Mosselen*
Octopus	*Inktvis*
Oysters	*Oesters*
Prawn	*Kreeft garnaal*
Roe Kuit (female),	hom (male)
Salmon	*Zalm*
Sardine	*Sardine*
Scallop	*St. Jabobsschelp*
Sea bass	*Zeebaars*
Sea devil	*Zeeduivel*
Shrimp	*Garnalen*

Smelt	*Spiering*
Sole	*Tong*
Squid, calamari	*Pijlinkvis*
Trout	*Forel*
Tuna	*Tonijn*
Turbot	*Tarbot*
Wolf fish	*Zeewolf*

Dairy Products

Butter, unsalted	Boter, *echte boter, roomboter (ongezouten)*
• Lightly salted	*Licht gezouten*
• Salted	*Gezouten*
• Herbed	*Kruiden*
• Frying	*Voor bakken en braden*
Buttermilk	*Karnemelk*
Cheese	*Kaas*
Coffee milk	*Koffiemelk*
Cream	*Room*
• Whipping	*Slagroom*
• Non-dairy whipping	*Klop Klop*
Custard/Pudding	*Vla, bavarois*
Ice cream	*IJs, roomijs*
Margarine	*Margarine*
• Frying	*voor bakken en braden*
Milk	*Melk*
• Whole	*Volle melk*
• Half fat	*Half volle*
• Skim	*Magere*
• Evaporated	*Geëvaporeerde volle melk*
• Powdered	*Melkpoeder*
• Sweetened condensed	*Gecondenseerde melk met suiker*
Sour cream	*Zure room*
Yogurt	*Yoghurt*

Fruits

Apples	*Appels*
Applesauce	*Appelmoes*
Apricots	*Abrikozen*
Bananas	*Bananen*
Berries	*Bessen*
• Blackberries	*Bramen*
• Blueberries	*Bosbessen*
• Currants, fresh	*Albessen*
• Raspberries	*Frambozen*
• Strawberries	*Aardbeien*
Cherries	*Kersen*
Currants, dried	*Krenten*
Dates	*Dadels*
Figs	*Vijgen*
Grapes	*Druiven*
• Grape leaves	*Druiven bladeren*
Grapefruit	*Grapefruit*
• Pink/red	*Rode/dubbele rode*
• Pomelo	*Pompelmoes*
Kiwi	*Kiwi*
Lemons	*Citroenen*
Limes	*Limoenen*
Litchee	*Lychee*
Mango	*Mango*
Melons	*Meloenen*
• Cantaloupe	*Cantaloup*
• Honeydew	*Suikermeloen*
• Watermelon	*Watermeloen*
Nectarine	*Nectarine*
Olives	*Olijven*
Oranges	*Sinaasappelen*
• Juice oranges	*Perssinaasappelen*
Papaya	*Papaja*
Passion fruit	*Passievrucht*
Peaches	*Perziken*
Pears	*Peren*
• Eating pears	*Handperen*
• Stewing pears	*Stoofperen*
Persimmons	*Kaki*
Pineapple	*Ananas*

English	Dutch
Plums	*Pruimen*
Pomegranate	*Granaatappel*
Prunes	*Gedroogde pruimen*
Raisins	*Rozijnen* or *Sultanas*

▸ Vegetables

English	Dutch
Artichokes	*Artisjokken*
Asparagus	*Asperges*
Avocado	*Avocado*
Beans	*Bonen*
• Black eyed peas	*Zwartoogboon*
• Broad or fava	*Tuinbonen*
• Brown	*Bruine bonen*
• Flageolet	*Flageolet*
• French, string or snap	*Sperziebonen (aka Prinsessenbonen or sla bonen)*
• Kidney	*Kidneyboon*
• Lima	*Boterboon*
• Mung bean	*Katjang idjo*
• Pinto	*Kievitboon*
• Runner bean	*Snijboon*
• Soy	*Soya*
• Wax or butter	*Boterboon/lima boon*
• White	*Witte*
• Yard long	*Kouseband*
Bean curd	*Tahoe, tofu*
Bean sprouts	*Bonenkiem*
• Alfalfa sprouts	*Alfalfa groenten*
• Bean sprout mix	*Kiemmix*
• Mung bean sprouts	*Taugé*
• Radish sprouts	*Radijs sla*
Beets (red)	*Bieten (rode)*
Broccoli	*Broccoli*
Brussels sprouts	*Spruitjes*
Cabbage	*Kool*
• Chinese	*Chinese kool*
• Curly kale	*Boerenkool*
• Green	*Groene*
• Red	*Rode kool*
• Sauerkraut	*Zuurkool*
• White	*Witte kool*
Carrots	*Wortel* or *peen*
• Winter carrots	*Winterwortelen*
Cauliflower	*Bloemkool*
Celery	*Selderij*
• Celery leaves, for soup	*Selderij*
• Celery root (celeriac)	*Knolselderij*
• Celery stalk	*Bleekselderij*
Chicory (endive)	*Witlof*
• Belgian endive (U.K.) or chicory (U.S.)	
• Escarole	*Andijvie*
• Curly endive (U.K.) or chicory (U.S.)	*Krul andijvie, frisée*
• Radicchio	*Radicchio* or *roodlof*
Corn	*Maïs*
• Sweet	*Zoete maïs*
• On the cob	*Maïskolven*
• Baby corn	*Babymaïs*
Cress, water	*Waterkers*
Cucumber	*Komkommer*
Eggplant	*Aubergine*
Fennel	*Venkel*
Garlic	*Knoflook*
Gherkins	*Augurken*
Kohlrabi	*Koolrabi*
Leeks	*Prei*
Lentils	*Linzen*
Lettuce (head)	*Sla (Krop)*
• Iceberg	*IJsbergsla*
• Leaf (butterhead)	*Kropsla*
• Red	*Rode sla*
• Oakleaf	*Eikenbladsla*
• Romaine	*Sla Romaine*
• Arugula	*Rucola*
Mushrooms	*Paddestoelen*

English	Dutch
• Button	*Champignons*
Okra	*Okra*
Onion(s)	*Ui(en)*
• Red	*Rode uien*
• Shallots	*Sjalotten*
Parsnip	*Witte peen or pastinaak*
Peas	*Erwten*
• Chick peas	*Kikkererwten*
• Green	*Groene erwten*
• Small green	*Doperwten*
• Snow peas	*Peultjes*
• Split peas	*Spliterwten*
Pepper, hot	*Spaanse peper/lombok*
• Green, red	*Groene, rode*
Pepper, sweet or bell	*Paprika*
• Green, red, yellow	*Groene, rode, gele*
Potatoes	*Aardappelen*
Pumpkin	*Pompoen*
Radishes	*Radijs*
• Large white	*Rettich*
• Small red	*Radijs*
Rhubarb	*Rabarber*
Rutabaga/Swedish turnip	*Koolraap*
Spinach	*Spinazie*
Squash	*Pompoen*
Sweet potatoes	*Zoete aardappelen*
Tomatoes	*Tomaten*
• Beefsteak	*Vleestomaten*
• Cherry	*Kerstomaten*
Turnip	*Raap*
Turnip leaves	*Raapstelen*
Zucchini	*Courgettes*

▸ Breads and Pastries

English	Dutch
Brown bread	*Bruin brood*
Currant bread	*Krentenbrood*
Danish pastries	*Koffiebroodjes*
French bread	*Frans stokbrood*
Dutch style	*Hollands stokbrood*
Dutch rusk	*Beschuit*
Raisin bread	*Rozijnenbrood*
Rolls	*Broodjes*
Soft rolls, round or oval	*Zachte broodjes, bolletjes, puntjes*
Hard rolls	*Harde broodjes*
Currant rolls	*Krentenbollen*
Rye bread	*Roggebrood*
White bread	*Wittebrood*
Round loaf	*Lampionnebrood*
Whole wheat bread	*Volkorenbrood*
Whole-grain	*Grof volkoren*

▸ Herbs and Spices

English	Dutch
Allspice	*Piment*
Anise	*Anijs*
Basil	*Basilicum*
Bay leaf	*Laurierblad*
Caraway seed	*Karwijzaad*
Cardamon	*Kardamon*
Cayenne pepper	*Cayennepeper*
Celery leaf	*Selderij*
Celery seed	*Selderij zaad*
Chervil	*Kervel*
Chili pepper	*Spaanse peper*
Chives	*Bieslook*
Cinnamon	*Kaneel*
Cloves	*Kruidnagel*
Coriander seed	*Koriander zaad*
Coriander leaves/ cilantro	*Koriander*
Cumin	*Komijn*
Dill	*Dille*
Fennel seed	*Venkelzaad*
Garlic	*Knoflook*
Ginger, root	*Gember, wortel*
Horseradish	*Mierikswortel*
Juniper berries	*Jeneverbessen*
Lemon balm	*Citroenmelisse*
Lemon grass	*Sereh*
Lovage	*Lavas*

Mace	*Foelie*
Marjoram	*Marjolein*
Meat tenderizer	*Vleesverzachter*
Monosodium glutamate	*Ve-Tsin*
Mint	*Munt*
• Peppermint	*Pepermunt*
• Spearmint	*Kruizemunt*
Mustard	*Mosterd*
Nutmeg	*Nootmuskaat*
Onion powder	*Ui poeder*
• Flakes	*Vlokken*
Oregano	*Oregano*
Paprika	*Paprikapoeder*
Parsley	*Peterselie*
Pepper	*Peper*
• Black	*Zwarte peper*
• White	*Witte peper*
• Green	*Groen*
• Pepper corns	*Peperkorrels*
• Pink	*Baies Frais*
Poppy seed	*Maanzaad*
Rosemary	*Rozemarijn*
Saffron	*Saffraan*
Sage	*Salie*
Salam leaf	*Daun Salam*
Savory	*Bonekruid*
Salt	*Zout*
Sorrel	*Zuring*
Mixed seasonings	
• Herb salt	*Kruidenzout*
• Italian	*Italiaanse*
• Poultry seasoning	*Gevogeltekruiden*
• Chili powder	*Chilipoeder*
• Curry powder	*Kerriepoede*
• Pickling spices	*Inmaakkruiden*
• Four spices	*Quatre épices*
Sesame seed	*Sesamzaad*
Star anise	*Steranijs*
Tarragon	*Dragon*
Thyme	*Thijm*
Turmeric	*Koenjit, kunyit, kurkuma*

Kitchen Supplies

Aluminum foil	*Aluminiumfolie*
Cocktail pick/ toothpick	*Cocktail prikker, tandestoker*
Deep freeze bags	*Diepvrieszakjes*
Food wrap	*Huishoudfolie*
Parchment paper	*Bakpapier*

Books and magazines directly imported from the UK and US
10% discount for students, teachers, 65+ and ABC discount card holders
ENGLISH DICTIONARY
UNSTUCK
CINEMA NOW
1001 BOOKS
MySQL
GHETTO
POSTCARDS
POP-UP SEA CREATURES
LOUIS VUITTON
GRAFFITI WORLD
FOOD BIBLE
LOVE CARDS
HISTORY OF TENNIS
the american book center
Spui 12, Amsterdam
Lange Poten 23, Den Haag
www.abc.nl

Chapter 16

Shopping

The Netherlands is a modern, industrialized nation and a member of the European Union (EU). In addition to domestic products, Dutch shops are stocked with a variety of wares from many other countries. Not only will you find most of your everyday necessities, but you will also encounter a wide range of exquisite treasures. It is just a matter of knowing what to look for and where to find it. Our **The Dutch Kitchen** chapter has an entire section devoted to demystifying the grocery shopping process.

The Netherlands has a Value-Added Tax, commonly known in English as VAT, which is abbreviated BTW (pronounced "Bay-Tay-Vay"). Currently, it is 19% for most items except food, medicine, passenger transport and hotel accommodation, which are 6%. Tax is included in the price of the product, so the price shown is the price paid.

Where to Shop

The center of each town or city (*centrum*) is the main shopping area, and is where you will find a large variety of stores, all within walking distance of each other. In addition, each little town, city or residential area has its own shopping streets where you will find many small specialty shops. One of the real pleasures of shopping is that you can find shops with household necessities right next to your favorite boutique. You can enjoy a leisurely shopping spree and not have to worry about making a special trip to get something for dinner. Just pick up something on the way home.

▸ Department Stores

Department stores in the Netherlands carry a full range of household items, including clothing and appliances, toys, DVDs and even groceries:

- **Vroom & Dreesman (V&D)** (*www.vd.nl*)
- **Bijenkorf** (*www.bijenkorf.nl*)
- **HEMA** (*www.hema.nl*)

▸ Air Miles *(www.airmiles.nl)*

In many supermarkets, department stores, gas stations and other shops, you can earn points for each purchase. You can redeem them for merchandise, airline tickets and theme park admission or designate a charity as the recipient of the points. Forms are available in any of the shops where you see the blue and white Air Miles signs such as Albert Heijn supermarket.

▸ When to Shop

The retail hours of a shop are limited by Dutch law, but owners can choose the times. Be sure to note the open hours printed on the front door of your favorite shops, and note especially if they will be open on the shopping night (*koopavond*). This is the one night per week when downtown shops stay open until 9:00 p.m.

In general, shops stay open until 6:00 p.m. and are closed all day Sunday and on Monday mornings. Shops in the *centrum* area of Amsterdam, Rotterdam and The Hague are generally open from 12:00 p.m. until 5:00 p.m. on Sundays. You may have to adjust your normal shopping routine; but, when desperate, remember that the shops in tourist and resort areas are usually open on Sundays and also on evenings during the summer. In larger cities, night-shops (*avondwinkels*), can be found which open after other shops close and stay open until late at night. Look in the Yellow Pages listed under *Avondverkoop*. You will also find shops open on weekends and evenings at Schiphol Airport and major railway stations.

If a shop is open until 6:00 p.m., don't go there at 5:45 p.m. and expect outstanding service. Frequently, the employees will already be sweeping the floors, and some sections of a shop may already be closed. The employees will usually want to walk out of the door at 6:00 p.m. sharp. Late customers prevent them from going home on time and will not be appreciated.

▸ Returns

Always inquire about the return policy. Many stores, even large department stores, can be reluctant to take back items for exchange or credit.

The Shopping Experience

▸ Shopping Etiquette

When you first enter a smaller shop, you will be greeted by one or all of the salespersons. He or she may be the owner and very interested in serving you. You should make eye contact and return the greeting in either Dutch or English.

▸ Browsing

Many people enjoy browsing and shopping without assistance. In fact, some even become annoyed when a salesperson takes too much interest in them. This can be avoided by telling the salesperson that you just prefer to look around. A handy phrase in Dutch is "*Ik wil een beetje rondkijken*" (I want to look around a little.)

▸ Customer Service

You may be familiar with the aggressive attitude of salespersons whose salaries are dependent on commissions; this is not the case in Europe. In most shops, the salesperson's income is not determined by the amount of sales made. Thus, you will be permitted to take as long as you like, try on as many outfits as you choose and even take the time to find coordinating accessories. Even if you decide not to purchase anything, the salesperson will generally smile, say thank you and invite you to come again—and actually mean it!

Should you have any questions or difficulties, most large shops have a Customer Service desk (*Klantenservice*) to assist you.

▸ Coping While Shopping

Psychologists have discovered that, in general, Americans need more personal space than people of other countries, including the Dutch. If you are an American, knowing this can help you be less irritated when you are jostled about by the hustle and bustle in the stores and market places of the Netherlands.

Remember—you and the Dutch are viewing everything through two different cultural lenses. A sense of humor will get you through most situations.

How to Pay

- Cash is the most common type of payment instrument
- PIN cards (ATM cards) are accepted at most stores
- Credit cards have limited acceptance, but are often accepted in major stores
- Chipknip has limited acceptance in stores

See the **Banking** chapter for more detailed information.

Bargain Hunting

Look on bulletin boards and in the classified section of newsletters of international clubs or schools for slightly used items being sold by members who are leaving the country. Some great bargains can be found.

Generally, the best store bargains, at prices reduced by 50% and more, can be found in January and July. When an item is advertised in a circular, there is no guarantee that it will be available when you get to the store. If you don't see it, ask a salesperson. If it is sold out, it is probably gone. If you have seen an advertisement with the deceptively simple "*OP = OP!*" it means you need to hurry down to the store, because when the item is sold out (*uitverkocht*), you will be out of luck. A rain check (*waardecheque*) allows you to purchase an item at the sale price when it is back in stock.

Sale Signs

Aanbieding	Special offer
Actieprijs	Special/advertised price
Afgeprijsd	Reduced in price
Korting	Discount
Op = Op	When it is gone, it is gone
Opruiming	Clearance
Reclame or *Reklame*	On sale
Twee Halen, Een Betalen	2-for-1
Uitverkoop	Going out of business

Clearance Racks

Many shops have clearance racks at times other than during the end-of-season sales. Keep in mind that sale items are not usually returnable. Look them over carefully before you buy. Don't be afraid to ask questions to avoid later embarrassment or frustration.

Outlet Shopping

Outlet shopping is also possible in the Netherlands:

- **Batavia Stad Lelystad** (*www.bataviastad.nl*)
- **McArthurGlen Designer Outlet Roermond** (*www.designeroutletroermond.com*)

Shopping Phrases

May I help you?	*Mag ik u helpen?*
Who is next?	*Wie is aan de beurt?*
What would you like?	*Zegt u het maar?*
Anything else?	*Anders nog iets?*
No, thank you.	*Nee, dank u.*
How much is it?	*Hoeveel kost dat?*
May I have a receipt?	*Mag ik een bonnetje?*

You will also often hear, "*Gaat het zo mee?*" which is difficult to translate literally. The salesperson wants to know if you are taking your purchase "just like that" or without a bag. If you do need a bag, then say, "*Mag ik een tasje?*" Depending upon the store, you may have to pay extra for it, usually €0,25. You may be asked if your purchase is a gift (*cadeau*), in which case it will be gift-wrapped.

What You Can Buy from A-to-Z

▸ Antiques *(Antiquiteiten)*

The best way to start your shopping for antiques in the Netherlands is to talk to others who have already researched various cities and shops, and have found the best buys. Begin by asking your acquaintances and inquiring at various clubs.

Auction houses are good places to find collectibles. **Sotheby's** (*www.sothebys.com*) and **Christie's** (*www.christies.com*) both have auction houses in Amsterdam. You can find others listed in the Yellow Pages under *Veilingen en Venduhuizen*. Check their websites or call to find out the sale dates and the pre-sale viewing times. Be aware, before you go, of the rules for bidding and what additional charges may be added to the price you offer.

An antique market is held in The Hague on the Lange Voorhout each summer. Well-known antique markets carrying high quality items can also be found in Amsterdam at the **RAI Center** (*www.rai.nl*). The **TEFAF Fine Arts Fair** (*www.tefaf.com*) in Maastricht is held annually in March and is arguably one of the finest in Europe. It is fun to visit this fair even if you're not buying.

▸ Art Work

You will find an abundance of art galleries and exhibition halls in the Netherlands, because art is a special part of Dutch life. Dutch artists are subsidized by the government, and you will find a large variety of work in all media and at varying price ranges. As always, you must be a discerning shopper. For art galleries look under *Galeries* in the Yellow Pages.

▸ Arts and Crafts Supplies

The selection and quality of materials for crafts (*kunstnijverheid*) is limitless. Choose your favorites from department stores, neighborhood specialty shops or street markets.

Drawing and Painting: For drawing and painting supplies (*tekenmaterialen*) look in the Yellow Pages under *Kunstenaars Benodigdheden*.

Scrapbooking: Most scrapbooking supplies are expensive in the Netherlands, but they can be found. **Pipoos** (*www.pipoos.nl*) has a good selection, and other small specialty shops exist. The largest store in the Netherlands is the **Scrapbookwinkel** (*www.scrapbookwinkel.nl*) in Heesch, which also offers online shopping.

Yarns and Embroidery: In addition to an unusually large selection of colors, styles and fibers, yarn shops also sell the hand-made sweaters that are on display in their shop windows at reasonable prices. If you see one you like, stop in and ask the price; you may be pleasantly surprised. Some stores allow you to return unused skeins of yarn for a refund if you have the receipt. Department stores also sell yarns, but for shops that specialize look under *Wolartikelen en Breiwol* in the Yellow Pages.

▸ Books and Newspapers

English-language books and newspapers are available in most book shops and newsstands, either interspersed with all the other selections or in a special section for English readers. You will find these shops under *Boekhandels* in the Yellow Pages. Street markets, major train stations and Schiphol Airport are also good sources for books.

Large Dutch shops that carry books in English include:

- **AKO** (*www.ako.nl*)
- **Bruna** (*www.bruna.nl*)
- **Paagman** (*www.paagman.nl*)
- **Selexyz Donner** (*www.selexyz.nl*)

The **American Book Center**, located in The Hague and in Amsterdam, offers a large selection of books and magazines. **Waterstone's Booksellers** specializes in books from the U.K. Both the American Book Center and Waterstone's are quite happy to place special orders.

American Book Center
Spui 12, 1012 XA Amsterdam
☎ (020) 625 55 37
Lange Poten 23, 2511 CM Den Haag
☎ (070) 364 27 42
www.abc.nl

Waterstone's Booksellers
Kalverstraat 152, 1012 XE Amsterdam
☎ (020) 638 38 21
www.waterstones.com

A large selection of used English-language books are available at a chain of Dutch bookstores called **De Slegte** (*www.deslegte.com*), which is an emporium for new and used books at discounted prices.

▸ Clothing *(Kleding)*

Children: See our **Children** chapter for children's clothing.

Adults: You will be able to buy clothing from all over Europe. Sizes will vary, as will quality so be sure to try clothes on. You may have difficulty finding women's smaller sizes (4, 6 and 8). Look for French, Italian or Belgian clothing for these petite sizes. If you are an average-size adult, you will find that the selection and quality of clothing is excellent. However, as the sizes go up, your selection gets smaller. American sizes 16 to 18 are about the maximum in most shops.

Alterations at good shops are offered for a nominal fee. You can rely on alterations to be done on time and to be of excellent workmanship. Ask what the charges will be before having anything done.

Adult Clothing Conversion Charts

Women's Clothing

USA	6	8	10	12	14	16	18
British	8	10	12	14	16	18	20
European	38	40	42	44	46	48	50

Stockings

USA	8	8.5	9	9.5	10	10.5
European	0	1	2	3	4	4

Men's Suits & Sweaters

USA/British	32	34	36	38	40	42	44 46
European	42	44	46	48	50	52	54 56
Universal	Small			Medium		Large	Extra-Large

Men's Shirts

USA/British	14	14 ½	15	15 ½	16	16 ½	17
European	36	37	38	39	41	42	43

Clothing Vocabulary

Bath robe	*Badjas*	Bra	*Beha (Bh)*
Panty hose	*Pantie*	Scarf	*Sjaal*
Bathing suit	*Badpak*	Cardigan	*Vest*
Rain coat	*Regenjas*	Shoes	*Schoenen*
Blouse	*Blouse*	Coat	*Jas*
Robe	*Ochtendjas*	Skirt	*Rok*

Dress	*Jurk*	Jeans	*Spijkerbroek*
Slacks	*Lange broek*	Sweater	*Trui*
Evening dress	*Avond jurk*	Necktie	*Das*
Slippers	*Pantoffels*	Trousers	*Broek*
Gloves	*Handschoenen*	Nightgown	*Nachtjapon*
Socks	*Sokken*	Tuxedo	*Smoking*
Jacket	*Jas*	Panties	*Slipje*
Stockings	*Kousen*	Underpants	*Onderbroek*

Electrical Appliances

There are many quality kitchen appliances, equipment and gadgets available in the Netherlands. Look in the Yellow Pages under *Warenhuizen* and *Huishoudelijk Apparaten en Artikelen*. For washers and dryers also look under *Wasmachines en Wasdrogers*.

Large Appliances: Reliable manufacturers include:

- **Atag** (*www.atag.co.uk*)
- **Bosch** (*www.boschappliances.com*)
- **Miele** (*www.miele.nl*)
- **Siemens** (*www.siemenshuishouden.nl*)
- **Whirlpool** (*www.whirlpool.nl*)

Small Appliances: Two of the best are:

- **Braun** (*www.braun.com*)
- **Phillips** (*www.philips.nl*)

Electrical Appliance Vocabulary

Blender	*Blender*	Kitchen scale	*Keukenweegschaal*
Coffee grinder	*Koffiemolen*	Knife sharpener	*Messenslijper*
Coffee maker	*Koffiezetapparaat*	Meat grinder	*Vleesmolen*
Deep fryer	*Frituurpan*	Microwave oven	*Magnetron*
Dishwasher	*Afwasmachine*	Oven	*Oven; Fornuis*
Dryers	*Wasdrogers*	Pressure cooker	*Hogedrukpan*
Food processor	*Keukenmachine*	Toaster	*Broodrooster*
Hand mixer	*Handmixer*	Waffle iron	*Waffelijzer*
Iron	*Strijkijzer*	Washing machine	*Wasmachine*
Juicer, electric	*Citruspers*		

Furniture and Furnishings

There are numerous furniture stores carrying everything you can imagine. Many of the shops are located in the same area, such as the **MegaStores** (*www.megastoresdenhaag.nl*) in The Hague. Look under *Meubelen* in the Yellow Pages. For porcelain and crystal, see *Glas, Porselein en Aardewerk*. For affordable furniture, **IKEA** (*www.ikea.com*) is headquartered in Delft and has some very large stores throughout the Netherlands.

Garden Centers *(Tuincentra)*

One of the delights of living in the Netherlands is the wonderful garden centers. They not only sell indoor and outdoor plants, but garden furniture, supplies and barbecues as well. Before Christmas many become emporiums for Christmas decorations. Look in the Yellow Pages under *Tuinartikelen* for garden supplies such as pergolas and dog houses, and under *Tuincentra* for flowers, plants, furniture, barbecues and gardening supplies. Some of the larger garden centers with locations throughout the Netherlands are:

- **EuropaTuin** (*www.europatuin.nl*)
- **Intratuin** (*www.intratuin.nl*)
- **Life & Garden** (*www.lifeandgarden.nl*)
- **Xotus** (*www.xotus.nl*)

Gifts and Souvenirs

There are hundreds of souvenir shops in the major cities, especially Amsterdam. Popular souvenirs are wooden cookie molds (*koekplanken*), cheese, stroopwafels, chocolates, ceramic and pewter canal houses, cigars, silver and pewter, Heineken articles, Dutch gin (*jonge jenever*), Delft pottery, diamonds and, of course, wooden shoes. Flower bulbs from the Netherlands are always a special gift idea. Be certain that bulbs to be exported to the U.S. have been inspected by the American Agricultural Service and have the necessary health certificates. These bulbs are available at the floating flower market in Amsterdam, at some large flower shops and at the airport.

Hardware Stores and Do-It-Yourself Shops

Hardware stores carry mostly hardware (*ijzerwaren*) and garden supplies while the do-it-yourself shops carry almost everything you need in terms of hardware, building and painting materials, tiles and bathroom fixtures. These are often very large establishments where you can find almost anything you need for your home. Look under *Doe-Het-Zelf-Artikelen en Materialen* in the Yellow Pages for shops which carry carpeting, kitchen articles, house and garden furniture, tools and garden supplies, just to name a few. If any of your projects require your wood to be cut to size, these shops can cut it for you. Just take accurate measurements (in centimeters) and explain what you need. A nominal fee may be charged for this service. You will find stores located in most major cities:

- **Gamma** (*www.gamma.com*)
- **Praxis** (*www.praxis.nl*)

- **Fixet** (*www.fixet.nl*)
- **Hubo** (*www.hubo.nl*)
- **Karwei** (*www.karwei.nl*)

Sewing

Most fabrics are made from natural fibers such as cotton (*katoen*), wool (*wol*), silk (*zijde*) and linen (*linnen*), but artificial fibers are increasingly popular, especially in blends. Be sure to check the fiber content and washing instructions before buying. Permanent press is not widely available. Vogue and Butterick patterns (*patronen*) are available in fabric shops. For fabric shops, look under *Stoffen* in the Yellow Pages. For fabric markets, go to *www.stoffenbeurs.nl*.

Shoes *(Schoenen)*

Most shoes available in the Netherlands are made of quality leather, which is often expensive. Children and men are generally able to find shoes that fit, but for women with narrow feet widths A and AA are difficult to find. Large shoe sizes are easy to find and the larger cities have specialty stores.

You can buy athletic shoes at almost any shoe store, but for a better selection, go to a shop featuring athletic equipment and accessories. Athletic shoe shops, such as Footlocker, also exist. Look in the Yellow Pages under *Sportschoenen Winkels* or *Sport- en Spelartikelen*.

Adult Shoe Size Conversion Charts

Women's Shoes

USA	6 ½	7 ½	8 ½	9 ½	10½	11½
British	4	5	6	7	8	9
European	37	38	39	40	41	42

Men's Shoes

USA	9 ½	10½	11½	12	13	14	15	16
British	8	9	10	11	12	13	14	15
European	43	44	45	46	47	48	49	50

Stationery

Stationery and office supply shops (*Kantoorboekhandel*) are located in almost every shopping area. They offer a huge selection of paper, writing instruments, desk-top accessories, correction tools, record-keeping supplies and organizational products.

Toiletries

Toiletries and famous-name cosmetics and perfumes can be found in supermarkets, at street markets and in drug stores (*drogisterijen*). Cosmetics and perfumes are also sold in perfume shops (*parfumerieën*). Remember, medicines and prescriptions are found at an *apotheek*, and not at a *drogisterij*. *Drogisterijen* do carry some over-the-counter pain killers, cold remedies and gastro-intestinal medications. See our **Health Care** chapter for more information.

Upholstery and Curtains

While the large department stores can supply everything you need for the interior of your house, such as carpets (*tapijten*), curtains (*gordijnen*), table and bed linens (*tafel en bedlinnen*) and upholstery (*meubelstoffering*), you might want to explore the shops that specialize in interiors. Look under *Woninginrichting* in the Yellow Pages. They do a wonderful job of measuring, sewing and installing curtains in your home.

Street Markets

One delight to be found in the Netherlands is the street market. Colorful market stalls are stocked by independent merchants who travel to different locations on a regular schedule. Budget-conscious homemakers have found that the farmer's market is an economical source of fresh fruits and vegetables, dried fruits and nuts, fish, cheese, pet food, plants and flowers, scarves, books and many other goods.

Most communities have at least one market day per week. Check with your neighbors or go to *www.hollandsemarkten.nl*, which lists all the farmer's markets in the country. In the larger cities they will be more or less permanent fixtures. As an example of what you can expect, below are a variety of markets in the major cities (hours are subject to change):

Amsterdam

- **Albert Cuypstraat** (*www.albertcuypmarkt.com*)**:** Monday–Saturday, 9:00 a.m.–6:00 p.m.
- **Biological Farmer's Market** (*www.boerenmarktamsterdam.nl*)**:** Saturday, 9:00 a.m.–4:00 p.m. at Noordermarkt
- **Floating Flower Market:** Monday–Saturday, 9:00 a.m.–5:30 p.m. and Sunday, 11:00 a.m.–5:30 p.m. at Singel
- **Waterlooplein Flea Market** (*www.waterloopleinmarkt.nl*)**:** Monday–Saturday, 9:00 a.m.–5:00 p.m.

Beverwijk

- **Flea Market & Grand Bazaar, De Zwarte Markt** (*www.debazaar.nl*)**:** Saturday & Sunday, 8:30 a.m.–6:00 p.m., Beverwijk Market Halls

Delft

- **Marktplein:** Thursday, 9:00 a.m.–5:00 p.m.
- **Brabantse Turfmarkt:** Saturday, 9:00 a.m.–5:00 p.m.

- **Curiosities & Antiques:** Saturdays in April thru September, 9:00 a.m.–4:00 p.m., at Voldersgracht and Hippolytusbuurt

Gouda

- **Markt Centrum:** Thursday, 8:30 a.m.–1:00 p.m. and Saturday 8:30 a.m. –5:00 p.m.
- **Cheese Market** (*www.goudakaas.nl*)**:** Thursday late-June until early-September, 10 a.m.–12:30 p.m. at Markt (main square)

The Hague

- **Haagse Market** (*www.dehaagsemarkt.nl*)**:** The largest market in the Netherlands, Monday, Wednesday, Friday & Saturday, 8:00 a.m.–5:00 p.m. at Herman Costerstraat / Hobbemastraat
- **Markt Scheveningen:** Thursday, 9 a.m.–4:30 p.m. at Stevinstraat
- **Antique & Book Market:** Mid-May through September, Thursday and Sunday, 10:00 a.m.–6:00 p.m. at Lange Voorhout
- **Antique & Book Market:** October through mid-May, Thursday, 10:00 a.m.–6:00 p.m., at Plein
- **Fish Market:** Monday–Friday, 7:00 a.m.–10:00 a.m. or until the fish are sold out, Scheveningen, Inner Harbor at Visafslagweg
- **Biological Farmer's Market:** Wednesday 11:00 a.m.–6:00 p.m. at Hofweg

Leiden

- **Centrum Market**: Wednesday & Saturday, 9:00 a.m.–5:00 p.m.

Rijswijk

- **Evenementen HAL** (*www.evenementenhalrijswijk.nl*)**:** Theme of market changes weekly, Saturday and Sunday 10:00 a.m.–5:00 p.m.at Volmerlaan 12

Rotterdam

- **Centrum Market** (*www.centrummarktrotterdam.nl*): Tuesday, 8:00 a.m.–5:30 p.m., Friday, 12:00 p.m.–6:00 p.m., Saturday 8:00 a.m.–5:00 p.m., Sunday, 12:00 p.m.–5:00 p.m.
- **Afrikanermarkt:** Wednesday, 8:00 a.m.–5:30 p.m., Saturday 8:00 a.m.–5:00 p.m. at Afrikaanderplein

Wassenaar

- **Market Wassenaar:** Tuesday, 9:00 a.m.–4:00 p.m.at Berkheiveld

Chapter 17
Housekeeping and Maintenance

If you are a veteran of several moves, you already know that the first few days in a new home can be quite challenging. If this is your first overseas move, you will soon discover that bewildering problems have a way of appearing out of nowhere and routine tasks can appear absurdly complicated, but do not worry! Armed with an abundance of patience, a Dutch dictionary and a sense of humor, it will not be long until you have a well-functioning household again, and you will really begin to feel "at home in Holland."

Electrical Issues

Power

Electrical power in the Netherlands and in most of Western Europe runs on a 50-cycle frequency and a voltage of 220 VAC (voltage, alternating current). North American power is supplied at 60 cycles, 110-117V. This means that most North American electrical appliances and machines will not work in the Netherlands unless they are used with a transformer.

Voltage: Voltage can easily be converted by the use of transformers. They are adequate for most appliances up to 1,000 watts and are frequently obtainable from people who are moving home. Read the "For Sale" sections of club and school newsletters and watch for ads on church and club bulletin boards among others. Transformers of up to 2,000 watts for high-wattage appliances such as deep fryers and mixers may be more difficult to find in the Netherlands.

Frequency: Frequency is often a problem for it can't be converted by using transformers. Clocks and timers on 60-cycle appliances will not work correctly. Furthermore, the motors may run hotter.

It is possible to convert some machines so they will run properly on 50 cycles by replacing motors or pulleys. Check with the equipment manufacturer or distributor to see whether it is possible or practical to replace them. Most computer equipment will have built-in frequency converters and some high quality audio/video equipment will as well. Check with the manufacturer before you pack these along just to be sure.

Electrical Helpers

Converters (*omzetter/omvormer*): Travel-sized converters up to 1,600-watt size are available in many luggage shops, electronics stores and duty free areas of airports. These converters are like oversized adapters and they reduce the voltage from 220V to 110V. They are great for contact lens cleaning kits, electric razors, curler sets and for anything with a built-in transformer plug that transforms down from 110V to about 10V. They are not suitable for refrigerators or clocks.

Adapters (*tussenstuk*): Universal adapter kits are difficult to find in the Netherlands. You will need universal adapter kits in order to use small appliances when traveling. Buy them in airport duty free shops, luggage shops or electrical supply stores in your home country. You can find plug adapters at the businesses listed at the end of this section.

Transformers (*transformator*): Transformers have a heavy metal core and they reduce the voltage from 220V to 110V. They are much heavier than the converters and are quite expensive. They are difficult to share between appliances because of their weight. You may need several: one or two in the kitchen for small appliances, one for the stereo, another for your sewing machine and so on. Be aware that the continual use of an appliance with a transformer may cause premature failure of the appliance; however many people have found that appliances last for a reasonable length of time if the appliance is used with the correct size transformer.

Appliances

Major Appliances

To Bring or Not to Bring: Think carefully before you bring your refrigerator, washing machine, clothes dryer or other large appliances. These appliances may create more problems than they are worth. Why?

- **Size:** European appliances are usually 60 centimeters wide (about 24 inches), and a standard space is allocated for these appliances in each Dutch home. Thus, appliances any larger in size might simply not fit in the kitchen of smaller Dutch houses.
- **Installation:** Installation of large appliances may present even greater problems.
- **Parts:** There are no local parts services for non-European appliances. If they break down, they could be difficult to repair.

Technical Considerations

Washers and Dryers: Washing machines manufactured in some countries require a hot water supply, while European washing machines heat their water internally. Thus, it is unlikely that your new Dutch home will have a hot water outlet in the laundry area.

Dryers pose a different kind of problem. Those manufactured in North America, for instance, require a very high wattage. Thus, you may not be able to use an American dryer because the power cables will not support it. You have a choice to do as many Dutch housewives do—hang your clothes outside to dry—or get accustomed to a smaller dryer.

Stoves: American electric kitchen ranges require extensive and expensive rewiring in order to be used in the Netherlands. In addition, many neighborhood power cables are overloaded and the addition of an electric range may create problems for the power company and, in turn, an additional expense for you.

Microwave Ovens: Regular, non-computerized microwave ovens will operate in the Netherlands on a large, 2,000+ watt transformer. However, the clocks will not be accurate and the cooking time must be increased substantially. Electronically programmed microwave ovens will operate, but permanent damage to internal chips may result. Their use is generally not recommended. Please check with the manufacturer.

Small Appliances

Our advice: bring the few small appliances you can't live without and buy the others new or used in the Netherlands (see the chapter on **Essentials to Bring**). All types of excellent quality appliances such as irons, alarm clocks, coffee makers and hair dryers are available. It is also possible to buy good used appliances from other expatriates who are leaving after their stay abroad.

Light Bulbs: Leave your old light bulbs behind. Replace all 110V light bulbs with European 220V light bulbs; both types have the same size base and thread. Better yet, consider using *spaarlampen*. These energy-saving light bulbs are available in various sizes, give the same amount of visible light, use less power and have a longer rated life, but generally have a higher purchase price.

Lamps: Lamps, on the other hand, are different. You may want to consider bringing your favorite lamps with you to the Netherlands because the wiring in lamps from other countries is adequate to handle European electrical current. You will just need to use a plug-adapter. Alternatively, you can convert lamp plugs by cutting off the plug end and replacing it with a Dutch plug, but remember to use Dutch light bulbs with it!

Pre-Converted Appliances: It is possible to buy appliances in North America which are designed for European 220V/50 cycle electrical current, and bring them with you. If this is your choice, look in the Yellow Pages under Appliances for shops that carry European appliances and transformers.

Dutch Electrical Supply Shops that Carry Adapters, Converters and Transformers:

Aurora Kontakt B.V.
Vijzelstraat 27-35, Amsterdam
Grote Marktstraat 32, Den Haag
www.aurora-kontakt.nl

Odemaere Radio & T.V.
Langstraat 160 2242 JZ Wassenaar
☎ (070) 511 51 01

Also look in *Gouden Gids* under electrical supplies and appliances (*huishoudelijk apparaten en artikelen*).

More Things Electrical

Fuses

All newer houses are equipped with circuit breakers. If part of your house is without electricity, it usually means that one of your circuit breakers has tripped. Unplug the cause of the power outage and move the circuit breaker back into position. Older houses still have fuses. Familiarize yourself with the types of fuses in your home and learn how to replace them. Keep spares on hand in the correct specifications. If your electricity goes out, check the fuses, replace any blown ones and reset your fuse box with the main switch. If the electricity does not go back on and yours is the only affected home in the neighborhood, the main fuse for your home has blown and will have to be replaced by the local emergency electrical service.

To avoid tripped circuit breakers or blown fuses take care not to overload a circuit. Like many older homes, many Dutch homes are not wired to handle more than one or two major appliances simultaneously on a given circuit. Never plug an electrical appliance designed for 110V directly into a 220V outlet. You will ruin the appliance and may seriously injure yourself.

In case of a major electrical failure, it is best to contact your electricity provider. Always keep a handy supply of candles and flashlights in case of an emergency.

Useful Telephone Numbers:
☎ (0800) 90 09 (Electric or gas queries)
☎ (079) 347 15 15 (Water queries)
☎ (0900) 88 96 (Cable TV queries)

▸ Ground Wires Required

Dutch law requires that larger appliances be grounded, so you may have to add a ground wire to some of your U.S. appliances. Consult a local dealer. Look under *Elektrotechnische Installatieburos* in the Yellow Pages if you need help with the servicing, conversion or repair of your appliances. This may come as a shock (so to speak), but as a safety precaution, normal electrical outlets are not allowed in Dutch bathrooms in homes or in hotels, however, special low-wattage outlets for electric razors can occasionally be found in bathrooms. Many Dutch bedrooms have a sink and mirror with a normal outlet nearby.

▸ Electrical Rates

There are variations between energy companies, but typically electrical rates are reduced weekday nights (Monday through Thursday at 9:00 p.m. or 11:00 pm to 7:00 a.m.), weekends (Friday at 9:00 p.m. or 11:00 p.m. until Monday at 7:00 a.m.) and most holidays. If you have a low-rate meter, you will save money by using your appliances during these cut-rate hours. You will be billed a fixed rate each month based on an annual estimate. Someone will come to read your meter or you will be asked to send in the meter readings in the fall, and the energy company will send you an adjusted invoice for your annual usage.

▸ Electrical Vocabulary

Electrical wire	*Kabel*
Single wire	*Draad*
Double wire	*Snoer*
Extension cord	*Verlengsnoer*
Fuse	*Zekering* or *stopzekering*
Fuse box	*Meterkast/Stoppenkast*
Grounding switch	*Aardlekschakelaar*
Light bulb	*Gloeilamp*
Double outlet extension cord	*Dubbele stopcontacten*
Triple outlet extension cord	*Drievoudige stopcontacten*
Outlet, power socket	*Stopcontact*
Plug	*Stekker*
Switch	*Schakelaar*

European Appliances

Before using your Dutch appliances, read the instructions. Have them translated if necessary. If an instruction booklet is not available, ask for guidance from your landlord or from the person who sold them to you. If you are purchasing new appliances, ask for instructions in English. They are in most cases available, but you may have to ask for them to be special ordered. You can also go a Google search with the make and model number of the appliance to see if a free downloadable manual is available.

Natural Gas *(Aardgas)*

Natural gas is almost always used in Dutch homes for central heating (*centrale verwarming*), water heaters (*geisers*), and cooking stoves (*fornuizen*). However, an ideal combination is a gas stove top and electric oven. Inquire at your *Gemeentelijk Gasbedrijf* before buying, installing or converting gas appliances.

Dual-System VCRs and DVD Players

It is possible to purchase DVD players that will allow you to watch American (NTSC) and European (PAL) DVDs on your European-bought television set. Ask at a large electronic goods store about "code free" or "region free" VCR/DVD players. It is still possible to find machines that will play video tapes, but they are becoming scarce.

Washing Machines *(Wasmachines)*

Proceed cautiously! European washers can heat water internally to nearly the boiling point (100°C/212°F) and cannot be opened mid-cycle. Make sure to set the correct temperature and cycle programs; most machines have a delicate cycle option. The wash cycle lasts about an hour. Most are front end loaders and do the job very well.

Dryers *(Wasdroger)*

Your European dryer may not be vented to the outdoors. If not, you can try tying a nylon stocking over the end of the outlet hose to help collect lint. Regularly empty the lint traps. If you have an internal water collector, empty it often for best performance. Don't be afraid to put up a clothesline and let your clothes air dry.

International Laundering Symbols

Most European fabric labels carry international garment care code symbols:

Machine wash	Bleachable
Wash up to 40° C	Do not bleach
Do not machine wash	Do not iron
Hand wash only	Dry clean
Iron at low heat	Do not dry clean
Iron at medium heat	Machine dry
Iron at high heat	Do not machine dry

Dishwashers *(Vaatwassers/Afwasmachines)*

Although expensive, dishwashers give excellent performance if used properly. In addition to having a detergent receptacle, all dishwashers have receptacles for:

- A salt-based product (*anti-kalkmiddel*) which prevents calcium deposits from forming on heating elements.
- A liquid drying agent or anti-spotting agent (*glansspoelmiddel*).

Refill these receptacles periodically. The salt will need to be added approximately every 20 washes. Alternatively, you can use a 3-in-1 dishwashing soap tablet. Suggested products are listed under *Household Cleaning Products*.

Household Help

Few expatriates living in the Netherlands have full-time household help, but if you have small children, do a lot of entertaining or hope to pursue outside interests, you may feel that some assistance is worth the expense. It is wise to ask your friends and neighbors about local customs as well as the current wage scale of domestic help.

▶ Responsibilities of the Employer

Depending upon the number of hours your household employees work, you may be required to contribute to several social insurance funds and to make deductions from the employee's salary for their share of the insurance. You must also provide your workers with paid annual holidays. Complying with the Social Insurance Acts in the Netherlands can be quite complicated. Proper handling of the many cards, work permits and other papers may be confusing. Some payments are made to the Trade Department for the Retail Trade and Professions (*Bedrijfsvereniging voor Detailhandel en Ambachten* or DETAM), and some to your local tax office. DETAM employs English-speaking workers who can answer your questions at ☎ (030) 284 42 42.

▶ Classifications of Domestic Help

Classifications of domestic help are more clearly drawn and more strictly observed in the Netherlands than in the United States. To aid you in determining the specific type of household help which will meet your needs, refer to these categories:

Babysitter	*Kinder oppas*
Housekeeper	*Huishoudster*
Cleaning woman	*Werkster*
Mother's helper	*Kindermeisje*
Cook	*Kok*

▶ Obtaining Help

The best way to obtain reliable help is by asking friends for recommendations. You may also place advertisements in newspapers by calling their advertising departments. Look under *Nieuwsbladen* and *Advertenties* in the *Gouden Gids*. Many local grocery stores also have bulletin boards for posting advertisements. Your advertisement, in English or Dutch, should include the type of help required, the number of hours per week, the days of the week, size of household, ages and gender of children, location (city and better yet, neighborhood), telephone number or newspaper reply address and possibly a request for an interview appointment (*afspraak*) and references (*aanbevelingen*). When you hire live-in help, it is advisable to prepare an informal contract covering issues such as working hours, salary, taxes, general duties, time off each week and vacation time.

▸ Special Part-time Help

Catering: Catering help may be obtained through a temporary employment office (*uitzendburo*) and via restaurants, hotels and ACCESS or look under *Cateringservice* in the *Gouden Gids.*

- Butler — *Butler*
- Waiter — *Ober*
- Waitress — *Serveerster*

Garden Care: Agree on the fees before committing your garden to anyone's care or services. If you need a horticultural expert, you will find two listings in the *Gouden Gids*:

- Landscape Gardener — *Tuinarchitect*
- Garden Upkeep & Layout — *Tuinaanleg en Onderhoud*

Helpful gardening vocabulary:

Bulbs	*Bollen*	Clipping or cutting	*Knippen, snoeien*
Peat moss	*Molm/Turfmolm*	Prune	*Snoeien*
Chemical fertilizer	*Kunstmest*	Hose	*Slang*
Rake	*Hark*	Seed	*Zaad*
Trowel	*Troffel*	Manure	*Mest*
Shovel	*Schop*	Soil	*Aarde*
Hedgeclippers	*Heggeschaar*	Mow	*Maaien*
Plant	*Plant*		

Household Cleaning Products

Cleaning products can be found in supermarkets, drugstores (*drogisterijen*) or in large department stores. Please follow the directions and use and store these products with care. Many are caustic and/or poisonous and are sometimes not available with child-safe caps. Many environmentally friendly (*milieu-vriendelijk*) products are available and highly recommended. Such products are for sale at health food stores (*reformhuizen*) and increasingly at mainstream grocery and drugstores.

Household Cleaning Product List

Any items that have a garbage container with an X through it are hazardous and clearly should be brought to a poisonous chemicals collection point or put into your *Chemobak* (bin for temporary storage of small chemical waste issued by some municipalities) for disposal. Look in the pink pages under *Gemeente instellingen, dienst stadsbeheer* and in our **The Environment** chapter. Municipal officials can tell you how to safely dispose of these things. They should not go into your trash!

Bathroom cleaner (*badkamer reiniger*): Use cleaning vinegar (*schoonmaakazijn*) or *Antikal* to remove hard-water calcium deposits.
Bleach (*bleekwater* or *bleekmiddel*): Chlorine (*chloor*) is no longer available. The *bleekwater* made by Loda is not recommended for clothes. It is used, for instance, in the bathroom to get rid of mildew stains.
Carpet cleaner (*tapijtreiniger*): Try Airwick Dry Magic, Sapur and K2R.
Cleaning/dusting supplies: broom (*bezem*), brush (*borstel*), chamois (*zeem*), mopping cloth (*dweil*), sponge (*spons*), dust pan and brush (*stoffer en blik*), dust cloth (*stofdoek*), dish towel (*theedoek*), hand towel (*handdoek*), dish brush (*afwasborstel*) and dish cloth (*afwasdoekje*).
Dish detergent (*afwasmiddel*): Use Brillo pads for hard to clean pots, pans and grill racks. For dish detergent try products such as Dreft or any of a number of store brands in supermarkets.
Dishwasher detergent (*machine afwasmiddelen*): Try Sun or Calgonit powder (*poeder*) or tablets (*tabeletten*). Both companies also make a good anti-spotting liquid (*glansspoelmiddel*). For a water softener, use Broxo Matic, a coarse salt that prevents calcium deposits from forming on your heating element.
Dry cleaning fluid (*wasbenzine*): This liquid is made for use at home. **Caution**: Do NOT use near an open flame.
Dryer sheets (*droogtrommel doekjes*): Use Robijn anti-cling dryer sheets.
Floor wax (*vloerwas*): HG and Johnson's Plavuis are used to clean and polish floors.
Furniture wax (*meubelwas* or *meubelolie*): These are furniture polishes. Try Pledge or Peli.
Laundry soap (*wasmiddel*): For hand wash, try Driehoek *zeep*, an all-purpose natural soap; Sunlight *zeep*, a mild bar soap and Woolite for wools and other fine fabrics.
Starch (*stijfsel*) and **sizing spray** (*strijkspray*): Crackfree and Jubilee are good sizing sprays. For starching, try Crackfree starch.
Laundry detergent (*wasmiddel*): There are several well-known brands of laundry detergents such as Persil, Dreft, All, Dixan and Ariel. These detergents might be for whites (*witwas*) or colored (*bonte was*). Most come in liquid (*vloeibaar*) or powder (*poeder*) form. BioTex is a prewash enzyme soak. You may also need blueing (*blauwsel*) that actually brightens whites.
Metal polish: Use a *koperpoetsmiddel* like Brasso for copper pans and a *zilverpoetsmiddel* like Silvo or Wrights for silver.
Oven cleaner (*oven reiniger*): Try Johnson's Muscle.

Stain remover (*vlekkenreiniger*): Use Shout or BioTex for tough stains on your clothes. Also try Driehoek *zeep*, an environment friendly soap, for stain removal on fabrics and carpeting. It comes in bars, liquid or gel. Citin also makes several stain removing products called *vlekkentovenaar* that are aimed at specific stains.
Tile cleaner (*badkamer reiniger*): For bathroom tile cleaners and for difficult spots try Jif, a liquid abrasive cleanser, or Vim, a cleansing powder (*schuurmiddel*).
Toilet bowl cleaner (*toilet reiniger*): Use any of the products such as Glorix and the decalcifiers mentioned above.
Window cleaner (*ruitenreiniger*): The Dutch have traditionally used ammonia dissolved in water to wash their windows. They dry them with chamois and a newspaper. No one has more practice than these folks, so give it a try. If you are still not convinced, there is always a window cleaner (*ruitenreiniger*) such as Glassex (similar to Windex), Ajax and Lustra sprays.

Household Services

The following is a partial list of some of the household services that may be of greatest importance to you at the beginning of your stay in the Netherlands. We recommend that you contact the publishers of the Dutch Yellow Pages (*www.goudengids.nl* or ☎ (020) 567 67 67) and request a copy of their current "Visitors Guide" for your area. This guide includes an index in English, German, French, Spanish and Italian, as well as other useful information in English.

▸ Household Services: A Yellow Pages Guide

Bicycle upkeep and repair (*Rijwielen en bromfietsen onderhoud/reparatie*)
Cabinet makers (*Meubelmakerijen*)
Cable TV (*Kabeltelevisie*)
Carpentry (*Timmerfabrieken* or *Timmerwerken*)
Chimney sweeping (*Schoorsteenvegen*): It is the responsibility of the householder to have chimneys cleaned once a year. Noncompliance may affect your insurance.
Dry cleaners (*Stomerijen*): Dry cleaning establishments post signs indicating that they are not responsible for loss or damage. Patronize a well-recommended cleaner, and even then proceed with caution. Dutch dry cleaners have a special finish called *speciale behandeling*, which allows you to remove spots easily. This finish is used most often on expensive items such as suits and winter coats.
Helpful Dry Cleaning Vocabulary:

- Mending, reweaving — *Stoppages*
- Mothproofing — *Motvrij maken*
- Press — *Persen*
- Starch — *Stijven*
- Steam cleaning — *Stomen*
- Suede cleaning — *Suedekleding reiniging*
- Waterproofing — *Vochtwerend maken*

Electrical services (*Elektrotechnische Installatieburos*)
Furnace installation & maintenance (*Centrale verwarming, installatie en onderhoud*): Your furnace should be cleaned once a year to keep the house clean, to save fuel and to prevent a fire hazard.
Glass and china repair: Inquire at an antique dealer (*Antiquiteiten*).
Gutter repair (*Loodgieters*): Plumbers do this work.
Hardware stores (*Ijzerwaren; Gereedschappen; Doe-het-zelf artikelen en materialen*): Do-it-yourself is your best bet to buy or rent a large selection of equipment and tools.
Knife sharpening (*Slijpen en polijsten*): Individuals that sharpen knives, sewing shears, pinking shears, lawn mower blades, pruning shears and nail scissors may visit your neighborhood. Be sure to ask the price before agreeing to the service offered.
Laundromats (*Wassalons* or *Wasserettes*): In some *wassalons*, you may even leave your laundry to be clean and folded within a couple of hours or the next day. Laundromats will wash and iron men's shirts very nicely, but they tend to use a lot of starch. You can request very light starch (*zeer licht stijven*).
Locksmiths (*Sleutels en sloten*)
Night watchman (*Bewakingsdiensten*): This service provides checks of your home at night which may prove invaluable during long absences.
Painters (*Schilders*)
Plasterers (*Stukadoors*)
Plumbers (*Loodgieters*)
Rentals (*Verhuur*): For rental of miscellaneous items, including: pianos, household goods and party needs. Check the following categories: Furniture (*Meubelverhuur*), Linen (*Linnenverhuur*), Radio and television (*Televisies en video-apparatuur, verhuur*), *DVDs*/video tapes (*Videotheken*), Washing machines (*Wasmachines en centrifuges, verhuur*)
Roofing (*Dakbedekkingen*)
Rug cleaning (*Tapijtreiniging*): Many drugstores and dry cleaners have excellent rug cleaning equipment for hire.
Sewing machine repair (*Naaimachinereparatie en Onderhoud*)
Shoe repair (*Schoenmakers*): Shoe repair stores fix shoes and most can make keys.
Upholstering (*Meubelstoffering*): It is difficult to hire an upholsterer that allows you to furnish the fabric. Upholsterers prefer that you choose one of their materials.
Wall paperers (*Behangers*)
Watch & clock repair (*Horloge en klokken onderhoud/reparatie*)
Window cleaners (*Glazenwassers*): Window cleaners can come to your home on a regular basis. They may also clean the gutters. Ask your neighbors.
Window repair (*Glashandel*)

▸ Municipal Household Services

Garbage pick-up: See **The Environment** chapter.

Pest control (*Ongediertebestrijding en Ontsmetting*): For eradication of rodents, insects and wood worms.

Public utilities: In some municipalities, gas, water and electricity charges are billed together. The White Pages heading is *Gemeente-instellingen* or *energiebedrijf.*

▸ Household Maintenance Vocabulary

Cement powder	*Cement voor metselspecie*	Natural gas	*Aardgas*
Charcoal	*Houtskool*	Oil	*Olie, smeerolie*
Coal	*Steenkool*	Plaster of Paris	*Gips*
Concrete block	*Blok beton*	Putty, planing knife	*Plamuur mes*
Fireplace wood	*Gekloofd hout/open haarden*	Sandpaper	*Schuurpapier*
Fuel oil	*Stookolie en Industrieolie*	Screws, nuts	*Schroeven*
Garden supplies	*Tuingereedschappen*	Steel wool	*Staalwol*
Glue	*Lijm*	Turpentine	*Terpentijn*
Gravel, sand	*Grint, zand*	Tools	*Gereedschappen*
Grease	*Vet, smeervet*	Wall paneling	*Wandbekleding*
Gutter	*Goot*	Weather stripping	*Tochtlat*
Matches	*Lucifers*	Wheelbarrow	*Kruiwagen*
Mole snare	*Klem voor mollen*	Wire	*Draad*
Nails	*Spijkers*	Wood	*Hout*

▸ Weather Information

If you are planning a day trip within the Netherlands or a longer trip elsewhere in Europe, you can call ☎ (0900) 123 45 70 for weather information. The information is delivered in Dutch and the temperatures are given in Celsius. You can also check the weather anywhere in the world at *www.weather.com.*

Useful Household Reference

Temperature Conversion

By Formula

- To convert Fahrenheit to Celsius:
  Temp in °F - 32) x 5/9 = Temp in °C
  subtract 32 degrees, multiply by 5 and divide by 9.
- To convert Celsius to Fahrenheit:
  (Temp in °C x 9/5) +32 = Temp in °F
  multiply by nine, divide by five and add 32

By Chart

°F	°C
0	-18
14	-10
32	0
40	4
50	10
60	16
70	21
80	27
90	33
100	38

For quick conversions of just about any kind, log onto *www.onlineconversion.com*.

Certificate

This is to certify that the Trees for Travel Foundation has offset the greenhouse gas emissions resulting from the printing of 3000 copies of the book:

At home in Holland

by

The American Women's Club of The Hague

A total amount of

2 tonnes of CO_2

has been absorbed by specially planted trees in Malaysia, which helps to curb global warming and protect the remaining tropical rainforest

TREES FOR TRAVEL

Dieren, 5 November 2008
Trees for Travel Foundation

drs. ing. W.R.G. Hagedoorn ,
chairman

www.treesfortravel.nl **Certificate number 00ZZ002/Z/081105**

Chapter 18

The Environment

The Dutch way is bicycling, recycling, wooden shoes in the garden, the use of sweaters instead of heaters and lots of plants in the houses. Much of it is earth-friendly and worthy of emulation. These habits arise from a genuine concern for the environment and from a strong tradition of thriftiness.

Below are all slogans you may see in various places throughout the Netherlands—on trams, in pamphlets, on billboards, in newspapers—and they all mean one thing: Take care of the environment!

Een beter milieu begint bij je eigen deur.	A cleaner environment begins at home.
Wilt u het milieu een handje helpen!	Lend the environment a hand!
Naar het werk? Beter op de fiets. Dan vervuil je niets!	Going to work? It's better to cycle. Then there is no pollution!
Meer milieu door minder energie.	Less energy waste means a better environment.
Afwassen is beter voor het milieu.	Dish washing is good for the environment (Do not use throwaways).

The Dutch are "grass roots" environmentalists. They believe that the road to a cleaner, more sustainable world is paved with all the individual steps each and every one of us takes.

Off to a Good Start

The Netherlands is a densely populated country and land is precious. With so many people in this small area, the environment becomes easily polluted. Each individual can, and should, do his or her share by taking an active role in pollution reduction. So use the opportunity to recycle and cycle, and become part of the Dutch landscape by contributing to a better environment (*een beter milieu*).

Keeping it Clean

For ecologically sound housekeeping, you can use non-toxic substances to keep your home and possessions clean. Lemon juice, cleaning vinegar (more concentrated than the cooking variety) and baking soda are effective and versatile agents.

Conserving Natural Resources

Bring your family's bicycles (or purchase one here second hand) and expect to use them. People of all ages use their bicycles for daily transportation. Bike paths make it easy and safe. In cold weather, the layered look is definitely "in." Put on a sweater instead of turning up the heat. Use less water and use electricity in the off-hours. Install water-conserving shower heads and purchase energy-efficient light bulbs. You will save money in the long run, too.

Have an Energy Audit

Your local power company (*gemeentelijk* or *gewestelijk energiebedrijf*) can help you conserve energy and save money. Most offer a free "energy audit" of your home that will examine areas where you could improve energy efficiency. Windows and doors are checked for heat loss, and hot water heaters and stoves are examined as well. These companies also sell energy-efficient light bulbs and water-conserving fixtures at advantageous prices.

The Department of the Environment

Each municipality (*gemeente*) has an environmental department (*reinigingsdienst*). This department is responsible for coordinating trash pick-up, hazardous waste disposal, street cleaning, recycling, environmental crises, etc. If you have old appliances, furniture or any other large debris such as tree branches, you can call this agency for an appointment to have it hauled away, sometimes for free. They will send a truck to your curb, have the debris hauled away and deal responsibly with its disposal. Once you have settled in, you will want to know:

- Where are the paper bins, glass bins and small chemical waste collection points in my neighborhood?
- Has the *gemeente* organized curbside pick-up for recyclables?
- Is a composting bin available for purchase or rental from the *gemeente*? (This is not the one for collection of compostable household waste, but one that will make compost for your garden.)
- Are there any car pool opportunities?
- Where is the closest recycling center? Is a pass needed?
- Does the *gemeente* have a bicycle (antitheft) registration program?

Refer to the phone book under *Gemeente Stadsbeheer*, *Milieu* or *Reinigingsdienst*.

Recycling

Part of the Dutch daily routine is recycling. Located near the main shopping street in every neighborhood, you will find various containers for recycling glass, paper, cardboard and old clothing. The Dutch collect and recycle just about everything that is conceivably recyclable: PVC plastics, old tires, scrap construction materials, etc.

Paper Recycling

Look for green bins in your neighborhood or at the shopping center. These bins are usually marked *papierbak* (paper bin). You can recycle:

- Advertising leaflets
- Books
- Cardboard boxes
- Computer paper
- Corrugated cardboard
- Paper bags
- Egg cartons
- Envelopes
- Gift paper
- Magazines
- Newspapers

Above all ensure that NO plastic or metal is left with the paper (for example: ring binders, file folders with metal bindings, staples, etc.). Sometimes egg cartons can be returned to the store where you purchased them and will be reused—the best kind of recycling.

Some areas have curbside pick-up. Call your *gemeente* or ask your neighbors if there is a curbside pick-up in your neighborhood. Ask the *gemeente* for a garbage collection schedule (*huisvuil kalender*) or deliver your paper to the local recycling center.

Glass Recycling

Ninety percent of nonreturnable glass is currently recycled by government mandate. In fact, there are more glass recycling bins than mailboxes. In most places you will find the glass recycling bins next to the paper bins. The glass bin is marked *glasbak*. There are usually two or three holes, each of which is clearly marked with words and colors for sorting glass. Remember, any container that has the word *statiegeld* on it, should be returned to the shop to obtain a refund of your deposit. Glass recycling guidelines:

- Remove all plastic or metal caps or wrappers, when possible.
- Never put old light bulbs or mirrors in the bin.
- Do not put any plastic, such as the bag in which you were carrying the glass, into the *glasbak*.

Battery Recycling

Used batteries should never be thrown in the trash. Any business that sells batteries, such as a grocery or electronic store, will have a bin shaped like a battery near the door or service desk for used batteries. The batteries will then be disposed of according to municipal instructions.

Metal & Plastic Recycling

There are no separate recycling bins for metal cans, so throw them in your regular trash. With the use of magnets, metals are separated from trash at the landfill. Plastic recycling is becoming more available in many places. Recycling centers now accept cans and plastic. Call your *gemeente* for the address of a drop-off center.

Household Goods Recycling

The next time you do your spring cleaning, please consider donating your old usable clothes, shoes, toys, furniture, etc. to the many charity shops and churches that will gladly take your donations. There is a Kringloop (*www.kringloopholland.nl*) or Salvation Army (*www.legerdesheils.nl*) shop in many towns; if your donation is large, they can usually send a truck for pick-up. Many charities regularly distribute plastic bags stamped with a pick-up day. If you fill your bag with clothing, shoes and linens, and set it out on the designated day, your old possessions will certainly find a new life. In addition, next to most glass recycling bins are special bins for clothes and shoes designated for a local charity or Amnesty International; remember to place all items in sealed plastic bags.

Recycling Center

Many cities have recycling centers so you can drop off your own waste. Some issue residents a dump pass (*stortpas*) to provide access; in other places anyone can drive in. Ask at your *gemeentehuis*. At these recycling centers, there are places to drop off appliances (such as refrigerators, freezers and air conditioners), building materials, large garden waste (like Christmas trees and fallen branches), paper, cardboard and large objects (such as chairs, sofas, etc.). There is usually someone there to direct you to the correct bins.

Compostable Recycling

If you opt not to have your own compost bin for your garden, you can have the city collect biodegradable waste. Many municipalities provide households with green trash bins (*groen afval bak*) and have regular curbside pick-up of the separated biodegradable waste. The containers belong to your home, not to you, so leave them behind when you move.

What SHOULD GO into a *groen afval bak*?
All organic matter, such as:

- Bread
- Cheese rinds
- Coffee filters & grounds
- Christmas trees (when cut into small pieces)
- Eggshells
- Fats (used cooking)
- Fish
- Flowers, old house plants
- Fruits, vegetables
- Grass, weeds, leaves, straw, other small garden waste
- Meat, bones
- Nutshells
- Solid waste from pets (except cats)
- Tea bags & leaves

What SHOULD NOT go into the *groen afval bak* or any other recycling bin? Items such as these should be disposed of in your non-recyclable waste:

- BBQ charcoal
- Boards and other wood
- Birdcage sand
- Cat litter
- Diapers
- Fireplace ash
- Grease from deep-frying
- Incandescent light bulbs
- Milk cartons
- Plastics (accept those with Statiegeld)
- Vacuum cleaner bags

Household Chemical Waste

▸ Disposing of Household Chemical Waste

There are several ways of disposing of your household chemical waste:

- Take it to a recycling center which accepts chemical waste.
- Take it to a location in your neighborhood which is a special collection point, such as a shop or Community Center (*Buurthuis*).
- Take it to a designated *Chemocar* stop or watch for an announcement of dates when a *Chemocar* will be in your neighborhood. *Chemocars* are specially manned and outfitted vehicles that pick up hazardous waste.

Many Dutch households are provided with special collection containers (*chemobox*) in which to temporarily store their hazardous waste. Please note that, while incandescent light bulbs go into your regular trash, compact fluorescent bulbs go into a *chemobox*.

What Constitutes Household Chemical Waste? Do you think that your household contains no chemical waste? Think again! The following items are hazardous waste (*milieuschadelijke afvalstoffen*):

- Acetone
- Ammonia
- Antifreeze
- Antioxidants
- Batteries
- Bleach
- Brake fluid
- Camphor spirits
- Caustic soda
- Chlorine
- Chrome polish
- Compact fluorescent bulbs
- Copper polish
- Copper products
- Cosmetics
- Degreasers
- Felt-tip pens
- Film & negatives
- Furniture polish
- Gasoline
- Glues
- Greases
- Herbicides
- Ink
- Insecticides
- Latex paint
- Lead
- Lye
- Medicines
- Mineral oil
- Motor oil
- Nail polish & remover
- Oil filters
- Oven cleaner
- Paint
- Paint rollers
- Paint thinner
- Pesticides
- Petroleum products
- Photographic chemicals
- Polishing cloths
- Printer inks, toner & cartridges
- Rust removers
- Silver polish
- Solvents
- Spray cans
- Thermometers
- Thermostats
- Turpentine
- Weed killers
- Whiteout & thinner
- Zinc

Stopping Junk Mail

The average household in the Netherlands receives more than 1,600 pieces (34 kg) of junk mail (*ongeadresseerd reclamedrukwerk*) each year. This huge waste of paper clearly causes unnecessary loss of the world's forests, contributes to global warming and is a general irritant. There is a national campaign against junk mail which encourages the use of "Nee/Nee" and "Nee/Ja" mailbox stickers, which are available at your local *gemeente*. The "Nee/Nee" sticker blocks all mail which isn't addressed to you, while the "Nee/Ja" sticker allows the delivery of free home-delivered newspapers.

Ecology Groups

▸ Greenpeace

Greenpeace is an international organization that is known for its confrontational, though non-violent, actions to alert the world to and protect the Earth from such things as the dumping of toxic waste and exploitation of Antarctica. Greenpeace volunteers also participate in oil spill cleanups.

Greenpeace Nederland
Jollemanhof 15-17, 1019 GW Amsterdam
☎ (0800) 422 33 44
www.greenpeace.nl

▸ Milieu Centraal

Milieu Centraal is a non-governmental organization (NGO) that specializes in providing environmental information to consumers. They operate a call center to answer questions.

Milieu Centraal
Herculesplein 357, 3584 AA Utrecht
☎ (0900) 1719 (€0,15/minute)
www.milieucentraal.nl

▸ Milieudefensie (Friends of the Earth Netherlands)

Meaning "Environmental Defense," this organization has many publications, several in English, which give valuable information about how to become greener in your daily routine. They can send you an information packet. You can also call with any question about the environment.

Milieudefensie
Nieuwe Looiersstraat 31, 1017 VA Amsterdam
☎ (020) 626 26 20
www.milieudefensie.nl

▸ Vogelbescherming

This organization is active in protecting bird habitats (both native and migratory birds) at the international, national and local levels. Members also help out when environmental disasters occur, such as oil spills. Organized walks and counts are held regularly, frequently in areas that are ordinarily off-limits.

Vogelbescherming
☎ (030) 693 77 00
www.vogelbescherming.nl

Helpful Vocabulary

Afdeling	Section, branch
Afval	Trash, garbage, refuse
Bak	Bin
Blik	Can, tin
Het Broeikaseffect	The greenhouse effect
CFKs	CFCs (chlorofluorocarbons)
Chemocar	Chemical waste collection vehicle
Chemohalt	Pickup point for a Chemocar
Compostbak	Compost bin
Dienst Stadsbeheer	Municipal Services Dept.

Glasbak	Glass recycling bin
Homeopatisch	Homeopathic
Kringlooppapier	Recycled paper
Kunststof	Plastic
Milieuvriendelijk	Environmentally friendly
Natuur	Nature
Ophaaldienst	Pickup & hauling service
Papierbak	Paper recycling bin
Reformhuis/Reformwinkel	Natural products shop
Reiniging	Cleaning
Statiegeld	Deposit

Chapter 19

Hobbies and Recreation

Leisure activities are an important part of both the Dutch and foreign communities in the Netherlands. You should be able to pursue most of your hobby and leisure interests during your stay in the Netherlands, as well as expand your horizons by developing new ones. International clubs and churches offer a wide variety of cultural and recreational activities. The American Women's Clubs of The Hague and Amsterdam have a constantly changing slate of activities ranging from bridge, tennis and travelling to lessons in art appreciation, languages and ethnic cookery. See our **Church and Community** chapter for a listing of these organizations.

Arts & Crafts

Many of the English-speaking churches sponsor craft guilds where you can learn a craft and, at the same time, provide items for fund raisers. Some museums, schools and many clubs also offer courses. Look in the Yellow Pages (*www.goudengids.nl*) under *Volksuniversiteiten* and *Vrije Academie* for institutions that offer courses. You can also ask at your city hall (*gemeente*) for they may sponsor some community classes.

The Arts & Crafts Club and Vernissage offer courses in upholstery, furniture restoration, water colors, paper English roses, *Tromp l'oeil*, decoupage, creative cards, flower pot decorating and flower arranging.

Vernissage has a children's studio on Wednesdays where children can learn to sculpt, make puppets and cook. They also give French, Italian, Thai and Latin American cookery lessons and arrange large parties for special occasions.

International Art Club Den Haag
Weimarstraat 49A, The Hague
☎ (062) 913 27 76
www.internationalartclubdenhaag.nl

Vernissage
Dr. Abraham Kuyperlaan 1A, Bussum
☎ (035) 691 67 88
www.vernissage.nl

Arts & Crafts Club – Koetshuis van Eyckenstein
Dorpsweg 195, Maartensdijk-Bilthoven
☎ (034) 621 26 30
www.topworkshops.nl

The Decorative and Fine Arts Society of The Hague
☎ (070) 387 26 06 Jane Choy
www.dfas.nl

Studio Jean Art Lessons
Thomsonlaan 65, Den Haag
☎ (070) 392 16 72
www.studiojean.nl

Bird Watching

For a country with so much water, it is understandable that bird watching, especially waterfowl, would be almost a national pastime. There are many wild bird reserves and many possibilities to see them. Contact your regional VVV for more information or contact BirdLife International in the Netherlands at *www.vogelbescherming.nl*. Guided tours of Wild Bird Reservations on the island of Texel and in Friesland can also be arranged through the VVV.

Bridge

Many of the social clubs—like the American Women's Clubs of The Hague and Amsterdam, the British Women's Clubs and the International Women's Clubs—have bridge groups. There are also many Dutch bridge groups, but their bidding is in Dutch and they mostly play the Acol system, so be prepared.

Dance Lessons

A wide range of dance instruction possibilities exists. Look in the Yellow Pages under *Dansscholen*. The Dutch terms for different dance styles are easy to understand, for example *tapdans*, *engelse wals* and *ballet* (*modern en klassiek*). Perhaps it is helpful to know that *gevorderden* means "experienced," i.e., not for beginners.

Flying

For schools that teach flying, look in the Yellow Pages under *Vliegscholen*. For all aviation-oriented information including a list of flight schools and clubs, see *www.aviation.nl*.

Gambling

The Netherlands has casinos in many larger cities that offer blackjack, poker, roulette, Punto Banco and several other games. Visit the website *www.hollandcasino.nl* or check with the VVV for addresses, opening times and more information.

Suitable dress may be required (jackets and ties for men), and players must show their passport and pay an entrance fee. Blackjack tables are limited in number, so you will usually need to make a reservation to sit at one after you arrive. Dutch rules allow standing players to bet on the hands of those seated. An English-language *Rules of the Game* is available.

Lectures

The John Adams Institute in Amsterdam promotes the exchange of culture between the United States and the Netherlands. It is one of Europe's leading lecture podiums, which brings top American thinkers and writers to speak in the Netherlands. Guests have included bestselling authors, Nobel laureates and recipients of the world's most prestigious literary prizes.

The John Adams Institute
West India House, Herenmarkt 97, 1013 EC Amsterdam
☎ (020) 624 72 80
www.john-adams.nl

The Library

▸ American Women's Club Library

The library of the American Women's Club of The Hague is one of the largest English-language, general interest libraries in the Netherlands. Library cards for the entire family are issued free with Club membership. Nonmembers must pay an annual user's fee. DVD rentals in both PAL and NTSC formats are also available. There is a 24/7 book drop for returning books and/or donating your old ones.

The American Women's Club of The Hague
Nieuwe Duinweg 25, 2587 AB Den Haag
☎ (070) 350 60 07
www.awcthehague.org

Dutch Public Libraries

Public Libraries (*Openbare Bibliotheken* or *Bibliotheek*) contain surprisingly large collections of English-language books including novels and children's books. Often, books can also be found in several other languages. Adults must pay an annual membership fee, but most libraries give children free borrowing privileges. Remember to take identification with you when you apply for your library card: i.e. your passport and proof of residency such as a bank statement or utility bill.

Most cities and larger towns have special music libraries which loan out sheet music and compact discs. Some libraries also lend out DVD's. These services are not always included in library membership and may involve an extra fee. Some libraries have computerized card catalogs and no access to the stacks. With your library card, you can order books and then pick them up at the counter after about 15 minutes. For more information visit the website at *www.bibliotheek.nl.*

The Royal Library

The Royal library (*Koninklijke Bibliotheek*) has many English-language art, literature and scientific research books. It is the Dutch version of the American Library of Congress. If you wish to use it, you must be 17 years or older and pay for a day pass or an annual user's fee.

Koninklijke Bibliotheek
Prins Willem Alexanderhof 5, Den Haag
☎ (070) 314 09 11
www.kb.nl

University Libraries

Some university libraries have a "good neighbor" policy and extend borrowing privileges to the community.

Live Performances

Performance Listings

Listings of all performances are regularly included in newspapers and in weekly brochures such as the *Weekprogramma* in The Hague, *Deze Week* in Rotterdam and *What's On* in Amsterdam. The VVV regularly publishes brochures which list activities for each day of the month (*Maandagenda*). Free newspapers delivered to your home also list the week's activities in your local town. All larger towns have websites dedicated to entertainment and special events, and some offer electronic newsletters that you can subscribe to:

- Amsterdam: *www.iamsterdam.com*
- The Hague: *www.thehagueonline.com*

- Ranstad: *www.expatica.com/nl*
- Rotterdam: *www.rotterdam.info/uk*
- Zuid-Holland: *www.zuid-holland.com*

▸ Buying Tickets

Tickets for the ballet, theater, concerts, festivals and other performances may be bought individually or by subscription (*abonnement*). They are available through reservation offices (*bespreekbureaus*), theaters, hotels, post offices, CD/DVD stores and most VVV Offices. It is wise to book in advance. Larger cities also may have an outlet that sells same-day tickets for 50% off.

The UitBuro
Hofweg 1, 2511 AA Den Haag
☎ (0900) 828 29 99 (€0,40/minute)
www.haagsuitburo.nl

Last Minute Ticket Shop
Leidseplein 26, Amsterdam
☎ (0900) 01 91 (€0,40/minute)
www.lastminuteticketshop.nl

▸ English-Language Theater

English-language performances are fairly common in major cities throughout the Netherlands.

In Players – International Drama Group
P.O. Box 11437, 1001 GK Amsterdam
www.inplayers.org

The Anglo-American Theatre Group
P.O. Box 10239, 2501 HE Den Haag
www.aatg.nl

For more information about theaters with international programs, inquire at the VVV. Ask for the NNTO (Netherlands National Tourism Office) booklet on the performing arts.

Movie Theaters and DVDs

Dutch movie theaters (*bioscopen*) show films in their original language with Dutch subtitles. Children's movies are often dubbed; the listing of the movie will show OV for the "original version" or NL for dubbed in Dutch. It is wise to arrive early on weekends unless you buy your tickets in advance either at the box office or online at *www.bios.nl* or *www.pathe.nl*.

Films are rated according to the minimum age at which children may be admitted, and limits are strictly enforced. "A. L." (*alle leeftijden*), means that there is no age restriction. It is the equivalent of the American "G" (general audience) rating. Americans may be surprised to discover that the Dutch will rate a movie strictly for violent content, but leniently for sexual content.

There are many video shops (*videotheken*) that rent DVDs of Dutch and foreign films with a large assortment of American films. The back of the case will show which languages are spoken and which subtitles are available.

Music Lessons and Choirs

Music schools and private instructors are numerous. Look in the Yellow Pages under *Muziekscholen* or *Muzieklessen (privé)* or contact the music department at an international school such as The American School of The Hague at ☎ (070) 512 10 79. The website *www.musicteachers.nl* is an online database of private teachers for the expatriate community and also has links to music clubs. In The Hague, the Royal Conservatory (*Koninklijke Conservatorium* at *www.koncon.nl*) offers bachelor's and master's degrees in music.

The Cecilia International Choir of The Hague (*www.cecilia-choir.com*) is an adult choir that performs four concerts per year. Sweet Adelines International is a worldwide organization of women singers committed to advocating the musical art form of barbershop harmony through education and performances. For more information, visit *www.sweetadelines.nl*.

Photography

Images International Photographic Club (*www.imagesphotoclub.com*) is an English-speaking international photography club for amateur photographers. It meets monthly in The Hague to exchange ideas and develop new skills. Members also benefit from field trips, exhibitions, workshops and newsletters. For photographic supplies, see *Fotozaken* in the Yellow Pages.

Sports and Active Hobbies

International clubs offer their members tennis and bowling leagues for all levels of ability. Additional sports information for the whole family can be found at the VVV as well as the following:

ABF International Sports Club
The ABF offers youth soccer (football), softball and basketball, and adult basketball.
Ammonslaantje 1, Wassenaar
☎ (070) 514 65 15
www.abfsport.nl

Dutch Sports Federation

The Dutch Sports Service has offices in various locations and can provide information regarding all sporting activities in their respective areas.

☎ (026) 483 44 00

www.sport.nl

Bowling

Bowling alleys (*bowlingbanen*) are found in many cities. Generally, shoes can be rented at a nominal fee, bowling balls are available at no charge, and lanes are rented by the hour. There is an active International Couples League at Bowling Scheveningen.

Dolfijn Bowling Scheveningen

Gevers Deynootweg 990-2 in the Palace Promenade, Scheveningen

☎ (070) 354 32 12

www.scheveningen-dolfijnbowling.nl

Camping

Camping is very popular in Europe. Camping equipment (*kampeerartikelen*) and trailers (*kampeerautos*) can be rented. For foreign camping advice and locations, contact the ANWB. For Dutch campsites, contact the VVV or:

Stichting Vrije Recreatie

☎ (018) 335 27 41

www.svr.nl

Climbing (Indoor)

There is no natural rock for climbers in the Netherlands, but there are over thirty rock climbing gyms (*klimhallen*). These gyms offer lessons for all ages and many also host birthday parties. To find a rock climbing gym near you, go to *www.klimgids.climbing.nl*

Cricket

There are several cricket clubs. Contact your *gemeente* to see if one exists in your area, check the listings on the Royal Dutch Cricket Board at *www.kncb.nl* or contact:

Voorburg Cricket Club

www.voorburgcc.nl

Hilversum Cricket Club

☎ (035) 544 57 01

www.hilversumschecricketclub.nl

De Kieviten Cricket Club of Wassenaar
www.kieviten.nl

Cycling

Bicycle paths (*fietspaden*) are everywhere. Given this feature, plus the decidedly horizontal lay of the land, cycling is a very popular and safe sport. The ANWB and VVV can supply you with information, maps and touring tips on biking. Bicycles may be rented at many train stations and at bicycle rental stores (*Fietsenverhuurwinkels*). Renting is a great option for guests and for weekend bicycle-touring trips in combination with the trains, but if you are staying a while you should definitely buy your own bicycle.

If you wish to participate in organized rides, there are cycling clubs in most towns. Each club has rides for various levels and interests, providing a place for the serious rider, the mountain biker, and the family tourist. See our **Transportation** chapter for more information about buying, renting, and transporting your bicycle plus some of the rules of the road.

Fishing

Fishing is a favorite pastime in the Netherlands. Everyone 15 years and older must have a fishing license (*VISpas*), obtainable when you join a sports fishing club. A limited fishing pass is available at the post office. If you want to fish on non-commercial inland waters, you will also need a permit from the local sport fishing club or permission from the owner. Fishing on the inland waters is mostly catch and release. The inland water fishing season lasts from June to mid-March, but deep-sea and coastal water fishing have no seasonal restrictions. For more information contact:

Sportvisserij Nederland
☎ (0900) 202 53 58 (€0,35/minute)
www.sportvisserijnederland.nl

Fitness Centers

Fitness centers have become very popular in recent years. Most have the full line of equipment and aerobics classes plus many have saunas. Many fitness centers require that you have shoes for indoor use only. Look under *Fitnesscentra* in the Yellow Pages.

Golf

The majority of golf courses (*golfbanen*) are private and expensive. However, nonmembers may play at most of these private clubs upon payment of green fees. A golfer must be able to prove his qualifications by showing a card equivalent to the Golf Proficiency Card (handicap card) called a *Golf vaardigheidsbewijs*. Membership in an overseas club will be sufficient. Examinations are offered by the golf clubs. You will need to undergo both a practical and a written exam. Golf clubs follow the Royal and Ancient Golf Club of St. Andrews and United States Golf Association rules. If you have clubs, bring them with you. For more information and a list of courses:

Nederlands Golf Federatie (Dutch Golf Federation)
☎ (035) 523 04 02
www.golf.nl

Golf Europe
www.golfeurope.com

Delfland Golfbaan
Abtsrechtseweg 1, Schipluiden
☎ (015) 380 17 96
www.delflandgolf.nl

Swingaway
Indoor golf and workout center
Binckhorstlaan 50a, Den Haag
☎ (070) 315 30 40
www.swingaway.nl

▸ Horseback Riding

Horseback riding is very popular in the Netherlands. The Royal Dutch Equestrian Federation, the KNHS (*Koninklijke Nederlandse Hippische Sportfederatie* at *www.knhs.nl*), has over 195,000 members. Much like you need a proficiency card to play golf, you need a rider's license (*KNHS Ledenpas*) to hire a horse independently for a ride on the beach or in the woods. You must be registered at a riding school (*manege*) and take lessons before you can join the riding federation. There is a five-star rating system for *manages* similar to hotel ratings, i.e. the higher number of stars the higher the *manege* is ranked.

▸ Ice Skating

Ice skating is a favorite Dutch winter sport. The *Elfstedentocht*, a race held between eleven cities in Friesland, is a national passion. This race is over 125 miles long and is scheduled only when weather conditions provide frozen canals, which has only happened 15 times since it began in 1909. Nonetheless, the entire nation hopes that conditions will be right each winter, because it is quite a sight to see. To participate in the competition, you have to be a member of the Frisian Eleven Cities Association.

Frisian Eleven Cities Association
☎ (058) 215 50 20
www.elfstedentocht.nl

There are both indoor and outdoor ice rinks (*ijsbanen*), and a cold winter will find crowds on the canals. If you get the chance, strap on a pair of old wooden skates—they really work! Ice shows and ice hockey are also popular. There is year-round indoor skating available throughout the country:

De Uithof
Jaap Edenweg 10, 2544 NL Den Haag
☎ (0900) 338 484 63
www.deuithof.nl

Nederlands Schaatsenrijders Bond (Dutch Skaters Federation)
☎ (033) 489 20 00
www.knsb.nl

To have your ice skates sharpened, look in the Yellow Pages under *Schaatsenslijperijen*.

▸ Rugby

International Rugby Club of Amsterdam
Sportlaan 25A, 1185 TB Amstelveen
☎ (020) 643 89 79
www.arcrugby.com

Te Werve RUFC International Rugby in The Hague
H.S.V. Celeritas Sportcomplex
Leyweg 1630, 2584 AE Den Haag
☎ (017) 429 51 51
www.rugby-tewerve.com

▸ Running or Jogging

The Hague Road Runners caters to all levels of experience and offers training groups for distances from 5K to marathon. In addition to weekly training sessions, the club organizes training weekends, group trips to runs and social events.

The Hague Road Runners Club
Groenendaal 11, Wassenaar
☎ (070) 328 10 25
www.hagueroadrunners.nl

To find an irreverent running group who mix socializing and running, contact the Hash House Harriers. They have groups worldwide and several local groups:

Amsterdam Hash House Harriers
www.harrier.nl

Hague Hash House Harriers
☎ (063) 867 34 47 Hans
www.haguehash.nl

Dutch Treat Family Hash House Harriers
Family-friendly trails in The Hague and surrounding towns
www.dutchtreathash.com

▸ Sailing and Boating

Boats of all sizes, with or without crew, may be rented by the day, month or season through the ANWB. The VVV has brochures on all types of water sports, including regattas, meets and races.

Nederlandse Watersport Verbond (Dutch Water Sport Federation)
☎ (030) 751 37 00
www.watersportverbond.nl

Koninklijke Nederlandsche Zeil & Roeivereeniging (Royal Netherlands Sail and Rowing Assocation)
☎ (029) 426 15 40
www.knzrv.nl

To take your own small flat-bottom boat out on one of the canals in The Hague, visit the Waterkant. It was built on the site of a WWII German bunker and sits on the bank of the beautiful canal at Westbroek Park. Check the website for specifics and hours of operation:

Waterkant
Westbroek Park at Haringkade, Den Haag
☎ (070) 350 28 63
www.dewaterkant.nl

▸ Scouting

English-language scouting groups can be located via the international schools, ACCESS or the following:

Scouting Nederland
☎ (033) 496 09 11
www.scouting.nl

Scuba Diving
Believe it or not, people do scuba dive in the canals and lakes of the Netherlands. There are dive shops in many larger cities. Ask at the:

Nationaal Duikcentrum (National Dive Centre)
www.ndc.nl

Skiing
If you have not already done so, try a ski holiday package. You can practice at several (artificial) Dutch ski runs.

Snow World
Buytenparklaan 30, Zoetermeer
☎ (079) 320 22 02
www.snowworld.nl

For ski courses, equipment and schools, look in the Yellow Pages under *Skibanen en scholen*. For more details on skiing, contact:

Nederlandse Ski Vereniging (Dutch Ski Association)
President Kennedylaan 15, 2517 JK Den Haag
☎ (070) 310 11 00
www.ski.nl

Soccer/Football
The Dutch call it *voetbal*, and it is the Dutch national sport. Both major and minor leagues exist. Even the smallest communities have soccer facilities and youngsters can participate from age four. Contact your local VVV or your *gemeentehuis* for more information. The ABF International Sports Club mentioned above offers children's soccer leagues. For more information on the Dutch National Team and the various city teams visit **Koninklijke Nederlandse Voetbalbond (Royal Netherlands Football Association)** at *www.knvb.nl*.

Squash
Many of the squash courts are associated with tennis courts and every community seems to have one. However, look under *Squashbanen* in the Yellow Pages or under *Fitnesscentra* or *Sportsscholen*. For clubs in the Netherlands, visit *www.squash.nl*.

Swimming

Living in a country where there is so much water, it is very important to know how to swim, and the Dutch have built many pools (*zwembaden*) for swimming instruction and recreation. Facilities and programs often include a sauna and a cafe/bar, lessons, family swim hours, hours for pregnant mothers, mother and toddler swims, lap swimming and recreational swimming. Season tickets are sold, as are discount cards; e.g., a '*12-badenkaart*' means 12 entries for the price of 10. For more information, contact your local *Zwembad*.

Beginner swimming lessons are quite different from lessons offered in U.S. The main focus is on survival skills including perfecting breast stroke, jumping/diving into the water fully dressed and doing long underwater swims. Diplomas are awarded as different skills are mastered at large ceremonies attended by the entire family.

A dip in the North Sea is a must, despite the frigid water. At many locations, beach chairs can be rented by the day or by the hour. Some beaches to visit are located at: Oostvoorne, Rockanje and Brielle, Hoek van Holland and Kijkduin, Scheveningen, Noordwijk aan Zee, Zandvoort and Ijmuiden, Egmond aan Zee, Schoorl and Julianadorp.

Tennis

Private clubs with both indoor and outdoor facilities can be found in almost all cities. Look in the Yellow Pages under *Tennispark* or *Tennisbanen*. Public courts are scarce and you may have to consider joining a club in order to play. Many of the international clubs offer daytime leagues for players of all levels. Consider getting tickets to the Dutch Open (*www.dutchopentennis.nl*) or the Dutch National Championship known as the Scheveningen Challenger (*www.siemensopen.nl*). Contact the VVV for more information or:

Koninklijke Nederlandse Lawn Tennis Bond (Dutch Tennis Association)
☎ (033) 454 26 00
www.knltb.nl

Walking

Walking (*wandelen*) is a favorite Dutch pastime, and there are many pedestrian paths in parks, dunes, gardens and woods.

Nederlandse Wandelsport Bond (Dutch Walking Association)
☎ (030) 231 94 58
www.nwb-wandelen.nl

Also contact *Natuurmonumenten* for information regarding parks and walking trails throughout the Netherlands. For a membership fee you get a pass and guide book with maps.

Vereniging Natuurmonumenten (Natural Monuments Association)
☎ (035) 655 99 11
www.natuurmonumenten.nl

The low-tide mud flats of the Wadden Zee may be crossed on foot between May and September. Called *Wadlopen*, you must have an experienced guide from the mainland to the islands of Schiermonnikoog, Ameland or Engelsmanplaat. Contact the VVV or:

Stichting Wadloopcentrum Pieterburen
Hoofdstraat 105, 9968 AC Pieterburen
☎ (059) 552 83 00
www.wadlopen.com

▸ Wind Surfing

This sport is enjoyed by an increasing number of people of all ages. Contact:

Nederlandse Watersport Verbond (Dutch Water Sport Federation)
☎ (030) 751 37 00
www.watersportverbond.nl

Holland Surfing Association
Visafslagweg 1, 2583 DM Scheveningen
☎ (065) 171 61 10
www.surfing-hsa.tk

Vacation Parks

Called "bungalow parks" in the Netherlands, many Dutch families go to vacation parks to relax. Many have swimming pools with courses in diving and swimming. They also may have saunas, bowling centers, miniature "midget" golf, squash and tennis courts, aerobics classes, water skiing, sailing, DVD rentals, roller skating and golf courses.

Center Parks
☎ (010) 498 97 54
www.centerparcs.com

Landal Green Park
☎ (070) 300 35 06
www.landal.nl

Chapter 20

Pets

Pets (*huisdieren*) of all shapes and sizes are extremely popular among the Dutch. As a result, pet products and services are plentiful, so you can rest assured that once here, your cat (*kat*) or dog (*hond*) will feel right at home. In order to ensure a smooth journey for your pet, be sure to have all the required documents in order before leaving your home country. General guidelines regarding veterinary certificates and vaccinations are provided in this chapter; however, specific requirements for your pet's health certificate should be obtained from a Dutch consulate in your home country.

Bringing Your Animal

▸ Import of Cats, Dogs and Ferrets

Veterinary Certificate: You will need a Veterinary Certificate issued by a veterinary surgeon whom has been officially recognized or admitted to practice. For American pets traveling with their owner, the certificate doesn't have to be certified by the U.S. Department of Agriculture or your "State Veterinarian." If your pet is traveling alone, it will be considered commercial trade and additional requirements apply (please see below for more information on commercial trade). A sample of the Veterinary Certificate may be found on the website of the Netherlands Embassy in Washington D.C. at *www.netherlands-embassy.org*. While it is not mandatory that this form be used, your Veterinary Certificate must contain all of the required information. Once issued the certificate is valid for a period of four months or until the expiration of the rabies vaccine, whichever is earlier.

The Veterinary Certificate must contain the following information:

- **Country of Dispatch**
- **Owner/Responsible Person:** Including name, address, country and telephone number.
- **Description of Animal:** Including species, breed, sex, date of birth, coat type and color. Note: Pit bull terriers and any pit bull terrier cross breeds are NOT allowed into the Netherlands.

- **Identification of Animal by Microchip Implant or Tattoo:** Including microchip/tattoo number, location of microchip/tattoo, and date of microchipping/tattooing. Computer technology has made it possible to permanently implant, under the skin of your pet, a microchip programmed with an ID number that can be read using a scanner. The ID number is linked to a database containing information about the animal, making it easier for the authorities to reunite a lost pet with its owners. While the microchips are safe, non-toxic, permanent and inexpensive to implant, not all veterinary offices are equipped to administer the implants, so plan ahead. Also, ask if the microchip meets the International Organization for Standardization (ISO) standards. If your pet's microchip is not in compliance with the ISO standards, you can bring your own reader. This will enable the Customs Authorities to identify the microchip number. A tattoo is currently accepted as an alternative method of permanent identification, although the microchip implant is the preferred method and the use of the tattoo is being phased out. Note: You will need to re-register the microchip with your new state/country when you move.
- **Rabies Vaccination Information:** Includes the date of vaccination, type of vaccine used and its expiration date, name of manufacturer and batch number. Dogs and cats less than 12-weeks-old may travel to the Netherlands without a rabies vaccination if the veterinarian declares that the animal resided at the birthplace until the travel date and has had no other contact with animals possibly infected with rabies. For animals vaccinated after reaching the age of three months, regulations in effect as of July 2004 state that the vaccination need not have been administered 30 days prior to entry in the Netherlands and the frequency of vaccination may be either one or two years depending on the type of vaccine and expiration date. Note that if the vaccination took place within the last 30 days or over a year ago, supporting documentation regarding prior vaccinations may be required. The Netherlands doesn't require your pet to have a serological test for rabies, a tick treatment or an echinococcus (tapeworm) treatment.

Certificate of Good Health: Most airlines require a Certificate of Good Health issued by a recognized veterinarian confirming that the animal has been examined and found free of disease. Requirements vary as to the date of the certificate. Check with your airline carrier for specific requirements.

No Quarantine: There are no quarantine requirements in the Netherlands if your pet is healthy and its vaccinations are up-to-date.

Commercial Trade: If your pet is traveling alone, it will be considered commercial trade. In addition to the above, additional requirements will apply. Pets must be clinically examined by a USDA-certified veterinarian within 24 hours before departure to the Netherlands and supporting documentation (health certificate) must accompany your pet. Please note: A veterinarian at Schiphol Airport in the Netherlands will examine your pet at the KLM Animal

Hotel. Since this is owned by KLM, if you are not traveling with KLM, a request must be made in writing for your pet to be seen.

▸ Import of Pets Other than Dogs, Cats and Ferrets

The regulations surrounding the importation of parrots, psittacine birds or other more exotic pets into the Netherlands have become quite detailed, particularly if your pet is listed under the Convention on International Trade of Endangered Species (CITES) or under the U.S. Endangered Species Act. Individuals interested in bringing a pet other than a dog, cat or ferret are advised to contact CITES at the website of the U.S. Fish and Wildlife Service at *www.international.FWS.gov*. You will need the scientific name of the animal you wish to import.

▸ EU Pet Passport

Legislation has been adopted by the member states of the European Union which attempts to standardize regulations for travel with your pet within the EU. Your pet must now be accompanied by an EU passport for travel within the EU. This document contains the animal's permanent identification information and description, owner's name and address and proof that the animal has a valid vaccination against rabies certified by an authorized veterinarian. Be aware that requirements still vary among the EU nations. The Netherlands, for example, doesn't require that the pet be treated for ticks and tapeworms nor is there a requirement for a rabies serological test to establish the presence of the anti-rabies vaccination in the blood. Other EU nations may require these tests and treatments. A pet passport (*dierenpaspoort*) is also required when leaving your pet in a kennel in the Netherlands. To find out how to get your pet's passport, contact a veterinarian (*dierenarts*) in your area.

▸ Your Pet, the Passenger

Once you have its rabies vaccination and Veterinary Certificate, it isn't difficult to bring your pet into the Netherlands. Careful planning, however, will help avoid the unexpected and unsettling problems which may occur during the flight or during transfers. Below are the most important steps to help you plan a safe and uneventful trip for your pet:

- Make sure you have the most recent information regarding pet travel to the Netherlands by checking with the Netherlands Embassy in Washington, D.C. at *www.netherlands-embassy.org*.
- If possible, fly your pet directly to the Netherlands. Otherwise your pet must comply with the specific regulations for each country through which it travels. Contact the individual consulates of each stop to ask about their particular regulations. Failure to do so may mean your pet will not be allowed to enter a country or it may be placed in quarantine.

- The most economical way to bring your pet to the Netherlands is to have it accompany you as excess baggage. Pet carriers that meet airline regulations can be purchased from pet shops and many discount stores. Check with your airline for specific requirements regarding pet carriers, including appropriate carrier size. Ask about temperature restrictions if you are traveling during the hottest or coldest months of the year. Mention any specific requirements your pet may have. Once you have chosen an airline, make the appropriate advance reservations. Also, be sure to inquire where your pet can be claimed at the end of the journey.
- Many Dutch hotels will allow you to keep your pet with you or you can make reservations, via your travel agent, for your pet to stay at the airport kennel. Confirm kennel reservations prior to your departure.

Once Your Dog is in the Netherlands

▸ Registration

Within 14 days of arriving, you must register your dog with your local city hall (*gemeente*) and pay a dog tax. (Cats don't need to be registered and are not taxed.) From that time on, you will automatically receive an annual tax bill (*hondenbelasting*). The tax increases considerably with each additional dog you own. Dogs are not required to have dog tags in the Netherlands.

▸ Dog Etiquette

Dogs must be kept on a leash if you see a sign reading, "*Honden aan de Lijn*" and are not allowed in areas posted with signs reading "*Honden Verboden.*" Signs are posted if dogs are permitted to run freely in a specified area of a park or if they may run freely on the beach and dunes during certain times of the year. Well-behaved and leashed dogs are frequently allowed in hotels, restaurants and many stores. Animals are permitted to travel with their owners on trams, trains and buses. Small animals which may be carried on or kept in a basket may travel at no charge. However, larger dogs are required to purchase a special reduced rate *strippenkaart* (good also for children!) on trams and buses and a Dog Day Travel Card on trains.

Caring for Your Pet

▸ Pet Food and Grooming

Pet stores, veterinarians, supermarkets, large garden centers, street markets and even your local butcher will carry a selection of pet foods and products. Prescription-diet pet foods and many of the same high-quality dog and cat foods found at home are available in the Netherlands. For pet grooming, look under *Hondentrimsalons* in the Yellow Pages (*Gouden Gids*).

Earth-Friendly Pet Care

Cat Litter: Although not exactly classified as toxic waste, kitty litter (*kattenbakvulling*) should not go into your compost bin. Dispose of it with your non-recyclable waste. The most environmentally friendly cat litter uses straw, wood chips or paper rather than clay. Try Victory Cat or Woody Cat.

Dealing with Fleas: One concern of pet owners is how to keep one's home and pets flea-free. Milieu Centraal (*www.milieucentraal.nl*), an organization that provides environmental information for consumers, produces an information sheet entitled "Conquering Fleas" or "*Vlooienbestrijding.*" Recommendations are thorough and include frequent vacuuming, feeding your pet garlic, using eucalyptus oil, feeding your pet ½ to 1 teaspoon of brewer's yeast or 25 mg of vitamin B (thiamine), or adding 1 teaspoon of vinegar to its drinking water—daily. Other products (sprays, powders, flea collars, citronella oil) are poisonous to people.

Dogs: The environmental department in your municipality will have prevailing rules on dogs. These will stipulate areas where dogs are not allowed unleashed or not at all, like some beaches. Cleaning up after your pet is a law in the Netherlands and not cleaning up after your dog will result in a fine. In addition, when walking your dog, you must carry an item to "scoop the poop," such as a paper/plastic bag or a small scoop. Failure to produce this item when asked will also result in a fine.

Veterinarians *(Dierenartsen)*

Veterinary care is generally excellent in the Netherlands. Veterinarians are well trained and use the latest information and technology available. Veterinarian specialists in eye care, orthopedics, oncology, etc., are also available, as is 24-hour emergency care. In most neighborhoods, a veterinarian is on-call for emergency service on weekends and holidays. The veterinarian's name and telephone number will be listed in your local newspaper on the same page as the on-call family practitioners and dentists. Be sure to check with your veterinarian about after-hour emergency services. Veterinary services can be located in the Yellow Pages under *Dierenartsen en Dierenklinieken*.

The Animal Ambulance *(Dierenambulance)*

In case of an emergency, the quickest and cheapest method is to safely drive your sick or injured pet to a veterinarian yourself. Another option is to call an animal ambulance. Find the number in the Yellow Pages under *Dierenambulance*.

Lost and Found

If you find an animal or your pet is lost, contact local animal shelters (*dierenasiel*). It is important to register your pet's microchip number with the Dutch Pet Database, *Nederlandse Databank Gezelschapsdieren* (NDG) at *www.databankgezelschapsdieren.nl*. All veterinarians, animal ambulances and animal refuges have a microchip reader to help reunite you with your pet.

▸ The Boarding Kennel *(Dierenpensions)*

Boarding kennels are found throughout the Netherlands. It is a good idea to make reservations well in advance, especially around holidays and school breaks. A reputable kennel will ask for your pet's passport (*dierenpaspoort*) showing that your pet's vaccinations are up to date. Dutch law also requires that animals boarding at a kennel be permanently identified by microchip implant or tattoo. Check with your veterinarian for local boarding kennels or animal shelters (many of which also have boarding facilities) in your town.

Pets may also be cared for in your own home while you are away. In-home care can be of great benefit for older or less social animals and your caregiver may provide additional services such as watering your plants and retrieving your mail. Look in the Yellow Pages under *Dierenhulp*.

▸ For More Information

For more information about issues regarding pets, contact:

Nationale Dierenzorg
Zijdeweg 56, 2245 BZ Wassenaar
☎ (070) 517 98 52
www.ndz.nl

Taking Your Pet with You

When it's time for your pet to leave the Netherlands, the process will be much the same as upon your arrival and the same care must be exercised. You may be returning home or going on to another international assignment. Globally the regulations for the import of pets vary greatly. To assure your animal travels safely, contact the consulate or embassy of your destination country as early as possible for applicable regulations.

For many readers, returning home means your pets' next stop will be in the U.S. Pets returning to the U.S. are subject to the same regulations as those entering the country for the first time. General information about bringing a pet into the U.S. is provided below, however regulations are subject to change and current information should be obtained. The Center for Disease Control (*www.cdc.gov*), U.S. Customs Service (*www.cbp.gov*) and the U.S. Fish and Wildlife Service (*www.fws.gov*) are concerned with the import of animals into the U.S. and their websites are sources of useful information. In addition, the Department of Agriculture in your destination state should be contacted for local restrictions on importing pets.

All dogs and cats arriving in the U.S. are subject to inspection upon arrival at the port of entry and must be free of evidence of any disease communicable to humans. If your pet is not in apparent good health, further examination by a licensed veterinarian may be required and the pet may be detained at the port of arrival at your expense.

While there is no requirement for a cat to have a rabies vaccination, you must have a valid rabies vaccination certificate for your dog. The certificate should be in English or accompanied by a translation. It must be signed by a licensed veterinarian and identify the animal, the vaccination date and the type, batch number and expiration date of the vaccination. If your dog arrives without valid proof of vaccination, it may be subject to quarantine. Keep copies of this certificate with other important paperwork.

While the U.S. government doesn't require general certificates of good health for pets, many airlines do. Check with your airline regarding health certificate requirements and any additional requirements regarding pet carriers, carrier size and restrictions on travel due to climate.

▸ Tough Love

The transition to living in the Netherlands is eased greatly by the lack of quarantine for your pet upon arrival. Depending on your destination, your pet may be subject to quarantine and confinement for an extended period of time. Do your research and carefully consider your best interests and, above all, the best interest of your pet. If you find that the welfare of your pet will be compromised by your new assignment, reach out to friends and neighbors to find your pet a new home. Alternatively, contact an animal shelter (*dierenasielen*) that will take your pet and try to locate new owners.

Chapter 21

Sightseeing

Although the Netherlands is a small country, it offers an amazing amount of diversity. You will marvel at the picturesque towns and villages, medieval cathedrals, 18th century windmills and thatched roof farms surrounded by lush green meadows. Black and white Holstein cows graze in meadows while rivers and canals are filled with barges and weekend boaters. The Dutch recognize their precious heritage and have done much to preserve it for future generations.

Because of their colorful history, creativity and energy, the Dutch have left a treasure house of great museums filled with priceless works of art painted by native sons: Rembrandt van Rijn, Vincent van Gogh, Johannes Vermeer, Frans Hals and many others. At last count there were over 1,200 museums in the Netherlands. There are also wonderful theaters, country markets, folklore festivals, flower parades, auctions and a host of other activities.

The casual tourist can hardly expect to scratch the surface, but as a resident you will have endless possibilities for sightseeing. Your biggest challenge, whatever the length of your stay, may be having enough time to see it all.

It is easy to tour the Netherlands. Language need not be a barrier since 75% of the residents speak English, many of the tourist pamphlets are available in English and assistance is abundantly available. Furthermore, there is an efficient public transportation system that can take you wherever you want to go.

Sources of Information

Before Arrival

The Netherlands Board of Tourism: Once you know that you are moving to the Netherlands, you may want to stop by your favorite bookstore and purchase some guide books and maps (see our **References** list at the end of this book.) The website *www.holland.com* has comprehensive tourism information for the entire country available in a wide variety of languages.

▸ Once in the Netherlands

The Local Tourist Offices – VVV: The **VVV** (pronounced vay – vay – vay) *Vereniging Voor Vreemdelingenverkeer* (*www.vvv.nl*) is available to assist you with over 400 local tourist information offices. These offices are located in or near train stations, in town centers, at border crossings, and at primary tourist attractions. The VVV will provide you with books and pamphlets (many of which are in English and are free) about hotels, restaurants and destinations including details for self-guided walking tours. Most offices will also assist you in making hotel and entertainment bookings for a small fee.

White VVV signs on a blue background only carry local information. The VVV with a small white "i" on a black or blue background alongside it means they have information on the entire country. While you are at the VVV, you may want to buy a **Museum Card** (*Museumkaart*) for one year's worth of free or reduced admission to over 400 state and municipal museums. If you plan to visit several museums or will be visiting the same museums several times with visitors or for special exhibitions, it is a great value. You may also purchase the museum card at most museums or online at *www.museumkaart.nl*.

Other Sources of Information: The Internet has a wide range of websites offering travel advice and suggestions. You can always check major sites which offer worldwide travel guides:

- Frommer's: *www.frommers.com*
- Lonely Planet: *www.lonelyplanet.com*
- TripAdvisor: *www.tripadvisor.com*
- WikiTravel: *www.wikitravel.org*
- Yahoo!Travel Guides: *www.travel.yahoo.com*

For a more local viewpoint, there are two websites that you might find particularly helpful:

- For 1,000 museums throughout the Netherlands with English pages for top 50 museums: *www.museum.nl*
- For day trip ideas in English: *www.daysout.nl*

For other tourist information, you can also pick up the weekly and monthly publications in the major cities or you can subscribe to electronic newsletters within a city or a geographic region:

- Amsterdam: *www.iamsterdam.com*
- The Hague: *www.thehagueonline.com*
- Rotterdam: *www.rotterdam.info/uk*
- South Holland: *www.zuid-holland.com*
- North Holland: *www.vvvweb.nl*.

Lodging

Although many of the Netherlands' sights are within a day's drive, if you have the weekend off, why not stay overnight? As mentioned above, the VVV has listings of hundreds of facilities:

- Hotels and motels
- Self-catering bungalows
- Bed and breakfasts
- Campgrounds
- Farm stays
- Hostels

You may want to ask the VVV about one of the 30 **Stayokay Hostels** (*www.stayokay.com*). These simple hostels are not only for young backpackers, but anyone from families to seniors looking for budget accommodations.

If you're daring, you can arrive in a town without a reservation and take your chances. Another option is to do the research yourself in advance. One wonderful website is *www.weekendhotel.nl* which features small charming hotels, luxury bed and breakfasts and unique apartments. For chain hotels, a good search tool is *www.kayak.co.uk* which allows you to book directly with the hotels. For reviews on hotels, *www.tripadvisor.com* is very handy.

One family of hotels that is prevalent throughout Europe is **Accor Hotels** (*www.accorhotels.com*). This corporation owns a wide range of hotels for every price range:

- Formula 1: budget travel along major highways
- Novotel: 3- and 4-stars with rooms designed for a family of 4
- Sofitel: 4- and 5-star luxury
- Club Med: all-inclusive resorts

Eating Out

Although the Netherlands does not enjoy the gastronomic reputation of its neighbor Belgium, there are still wonderful places to dine. You will find all sorts of restaurants serving ethnic foods such as French, Indian, Greek, Italian, Indonesian, Chinese, Japanese, Thai and Vietnamese.

What you will not find much of is Dutch food, since the Dutch can cook it at home and want to try other cuisines when they eat out, although formal Dutch restaurants are in many large city tourist areas. Most cities have pancake (*pannekoeken*) houses that serve enormous platters of these delicious Dutch treats, which come in sweet or savory, as well as sweet mini puffed pancakes (*poffertjes*).

A unique dining experience in the Netherlands is the famous *rijsttafel* meal served in Indonesian restaurants. You will not see restaurants like this anywhere else, not even in Indonesia. *Rijsttafel* is a name given to the enormous buffets the Dutch used to eat when Indonesia was the Dutch East Indies. Rice *(rijst)* is central to the meal and there are many side dishes. They are served at your table and the meal itself can range from 13 to 21 dishes.

Restaurants are obliged to display their menus with prices outside the restaurant entrance, so it is easy to see if the menu appeals to you and is in your price range. Smoking is prohibited indoors at all restaurants. The VVV will have listings of restaurants, but can't make recommendations. In addition, you may find one of the restaurant guides helpful such as IENS, an English language guide for various regions throughout the Netherlands. There are also websites that allow you to search by cuisine which have menus and reviews for restaurants in large cities:

- *www.iens.nl*
- *www.dinnersite.nl*

When the Dutch dine out, they usually make an evening of it unless, of course, they eat in a fast food, pizza or pancake restaurant. Dining out is an experience not to be rushed and, as in much of Europe, the table is yours for the evening. Reservations are often recommended.

When you go out to dinner, you have a choice of ordering "a la carte" or "fixed price" (known as the "tourist menu" or simply "menu"). Typically, this option gives you a choice of a three or four course meal. The choices may be from the regular menu with several options for each course or they might be special courses that the chef makes in limited amounts.

In some countries, the house wine is of poor quality. Fortunately, the house wine in the Netherlands tends to be very good. The chef takes pride in selecting it for its quality and value as it represents his/ her restaurant. Most of these wines are not ones you will find in a shop, but rather are special labels that vineyards make available to restauranteurs.

What to See in the Big Cities

Like most tourists, you will probably want to start your Dutch adventure in the big cities such as Amsterdam, The Hague or Rotterdam before branching out into the countryside. Below are some of the big city sights along with abbreviated itineraries. It is always best to check websites for each individual attraction for the latest information including opening times and days.

▸ Amsterdam *(www.iamsterdam.com)*

This is the cultural capital of the Netherlands and is an interesting mixture of historic glory and modern sophistication. Its tree-lined canals, gabled houses, bridges and museums attract millions of tourists from all over the world. The easiest way to access Amsterdam is by train, which stops in the heart of the city at Centraal Station. Just outside the station, you can stop by the Dutch Tourist Office, the largest VVV in the Netherlands, for detailed information on tourist attractions and walking tours within the city of Amsterdam and its surrounding areas. An option before going is to visit the Amsterdam tourism website at *www.amsterdamtourist.nl*.

This city is where the Golden Age of trading and exploration began and where most of the money made from these ventures was invested. Take a **canal boat ride** to get a brief orientation of the city. You will spend about an hour traveling the waterways in a glass-roofed boat with a multilingual commentary. There are also **museum boats** that stop in front of the Station and then at the major museums including the **Anne Frank House**, the **Rijksmuseum** and the **Van Gogh Museum**. You can get on and off these boats throughout the day with a day pass.

Walk up Damrak to **Dam Square**, the site of the original dam across the Amstel River. Here you can see the **Royal Palace**, which is open afternoons in the summer, the **National War Monument** and a variety of unusual characters who are relaxing, performing or sightseeing—just like you.

From **Dam Square** it is only a short way to the 17th century church, **Westerkerk**, on the Prinsengracht. This magnificent church, topped by the crown of the Holy Roman Empire, is the burial site of one of the Netherlands' most famous residents, Rembrandt van Rijn, and it was the wedding chapel of Queen Beatrix and Prins Claus.

Next to **Westerkerk** is the **Anne Frank House**. It was here that a young Jewish girl wrote her diary describing life during the Nazi occupation of Amsterdam. The rooms of this building remain as they were during World War II, although without furniture. Be patient and allow enough time as lines can be very long. It is best to go early to avoid the crowds.

Take the tram or museum boat to the world-famous **Rijksmuseum** which houses a large collection of Dutch paintings from the 15th to the 19th centuries. Don't miss Rembrandt's *The Night Watch* with its marvelous panel-by-panel explanation in English. Nearby is the **Van Gogh Museum** housing the colorful collection of Vincent van Gogh.

If you are visiting without children, consider going to such tourist attractions as the **Xtracold Ice Bar** (*www.xtracold.com*), **House of Bols** (*www.houseofbols.com*) or **Heineken Experience** (*www.heinekenexperience.com*). You can also stop at one of Amsterdam's 1,500 cafés or bars. Most famous are the brown cafés (*bruin cafés*) that are so-called because of their brown chairs, wood paneled walls and ceilings that are brown with age and hundreds of years of tobacco smoke (although smoking indoors is now prohibited.) You will, of course, have heard about the coffeehouses where the customers smoke cannabis. You will recognize them by the smoke, the loud music and their often creative decor. They are technically illegal, but are tolerated.

Anne Frank House	**Rijksmuseum**	**Van Gogh Museum**
Prinsengracht 267	Jan Luijkenstraat 1	Paulus Potterstraat 7
☎ (020) 556 71 00	☎ (020) 674 70 00	☎ (020) 570 52 00
www.annefrank.org	*www.rijksmuseum.nl*	*www.vangoghmuseum.nl*

▸ The Hague *(www.denhaag.com)*

The Hague is the seat of Parliament and is the center for all diplomatic missions; however, it is the administrative capital of the country while Amsterdam is the official capital. The main government buildings, the **Binnenhof – Inner Court** and the **Ridderzaal – Knight's Hall** date back to the 13th century and like most interesting historic and architectural sights in the cities, are located right in the centrum (city center). The **Binnenhof** and **Ridderzaal** are separated from the city by a huge moat, the **Hofvijver**, which is illuminated at night.

Located on the **Hofvijver** is the **Mauritshuis**. This royal picture gallery is one of the greatest art museums in all of the Netherlands and, for that matter, the world. It is relatively small, but all paintings are by Dutch and Flemish masters: Rembrandt, Vermeer, Frans Hals, Rubens, Hobbema, Ruysdael, Holbein and van Dyck. Three of the world's most famous paintings, Rembrandt's *Anatomy Lesson* and Vermeer's *View of Delft* and *The Girl with the Pearl Earring*, hang here along with other masterpieces. Audio guides specifically designed for children are available in English.

Nearby in the Lange Voorhout Palace is the **Escher Museum**, which opened in 2002 and features a large collection of works by M.C. Escher. Children will especially enjoy the interactive activities on the top floor and the fascinating chandeliers designed by Hans van Bentem.

You might also want to visit the **Peace Palace (*Vredespaleis*)** which houses the International Court of Justice and the Permanent Court of Arbitration. Call first for a tour appointment as tours are only available when court is not in session. Tours are in English, Dutch and German.

Just west of The Hague on the coast of the North Sea is the old fishing village of **Scheveningen,** which now has a modern harbor and very popular beaches. In the center of **Scheveningen**, the **Kurhaus Hotel** is a national monument in its own right. Built in 1885, the hotel has a beautiful ceiling in its main restaurant. On each side of the hotel, bordering the long expanse of beach are many restaurants and shops along the **Promenade**, including a mall which is open on Sundays. From Easter to early October, you can enjoy everything from a cup of hearty Dutch coffee to a sumptuous buffet in one of the outdoor beach pavilions. The many cafés along the promenade remain open throughout the winter as well. Or stroll out on the famous Pier where you can even go bungee jumping!

Nearby is **Westbroek Park** with finely manicured gardens, an award-winning rose collection, Japanese Garden, restaurant and miniature (*midget*) golf course. A visit to **Madurodam** will definitely be a hit if you have children with you. It is great fun to see the Netherlands in miniature with detailed replicas of historical buildings and airports, trains, harbors and more.

Panorama Mesdag is a painting-in-the-round of Scheveningen as it appeared in 1881 when it was painted in this purpose-built building. Several painters worked on it, including Sina and Hendrik Willem Mesdag. It is the biggest painting in the Netherlands at 14 meters high and 120 meters in circumference. Other works by Mesdag are also featured in this museum.

Escher Museum
Lange Voorhout 74
☎ (070) 427 77 30
www.escherinhetpaleis.nl

Mauritshuis
Korte Vijverberg 8
☎ (070) 302 34 56
www.mauritshuis.nl

Peace Palace
Carnegieplein 2
☎ (070) 302 42 42
www.vredespaleis.nl

Madurodam
George Maduroplein 1
☎ (070) 416 24 00
www.madurodam.nl

Panorama Mesdag
Zeestraat 65
☎ (070) 364 45 44
www.panorama-mesdag.com

Rotterdam (*www.rotterdam.info/uk*)

In sharp contrast to the charming Dutch style of Amsterdam and The Hague is the thoroughly modern city of Rotterdam. It was bombed heavily during World War II and so lacks much of its original charm. You can get an orientation of the city by taking a relaxing **Spido** harbor tour of **Europort**, an important gateway to Europe and the world's largest container port, or soar to the top of the **Euromast Tower** for a bird's-eye view of this bustling city.

You may want to visit the **Museum Boijmans Van Beuningen**. Besides Dutch masters, it has an impressive collection of modern art and is dedicated to helping visitors understand and appreciate the works of Dalí, Picasso, van Gogh and others. Nearby, you can visit the information center at the **Maeslant Storm Surge Barrier** in Hoek van Holland to see how the Dutch hold back the North Sea.

Euromast Tower
Parkhaven 20
☎ (010) 436 48 11
www.euromast.com

Museum Boijmans Van Beuningen
Museumpark 18-20
☎ (010) 441 94 00
www.boijmans.nl

Maeslant Storm Surge Barrier
Harbour Number 882, Hoek van Holland
☎ (017) 451 12 22
www.keringhuis.nl

Spido Harbor Tours
Willemsplein 85
☎ (010) 275 99 88
www.spido.nl

What to See in Towns, Villages and the Countryside

▸ Aalsmeer, Alkmaar, and Zaandam

Travel to the **Aalsmeer Flower Auction**, the largest flower auction in the world. It is open Monday through Friday only in the mornings; visiting before 8 a.m. is recommended. Go to the **Alkmaar Cheese Market** on a Friday between 10:00 a.m. to 12:30 p.m. from late-March to early-September. Explore the Cheese Market and Cheese Museum, then stroll around the old town and have lunch. Return via Zaanstreek and Zaandam. Stop at **Zaanse Schans**, an old windmill village where various mills are still working. Here you can watch cheese making and wooden shoe carving, and take a close look at a working windmill.

Aalsmeer Flower Auction
Legmeerdijk 313
☎ (029) 739 70 00
www.flora.nl

Alkmaar Cheese Market
Waagplein
www.kaasmarkt.nl

Zaanse Schans
Schansend 7, Zaandam
☎ (075) 616 28 62
www.zaanseschans.nl

▸ Apeldoorn and Hoge Veluwe Park, Arnhem

Travel to Apeldoorn to visit **Paleis Het Loo**, the traditional home of the Royal Dutch family. Continue on to the **National Park Hoge Veluwe** where you can have lunch at the famous **Kröller-Müller Museum** with its large collection of Vincent van Gogh paintings and an outdoor sculpture garden. Pick up some white bicycles at the gate which are available for touring the park. Continue to Arnhem and tour the **Open Air Museum**.

National Park Hoge Veluwe
Houtkampweg 9, Otterlo
☎ (0900) 464 38 35 (€0,20/minute)
www.hogeveluwe.nl

Open Air Museum
Schelmseweg 89, Arnhem
☎ (026) 357 61 11
www.openluchtmuseum.nl

Paleis Het Loo
Koninklijk Park 1, Apeldoorn
☎ (055) 577 24 00
www.paleishetloo.nl

▸ Delft (*www.delft.com*)

You can easily spend a day in this beautifully preserved, historic city. Visit the factory and showroom of **Royal Delft** to see how the world-famous, hand-painted Delftware is made. See the **Oude Kerk** (old church) and the **Nieuwe Kerk** (new church). You can buy one ticket to get into both churches. Also visit the **Museum Het Prinsenhof** where William of Orange was assassinated.

Museum Het Prinsenhof
Sint Agathaplein 1
☎ (015) 260 23 58
www.prinsenhof-delft.nl

Oude Kerk
Heilige Geestkerkhof 25
☎ (015) 212 30 15
www.oudekerk-delft.nl

Nieuwe Kerk
Markt 80
☎ (015) 212 30 25
www.nieuwekerk-delft.nl

Royal Delft
Rotterdamseweg 196
☎ (015) 251 20 30
www.royaldelft.com

▸ Friesland Lakes

Travel to the old Frisian cities of **Bolsward**, **Makkum** (see the old-style Dutch tiles being made), **Workum**, **Hindeloopen** (home of the famous Hindeloopen painted furniture), **Sloten** and **Joure** (see the famous village churches.) Have a fish lunch at the costumed village of **Urk** (the village virtually closes down on Sunday) and return via **Giethoorn**, the sleepy mini-Venice of the Netherlands. There are no roads in the village, only walking paths and canals. Boat tours are available.

▸ Gouda (*www.vvvgouda.nl*)

Stop in **Gouda**, which is famous for its cheese and its lovely town square. The **Cheese Market** is held on Thursday mornings from late June until early September. The **Gouda Stadhuis** is one of the oldest and most beautiful city halls in the Netherlands. Also visit **Sint-Janskerk**, a church remarkable for its stained glass windows, and **Het Catharina Gasthuis**, a museum that was first a 14th century traveler's hospice, then an almshouse and then housed an apothecary until it became exclusively a museum in the 1960s.

Cheese Market
www.goudakaas.nl

Het Catharina Gasthuis
Achter de Kerk 14
☎ (018) 233 10 00
www.museumgouda.nl

Sint-Janskerk
Achter de Kerk 16
☎ (018) 251 26 84
www.sintjan.com

▸ Haarlem (*www.vvvzk.nl*)

Stroll around the old city. A visit to the **Corrie ten Boom Museum** will allow you to experience the heroic efforts of the ten Boom family during World War II. Their story is re-enacted in the film and book, *The Hiding Place*. Also visit the **Frans Hals Museum** to see an impressive collection of 17th century paintings, **Teylers Museum** to visit the Netherland's oldest museum, and **Grote Kerk** to see where ten-year-old Mozart played the magnificent organ.

Corrie ten Boom Museum
Barteljorisstraat 19
☎ (023) 531 08 23
www.corrietenboom.com

Grote Kerk of St. Bavo
Oude Groenmarkt 23
☎ (023) 553 20 40
www.bavo.nl

Frans Hals Museum
Groot Heiligland 62
☎ (023) 511 57 75
www.franshalsmuseum.com

Teylers Museum
Spaarne 16
☎ (023) 516 09 60
www.teylersmuseum.nl

▸ Keukenhof Gardens and the Bulb Route

From late March through mid-May, starting from either Leiden or Haarlem, you can cycle or drive the **Bulb Route** *(Bollenstreek)* to the world-famous **Keukenhof Gardens** where you can enjoy seeing millions of bulbs in bloom. Pack a picnic or visit one of the restaurants. Visit **Panorama Tulipland** to see an impressive work of art of the bulb fields and the **Museum De Zwarte Tulp** (Black Tulip Museum) to learn more about the history of the bulb district.

Keukenhof Gardens
Stationsweg 166a, Lisse
☎ (025) 246 55 55
www.keukenhof.nl

Museum De Zwarte Tulp
Grachtweg 2a, Lisse
☎ (025) 241 79 00
www.museumdezwartetulp.nl

Panorama Tulipland
Jacoba van Beierenweg 79, Voorhout
☎ (025) 222 27 77
www.tulipland.nl

▸ Kinderdijk

Travel to **Kinderdijk** near Rotterdam to see the largest concentration of wind-driven water mills in the Netherlands. Walk along the dike to view this UNESCO World Heritage Site of nineteen mills and tour some of the mills if they are open during your visit. Boat rides are available during the summer. Take a leisurely drive via Albasserdam and Nieuw Lekkerland to see old Dutch farm houses along the dikes and in the polders.

Kinderdijk
Molenstraat, Kinderdijk
www.kinderdijk.com

▸ Leiden (*www.hollandrijnland.nl*)

With its historic district full of canals, 17th century buildings and outstanding museums, the university city of **Leiden** has the charm of Amsterdam, but on a smaller and less hectic scale. Saturdays are an excellent day to visit to wander through the farmer's market and to visit the **De Valk Windmill Museum**. In addition to being the birthplace of Rembrandt, it also has a connection with American history as the Pilgrims lived here from 1609 until 1620 when they left for their famous journey to the New World. You can visit the **Leiden Pilgrim Archive** and the **Leiden American Pilgrim Museum.**

Molen "De Valk"
2e Binnenvestgracht 1
☎ (071) 516 53 53
www.molenmuseumdevalk.nl

Leiden Pilgrim Archive
Vliet 43
www.pilgrimarchives.nl

Leiden American Pilgrim Museum
Beschuitsteeg 9
☎ (071) 512 24 13
www.rootsweb.ancestry.com/~netlapm

▸ Maarsbergen, Doorn and the Betuwe Region (*www.vvvdoorn.nl*)

Visit the center of the Netherlands. Travel to **Maarsbergen** to visit **De Weistaar,** a working cheese farm. See a film presentation on the making of cheese. Stroll through the adjacent Cheese Museum. Visit **Huis Doorn**, a small palace where Kaiser Wilhelm of Germany lived in exile from 1920 until his death in 1941. Have lunch in **Doorn** or picnic in **Tiel**, a major fruit growing area. Cycle or drive the well-marked blossom route that starts in **Tiel** during May.

▸ Maastricht (*www.vvv-maastricht.eu*)

Maastricht was founded by the Roman Legions and you can still see the old Roman quarters. Visit the ancient **Basilica of St. Servatius** and the **Basilica of Our Beloved Lady**. Explore the famous **St. Pietersberg Caves**, which are a result of centuries of stone excavations. Tours in English are available during the summer. Be sure to dine in one of the many excellent restaurants or cafes. The food in South Limburg is considered to be the best in the country.

Basilica of Our Beloved Lady
Onze Lieve Vrouweplein 20
☎ (043) 325 18 51
www.sterre-der-zee.nl

Basilica of Saint Servatius
Keizer Karelplein 6
☎ (043) 343 28 52
www.sintservaas.nl

St. Pietersberg Caves
www.maastrichtunderground.nl

▸ Muiden and the Vecht (*www.vvvhollandsmidden.nl*)

Visit the 13th century castle **Muiderslot** via the Loosdrecht lakes. Tour one of the Netherlands' most beautiful routes along the Vecht River by car or boat to see the old mansions along the waterfront.

Muiderslot
Herengracht 1, Muiden
☎ (029) 425 62 62 – *www.muiderslot.nl*

▸ South Limburg (*www.vvvzuidlimburg.nl*)

Enjoy the morning with a leisurely ride through the beautiful Limburg countryside. Stop at **Valkenburg** then drive from **Oud-Valkenburg** to **Wittem**, **Vaals**, **Drielandpunten** (where the Netherlands, German and Belgian borders meet), then **Vijlen**, **Epen**, **Slenaken**, **Euverem** and **Gulpen.** See the castles, an old water mill and the American Military Cemetery at **Margraten**. Stay at one of the rural inns. Spend a relaxing day at the **Thermae 2000** that has thermal baths in and outdoors, saunas and a gymnasium, and have a massage.

Thermae 2000
Cauberg 25, Valkenburg aan de Geul
☎ (043) 609 20 00 – *www.thermae.nl*

▸ Utrecht (*www.utrechtyourway.nl*)

Utrecht is a vibrant, university city with a quant historic district to explore and some very unique museums. It is also one of the few cities with a large indoor shopping mall right at the main train station. Climb the **Dom Tower** and visit one of Utrecht's excellent museums. Your kids will especially love the **Railway Museum** and will be surprised at how much they enjoy the **Speelklok Museum** which features automated musical machines and instruments. During the summer, rent a kayak to explore the canals or dine at one of the restaurants at the water's edge. Outside the city, visit the beautiful **De Haar Castle** and tour the castle with a guide (English tours are limited—check the website for times) and then visit the French Baroque-style gardens.

De Haar Castle
Kasteellaan 1, Haarzuilens
☎ (030) 677 85 15
www.kasteeldehaar.nl

Dom Tower
Domplein 9
☎ (030) 236 00 10
www.domtoren.nl

Railway Museum
Maliebaanstation
☎ (030) 230 62 06
www.spoorwegmuseum.nl

Speelklok Museum
Steenweg 6
☎ (030) 231 27 89
www.museumspeelklok.nl

Volendam and Marken (*www.vvv-volendam.nl*)

Enjoy the sights in **Volendam**, a charming (*gezellig*) Roman Catholic fishing village, and have a picture taken of the whole family dressed in traditional Dutch clothing. Then enjoy a boat trip to the neighboring **Marken**. This fishing village with its green and black timbered houses is Protestant and it's interesting to see the differences from Volendam.

Open-Air Markets

For a real taste of daily life, try the colorful street markets (*markten*). Budget-conscious shoppers find these traveling markets an economical source of fresh fruits and vegetables as well as flowers, breads, meat, fish, poultry, cheese, clothing, fabrics and a huge variety of other goods. See our **Shopping** chapter for a listing of some major markets. Go to *www.hollandsemarkten.nl*, which lists all the farmer's markets in the country, or visit the VVV for information about markets in your area.

Yearly Events Calendar

There is always something going on in the Netherlands. Since many events happen only during certain times of the year, you'll find some of these activities highlighted below. For further events information, consult your local VVV or websites for the area you're interested in as suggested earlier in this chapter.

January

For the Dutch, the New Year literally begins with a bang. On **New Year's Eve** and well into the wee hours of the morning, the Dutch create a tremendous amount of noise and excitement with fireworks. Then, on January 1st take a cold dip in the North Sea (***nieuwjaarsduik***) to welcome in the New Year with thousands of Dutch swimmers.

As everything begins to wind down after the hectic holidays, you can look forward to browsing through the terrific January sales. This is also a perfect time to spend a relaxing afternoon at one of the museums. It might surprise you to discover that on Sundays, if it's not raining, you'll find large numbers of people strolling along the beach.

February

Look for **Carnaval** (the Dutch version of Mardi Gras) activities in North Brabant and Limburg on the Saturday through Tuesday before Ash Wednesday. Enjoy the **Holland Flowers Festival** in Zwaagdijk-Oost (*www.hollandflowersfestival.nl*).

March

During March there are many special **antique shows** and fascinating **art exhibitions** throughout the Netherlands. Of particular interest is the **TEFAF Fine Arts Fair** (*www.tefaf.com*) in Maastricht which is arguably one of the finest antique shows in Europe. Spring arrives and over 18,000 runners participate in The Hague's annual **City-Pier-City Road Race**.

The Gardens Keukenhof (*www.keukenhof.nl*) opens in late March with over six million flower bulbs resulting in a dazzling display of colors and fragrances.

April

The Netherlands celebrates **Queen's Day (*Koninginnedag*)** on April 30th with a national holiday. It is in fact the Queen Mother's birthday, but Queen Beatrix kept the celebration on this day. There are special festivities all over the Netherlands including ***Vrijmarkt*** (Free Market) and concerts. The **Netherlands Bach Society** (*www.bachvereniging.nl*) performs St. Matthew's Passion during the Easter season in The Hague, Rotterdam, Amsterdam and Naarden.

Keukenhof (*www.keukenhof.nl*) continues with a spectacular display of daffodils, tulips, hyacinths and crocuses. The ***Bloemencorso*** (flower parade: *www.bloemencorso-bollenstreek.nl*), with flower-laden floats begins in Noordwijk and travels 40 kilometers to Haarlem. Floats are typically on display in Haarlem the night of the parade.

May

A solemn **American Memorial Day Service** is held the last Monday of May in the city of **Margraten** at the U.S. Cemetery. Throughout the Netherlands, the Dutch observe May 4th as **Remembrance of the Dead (*Dodenherdenking*)** to honor all who have died in wars since the outbreak of World War II. The following day is **Liberation Day (*Bevrijdingsdag*)**, which is celebrated each year on May 5th to mark the end of the German occupation during World War II. Additional **Liberation Days** from Spanish occupation in the 16th century are celebrated on different days throughout the country. **Windmill Day (*Molendag*)** is celebrated on the second Saturday in May throughout the country and most windmills are open to the public for a tour. **The Hague Jazz** (*www.thehaguejazz.com*) is a festival held at the World Forum in late May. The **North Sea Regatta** (*www.nsr.nl*) is a fun event for sailing enthusiasts in Scheveningen.

June

The **Holland Festival** (*www.hollandfestival.nl*) in Amsterdam runs for most of the month and is the Netherlands largest international performing arts festival featuring opera, theater, music, dance and film. **Flag Day (*Vlaggetjesdag*)** in early June marks the opening of herring season at Scheveningen Harbor (*www.vlaggetjesdag.com*). The delicious food, fun and festivities are not to be missed. Don't forget to try the herring (*haring*)! Check out The Hague's outdoor **summer sculptures** (*www.denhaagsculptuur.nl*) on the Lange Voorhout from June through August. There are a wide variety of activities at beaches throughout the Netherlands all summer long. For events such as concerts, sand sculpture festivals and fireworks visit *www2.holland.com/denhaag* for **Scheveningen** and **Kijkduin** and *www.vvvzandvoort.nl* for **Zandvoort**.

July

The internationally celebrated **North Sea Jazz Festival** (*www.northseajazz.com*) is held in Rotterdam. The **International Rose Competition** is held at the Rosarium in Westbroek Park.

▸ August

The **Bloemencorso** (flower parade: *www.rijnsburgscorso.nl*), with flower-laden floats, begins in Rijnsburg and travels to Leiden. **Scheveningen International Fireworks Festival** is held on the beach with competitors from all over the world. Visit **Kinderdijk** (*www.kinderdijk.com*) on Saturdays in August to see all nineteen windmills whirling at once. Amsterdam hosts Europe's most popular **Gay Pride Parade** (*www.amsterdamgaypride.nl*) with a large Canal Parade as the highlight.

▸ September

The 2nd weekend is **Open Monument Days** (*www.openmonumentendag.nl*). Many historic buildings, windmills and archeological sites throughout the land—many of which are not ordinarily open to the public—can be toured on this special weekend. The **International Kite Festival** (*http://vliegerfeestscheveningen.nl*) for three days in Scheveningen is quite a sight to see. Each year on the third Tuesday in September is **Prinsjesdag** (Day of Princes) when the Queen reads the State of the Union Address and officially opens Parliament. You can watch the royal procession as she rides in a golden carriage through the streets of The Hague from the Noordeinde Palace to the Binnenhof.

▸ October

Leidens Ontzet (Leiden's Relief: *www.3october.nl*) is the annual celebration on October 3rd of the liberation of Leiden from the Spanish siege. The celebration includes parades, music, a fair and white bread and herring.

▸ November

An **American Thanksgiving Day Service** is held in the Pieterskerk in Leiden. ***Sinterklaas*** arrives after a long trip from Spain and in mid-November he sails into Dutch cities. While his arrival is broadcast on television, if you have kids it's definitely worthwhile to take them to see the spectacle in your local town. See further details about the legend of *Sinterklaas* in our chapter on **Customs and Etiquette**.

▸ December

December 5th marks the day that ***Sinterklaas*** visits the homes of all well-behaved Dutch children in celebration of St. Nicholas' birthday. It is an important family celebration, so don't choose this day to drop in on your Dutch neighbors. **Gouda by Candlelight** (*www.goudabijkunstlicht.nl*) in mid-December is always a special way to celebrate the holiday season. The entire city is illuminated by candles, and choirs sing as the huge Christmas tree in the market square is lit up. Many cities set up outdoor ice skating rinks and some have small Christmas markets.

thorough
reliable
customer focus
UniGroup Worldwide UTS
Voerman International
Your helping hand for your international move
Moving to another country. That's something you want organized down to the last detail. Voerman International can be your helping hand. Before, during and after the move. Every time, anywhere.
Please visit www.voerman.com or call +31 70 301 13 01. We will be happy to be of service!
www.voerman.com
Omni
FIDI

relocating
people
people
Immigration service • Home finding • Orientation tours • Financial management • Settling-in services
International transferees and expatriates deserve a professional guidance during their transfer. EuroHome Relocation Services assists both the employee and his/her family during the entire process and renders all the help that is often so desperately needed.
More information +31 (0)70 301 13 66 or go to our website.
Offices in The Netherlands, Czech Republic, Poland, Russia and other countries in Central and Eastern Europe.
EUROHOME Relocation Services
EURA
MEMBER WORLDWIDE ERC
www.eurohome-relocation.com

Chapter 22

Repatriation

I long, as does every human being, to be at home wherever I find myself. Maya Angelou

It is likely that your time in the Netherlands is temporary. Your posting might have been for five years, but got cut short after just two. Your posting might have been for three years and after ten, you're ready to move on. You might be leaving voluntarily to head to an exotic location, or dreading moving to a posting less desirable, or be excited to repatriate to your home country. Whatever your situation, you will again have to adjust to a new lifestyle.

This chapter will give you some food for thought before you plan your departure from the Netherlands. It provides a useful checklist of things you need to do when departing, whether you are going on to another foreign assignment or returning to your home country. By being informed, you will know what to expect, be able to recognize your feelings and some of the causes, and be able to meet your new challenges with confidence.

Reverse Culture Shock

You may be surprised to discover that returning home may be one of the hardest moves you will make. This is largely due to having unrealistic expectations. The vision of reuniting happily with family and friends may be based on what is remembered, but might have little to do with what is likely to actually happen.

Just as when you came to the Netherlands, you can again expect to experience the different stages of culture shock. This is sometimes known as "reverse" culture shock.

Stages of Reverse Culture Shock

- Initial Euphoria
- Irritability and Hostility
- Gradual Adjustment
- Adaptation

Your expectations may be high for an easy reintegration when returning home. If feeling frustrated and irritable is unexpected, this can make the process of adjustment more difficult.

While abroad, you and your family have changed. While you were away from home, those you left behind have changed, too. Their lives continued on without you, just as your life continued without them. Because you will not be going back to exactly the same situation that you left, the same pioneering spirit you showed when you moved abroad will be required when you return home.

You will take home a variety of impressions and experiences to which the folks at home can't relate. Don't be disappointed that friends and family may show little or no interest in your adventures. They may also feel intimidated by your knowledge, and even react negatively to your enthusiastic accounts of your experiences.

Your relatives and friends will probably expect you to be interested in the same things you were interested in before you left. Perhaps the best way to relate at the very beginning is to ask questions about all the current aspects of life; find out what is "in" and what is "out," which are the favorite movies, sports teams, television shows, etc. Showing an interest in the things that interest your peers may help you to adjust more easily and feel comfortable again back at home.

You should expect to find a few stumbling blocks along the way to readjusting. The scope of your interests has probably been broadened by your overseas experience. Returning Americans may be disappointed in the lack of international news coverage in the U.S. The local newspaper may only skim over events which Dutch newspapers and the *International Herald Tribune* would have as lead articles. Television news coverage of international events may also be very sketchy and leave you wondering just what is going on in the world you recently knew so well. You may also be surprised that your understanding of—and interest in—world affairs has grown disproportionately to that of your old friends.

While living in the Netherlands, you may have discovered some things abroad that you prefer to those of your home country. You've learned that there may be other ways to do things, which might be counter to how your family and friends think. There may be things that you previously did not notice in your home country that now annoy or disappoint you. Some examples may be differences in dress, shopping, food, restaurants, television programs and commercials, public transportation and the like. When you return home, you may encounter some who consider such thinking as disloyal.

If you considered your posting abroad to be a career promotion, you may find it difficult to adjust to the loss of perks, prestige and responsibility when returning home. You may feel frustrated because many of the skills and experiences developed while abroad may not be relevant to the new job at home.

You may feel a need to establish yourself in the community by doing something you consider important or by doing something to distinguish yourself among your peers. This takes time. Be patient and confident that with time you will succeed in this effort.

No doubt, there are many positive aspects to moving home. You will find that you appreciate some things more now that you may have taken for granted before such as:

- Being able to speak and understand the local language
- Having familiarity with the local customs and culture
- Finding housing
- Using appliances to which you were accustomed
- Living in close proximity to friends and family
- Having the ability to participate in partisan politics more actively than just voting from abroad

What You Can Do to Make the Transition Home Easier

- Talk about the move with your immediate family. You may want to discuss what each member of the family will miss most from the Netherlands. Be sure to let your children know how and when the move will take place.
- It is important to take the time to say goodbye to your friends and associates. It is not an unusual response to this phase of transition to start to withdraw from social engagements. Failure to say goodbye to friends can result in guilty feelings that you have let someone drop out of your life as though you had not cared for their friendship. It is good to dream and make plans for the future, but try to stay involved with your current circle of friends for as long as you can.
- Start as early as possible to find out about your new (or old) home town. Read the news from the local newspaper (most are available online).
- Write to old friends to say you are coming home and correspond to catch up on each other's lives.
- Be sure to contact schools, sport clubs and social organizations so that you and your children can continue your activities.
- Keep your sense of humor and be prepared to laugh at yourself as you have to relearn how to live in your home country

For Americans, the Federation of American Women's Clubs Overseas (FAWCO) has an alumnae association FAUSA that helps to bring together people who have lived abroad and who now live within a reasonable distance of one another in the U.S. It can be refreshing during a period of transition to talk to someone who has had experiences similar to yours.

For more information about the alumnae association go online to *www.fausa.org*. This website also has some excellent articles about repatriating.

Teenagers and the Move

Teenagers returning home may encounter special difficulties. Peer acceptance is extremely important during the high school years. The high school in your new community may be many times larger or perhaps smaller than the school your child attended in the Netherlands. The schools which most expatriate children attend in the Netherlands tend to have a more transient student body, which means that new students are more quickly accepted. At home, you may find that social groups are already formed and your teen is more likely to find it difficult to fit in, especially if you move mid-year. It may also be more difficult to get a spot on a sports team, in a school play, band or other extracurricular activity. Further, you and your teen may have become accustomed to the freedom of autonomous mobility here via bicycle and public transportation, which you may not have access to back home. Your teen may also have enjoyed an occasional beer due to the lower drinking age in the Netherlands and will have to adjust to more stringent laws at home. Bear in mind that your teen will be experiencing many of the same aforementioned feelings and stresses that you will.

The ABCs of Moving

The following is a checklist of things to do before you leave the Netherlands:

▸ Automatic Bank Transfers

If you have authorized any agency to make automatic withdrawals, such as the telephone company, landlord or utilities, then file a cancellation form with the authorized party. At the same time, notify your bank to stop any automatic payments you set up online or directly with your bank.

▸ Automobiles

To move a car overseas, call a mover to make arrangements and get the proper forms. Visit the website for the Department of Homeland Security (*www.cbp.gov*) to read about the requirements to return a car to the U.S. For those going to Great Britain, visit the website for the UK Department of Transport (*www.vca.gov.uk*.) To sell a car in the Netherlands, accompany the purchaser to the post office, taking along your passport, Dutch driver's license and the title paper (*overschrijvingbewijs*). At the same time, you can request a refund of the unused portion of your road tax, cancel your car insurance and ask for a refund of premiums.

▸ Banking

You may need to keep your Dutch checking account open for a while after you leave in order to make bank transfers to pay your closing utility bills and to receive refunds. Online banking should help make this easy from your new home. Discuss the details with the branch manager or your preferred banker and file a change of address form. If you have no final transactions to resolve, you will want to close out your accounts and make arrangements to transfer the funds abroad.

▸ Change of Address Notices

Think not only of family and friends, but also of periodical subscriptions. Some companies offer online services to make the necessary changes.

▸ Clubs

If you belong to any clubs, you should write a letter of resignation to the club before the next year's payments fall due. Also file a change of address since you may still be entitled to receive the club's publications.

▸ Dutch Taxes

Remind your employer to have your taxes assessed for you. If you have paid into a Dutch pension fund and have no intention of ever using it, you may be entitled to a refund. Discuss this with your employer.

▸ Gas and Electricity

To arrange for a meter reading, cancellation and final billing, call your local *energiebedrijf* at least two weeks prior to departure. Under certain circumstances, the utility companies may not turn off the power or water to your home without written consent of the primary account holder, which might be your spouse. Therefore, if your spouse is returning ahead of you, the company may require a signed statement and copy of his/her passport.

▸ Hotel

Make reservations as far in advance as possible if you need to stay in a hotel in either the Netherlands or your new city because of timing of your shipment, and be sure to mention any special needs (children, pets, etc.).

▸ Household Goods

Contact a moving company to make an appointment to assess your shipment and to discuss packing details. You will have to select a reliable international moving company to pack your household goods. Many movers call themselves "international," although there are just a handful who truly are. These can be recognized by their FIDI FAIMISO certification. This certification guarantees that a moving company meets the minimum criteria to professionally handle an international move. Make sure you select a mover with a solid global and quality driven network because that company will be the one to select local partners to handle the local move. Before issuing a quotation, the mover will do a Pre-Move Survey at your residence in order to determine the volume and weight of your belongings. This service is free of charge and also allows you the get a good personal impression of the professionalism of the mover. You or your employer can then make the choice based on this evaluation and the quotations. Obtain appropriate customs declaration forms. Those bound for the U.S. may also download the useful pamphlet *Know Before You Go* from the Department of Homeland Security at *www.cbp.gov*. Other nationalities will want to contact their Consular Offices for specific customs information. Verify insurance of goods and cancel local insurance as needed.

▸ Housing

If you are renting, notify your landlord as soon as possible. Remember that most diplomatic clauses require at least 60 days notice. Provide banking information to arrange for the return of your deposit. If you own your home, prepare your home for sale or to become a rental property.

▸ Immigration and Naturalization (Immigratie en Naturalisatiedienst or IND)

On the day before your departure from the Netherlands, go to the police station and turn in your residence permits. Take along all passports of your family members and your certificate of de-registration (see Residency De-registration below).

▸ Mail

File a *verhuisbericht* form at the post office or online at *www.tntpost.nl*. Mail can be forwarded within the Netherlands or internationally for a monthly fee.

▸ Medical Records

Contact your doctor and dentist about picking up your records, and pick up any x-rays from hospitals.

▸ Passports

Make sure your passport is in order. If it expires prior to your departure, by all means get it renewed at a consulate. Americans can get detailed information under the U.S. Citizen Services section at *http://amsterdam.usconsulate.gov*.

▸ Pets

If you plan to take your pets with you, contact your airline for specific pet handling requirements, make shipping reservations and obtain the necessary vaccinations and health certificates from your *dierenarts*. While at the town hall (see Residency De-Registration below) inquire about a refund of the *hondenbelasting*. If you plan to leave your pets behind in the Netherlands (see our **Pets** chapter for more information), try to place them in their new home several weeks before you depart. This way, you and your children may visit them in their new home and your children won't have to leave both their pets and their home at the same time.

▸ Residency De-Registration

Go to the town hall about one week prior to your departure and notify them that you are leaving. Take the passport of each member of your family with you. You may need proof of de-registration in order to complete your departure formalities with the IND. Americans who have registered with the U.S. Consulate should inform them of their departure.

▸ Schools

Notify school officials of your departure well in advance as many require at least one term's notice. Request copies of school records.

▸ Telecommunications (Land Line, Mobile Phone, Internet and Cable TV)

Cancel your service at least 30 days in advance and give a forwarding address for billing purposes. Realize that if you are breaking an annual contract, you might have to pay heavy penalties.

▸ Water

Arrange for a meter reading and final billing by contacting your local water authority.

▸ Want Ads

If you wish to sell your used furniture, car, appliances, etc. via a published advertisement, allow a good month of lead time. You may also want to use church or club bulletin boards, school newsletters or online exchanges. Make an appointment for the Kringloop to pick up any unsold items for donation before your movers arrive.

▸ Work Permit

Remind your employer to cancel this for you.

Resources

▸ Resource Information

TCKid
www.tckid.com
A community website for Third Culture Kids (TCKs), Adult Third Culture Kids (ATCKs), and Cross Cultural individuals, dedicated to provide a safe and open environment for interaction, information, and support on TCK-related issues

Interaction, Inc.
☎ (630) 653-8780
www.interactionintl.org
Conducts re-entry seminars in the U.S. and sells publications.

Transition Dynamics
Barbara F. Schaetti
2448 NW 63 Street, Seattle, WA 98107
☎ (206) 789-3290
www.transition-dynamics.com
A consultancy committed to servicing men, women and children for whom international mobility and cultural transitions are a part of daily life, including re-entry.

▸ Books

The Third Culture Kid Experience by David C. Pollack and Ruth E. Van Reken
Addresses the challenges and rewards of the nomadic life of being a Third Culture Kid.

The Art of Coming Home by Craig Storti
www.interculturalpress.com
Details the re-entry process after a cross-cultural experience.

A Moveable Marriage by Robin Pascoe
www.expatexpert.com
Candid talk about the stress on relationships created by children, careers, money, sex, etc. This book is for couples who know that moving isn't all about furniture.

Homeward Bound by Robin Pascoe
www.expatexpert.com
A spouse's guide to repatriating.

Is it time to go home yet? I keep clicking these damn shoes, but nothing happens. Robin Hecht

Tot ziens!

References

ACCESS

Contact Details and Information Helpline

Stadhuis, Spui 70 Den Haag
☎ (070) 346 25 25
Prinses Irenestraat 59, 1077 WV Amsterdam
☎ (020) 423 32 17
www.access-nl.org

Books and Information Published by ACCESS

- *ACCESS Magazine*
- *The ACCESS Guide to Health Care in the Netherlands*
- *The ACCESS Guide to Working in the Netherlands*
- *ACCESS Information and Planning Calendar*
- *Babies and Toddlers: The ACCESS Guide to Having and Caring for Children in the Netherlands*

Cookbooks

Once you have learned a little Dutch, a whole new world of cooking will be open to you. *Lekker* magazine has delicious recipes for Dutch ingredients. Albert Heijn also publishes a monthly cooking magazine, *Allerhande*, in Dutch, which is free to shoppers.

- *Art of Dutch Cooking*, by Cornelia van Limburg Stirum
- *Netherlands Cookbook*, by Heleen A.M. Halverhout
- *Indonesian Cooking: Salamat Makan*, by Ina den Hartog
- *The Netherlands Days, A Collection of American and Other International Recipes Adapted for the Dutch Kitchen*, by The American Women's Club of Amsterdam.

Culture and History Books

- *Anne Frank – Life in Hiding*, by Johanna Hurwitz
- *Dealing with the Dutch*, by Jacob Vossestein of the Royal Tropical Institute
- *The Dutch Republic: Its Rise, Greatness and Fall 1477–1806*, by Jonathan Israel
- *The Embarrassment of Riches*, by Simon Schama
- *Europe and Europe: Road to Unity*, by Flora Lewis
- *First Salute*, by Barbara Tuchman
- *The Hiding Place*, by Corrie ten Boom (Movie version available on DVD)
- *The Low Sky: Understanding the Dutch*, by Han van der Horst
- *Patriots and Liberators, Revolution in the Netherlands*, by Simon Schama

- *Rembrandt A & I*, by Mariët Westermann
- *Soldier of Orange*, by Erik Hazelhoff-Roelfzema
- *The Undutchables*, by Colin White and Laurie Boucke

Dictionaries (*Woordenboeken*)

- *Dutch-English/English-Dutch Concise Dictionary*, by Davidovic Mladen
- *Dutch Phrase Book and Dictionary*, by Berlitz
- *Dutch Phrase Finder*, by Collins Gem
- *Prisma Woordenboek*
- *Van Dale Woordenboek*
- *Wolter's Handwoordenboek*

Expatriates Abroad

- *A Portable Identity: A Women's Guide to Maintaining a Sense of Self While Moving Overseas*, by Debra R. Bryson & Charise M. Hoge
- *After the Boxes are Unpacked; Moving on After Moving In*, by Susan Miller
- *Do's and Taboos around the World for Women in Business*, by Roger Axtell with Tami Briggs, Margaret Corcoran and Mary Beth Lamb
- *The Expert Expat, Revised Edition: Your Guide to Successful Relocation Abroad*, by Melissa Brayer Hess and Patricia Linderman
- *Holland Handbook*, by Xpat Media
- *Where in the World Are You Going*, by Judith M. Blohm
- *Women's Guide to Overseas Living*, by Nancy J. Piet-Pelon and Barbara Hornby

For other titles, contact:

Interculture Press
☎ (617) 523 38 01
☎ 888) 273 25 39 Toll free from U.S.
www.interculturalpress.com

Food

- *The Food Shoppers' Guide to the Netherlands*, by Ada Henne Koene

Language Courses on CD

- *Conversational Dutch*, from Pimsleur Language Programs
- *Dutch in Three Months*, from Hugo's Language Institute
- *Teach Yourself Dutch Complete Course*, by Gerdi Quist and Dennis Strik
- *Teach Yourself Beginner's Dutch*, by Gerdi Quist and Dennis Strik

Legal

For answers in English to legal questions concerning Dutch law, go to **GMW Advocaten** at *www.gmw.nl/en.*

Newspapers and Periodicals

The Hague/Amsterdam Times
☎ (020) 584 90 20

International Herald Tribune
www.iht.com

The Xpat Journal – Xpat Media
☎ (070) 306 33 10
www.xpat.nl

Travel and Guide Books

- *DayTrips - The Netherlands, Belgium and Luxembourg*, by Earl Steinbicker
- *DK Eyewitness Travel Guides – The Netherlands* published by Dorling Kindersley
- *DK Eyewitness Top 10 Travel Guides – Top 10: Amsterdam* published by Dorling Kindersley
- *Frommer's Irreverent Guide to Amsterdam*
- *Here's Holland*, by Sheila Gazaleh-Weevers
- Michelin Guides
- *Netherlands*, Lonely Planet

Websites

Basics about the Netherlands

- *www.expatica.com/nl*
- *www.hollandsouth.angloinfo.com*
- *www.xpat.nl*

Business

- **American Chamber of Commerce** (AmCham)
  www.amcham.nl
- **Dutch Business Index**: A business-to-business database of more than 250,000 companies in the Netherlands
  www.abcdirect.nl
- **Dutch Ministry of Economic Affairs:** For information on regulations and implementations of economic policies
  www.minez.nl

Entertainment

- **Museum Listings:** *www.museum.nl*
- **Movie Listings:** *www.belbios.nl*
- **Online TV Guide:** *www.tvgids.nl*
- **Theater Listings:** *www.theater.nl*

Expatriate Information

- **Outpost:** A compilation of resources for the Netherlands and around the world, including education, expatriate groups, local organizations, health and safety, tourist boards, etc.
  www.outpostexpat.nl
- **Federation of American Women's Clubs Overseas:** Has information about 75+ American Women's Clubs around the world
  www.fawco.org
- **Expat Life:** Informs, advises and offers English language local news
  www.expatica.com/nl
- **Expat Expert:** Informs, advises and offers online friendship to relocating expatriate spouses and families, by bestselling author Robin Pascoe
  www.expatexpert.com

Government

- **Dutch Ministry of Foreign Affairs:** The international home page features general country information, maps, statistics, and links to other English language websites with text on Dutch society and other topics
  www.minbuza.nl
- **Local Government Offices:** Most Dutch towns and cities have a variety of information online. If your town is not listed below, try *www.insertyourtownnamehere.nl* (for example, *www.utrecht.nl*). Most sites have Dutch and English language options.

City Name	Website
Amsterdam	*www.amsterdam.nl*
The Hague	*www.denhaag.nl*
Leidschendam-Voorburg	*www.leidschendam-voorburg.nl*
Rotterdam	*www.rotterdam.nl*
Wassenaar	*www.wassenaar.nl*

- **The Royal Family:** Official website
  www.koninklijkhuis.nl
- **U.S. Government Sites:**
  - **Internal Revenue Service:** *www.irs.gov*
  - **Social Security Administration:** *www.ssa.gov*
  - **U.S. Bureau of Consular Affairs/ U.S. Department of State:** *www.travel.state.gov*
  - **U.S. Consulate General Amsterdam:** *http://amsterdam.usconsulate.gov*

- **U.S. Embassy in The Hague:** *http://thehague.usembassy.gov*
- **U.S. Postal Service:** *www.usps.com*

Miscellaneous

- **American Book Center:** *www.abc.nl*
- **Learn to Speak Dutch:** *www.taalthuis.com*
- **Maps:** *www.maps.google.nl*
- **Metric Converter:** *www.onlineconversion.com*
- **Translate Dutch-English/English-Dutch:** *www.translate.google.com*

News

- International News
  - *www.cnn.com*
  - *http://news.bbc.co.uk*
  - *www.pri.org* (Public Radio International)
- Dutch News in English
  - *www.dutchnews.nl*
  - *www.nrc.nl/international*
  - *www.radionetherlands.nl*
  - *www.thehagueonline.com*

Sports

- **ABF International Sports Club:** *www.abfsport.nl*
- **Dutch Bicycle Routes:** *www.fietsen.123.nl/fietsroutes.htm*
- **Dutch Indoor Climbing Gyms:** *www.climbing.nl*
- **Soccer/Football:** *www.knvb.nl* or *www.the-football.com/holland.html*

Telephone Listings and Yellow Pages in English

- National Telephone Book
  - *www.whitepages.nl*
  - *www.detelefoongids.nl*
- National Yellow Pages
  - *www.goudengids.nl*
- National Service Listing
  - *www.markt.nl*

Tourism and Travel – The Netherlands

- **KLM Royal Dutch Airlines:** *www.klm.com*
- **Nederlandse Spoorwegen (NS):** *www.ns.nl*
  Dutch train service includes train trip planning in English
- **Netherlands Board of Tourism:** *www.holland.com*
- **Schiphol Airport Information:** *www.schiphol.com*

Tourism and Travel – Worldwide

- **Currency Conversion:** *www.xe.com/ucc/*
- Search Engines for Airline Tickets and Hotels
  - *www.expedia.com*
  - *www.kayak.com*
  - *www.travelocity.com*

- **Tips for Travelers World-Wide**
  - *www.concierge.com*
  - *www.fodors.com*
  - *www.frommers.com*
  - *www.lonelyplanet.com*
  - *www.ricksteves.com*
  - *www.roughguides.com*
  - *www.tripadvisor.com*
- **Travel Auction Sites**
  - *www.bid4travel.com*
  - *www.priceline.com*
- **Worldwide Events**
  - *www.festivals.com*

Transportation

- **ANWB:** *www.anwb.nl*
- **Deutsche Bahn AG** – German train service: *www.bahn.de*
- **Eurostar** – High speed train service to the U.K.: *www.eurostar.com*
- **Ferry service to the U.K.:** *www.stenaline.co.uk*
- **High Speed Trains:** *www.nshispeed.nl*
- **Nederlandse Spoorwegen (NS)** – Dutch train service: *www.ns.nl*
- **Public Transportation:**
  - **Amsterdam:** *www.gvb.nl*
  - **The Hague:** *www.htm.net*
  - **Rotterdam:** *www.ret.nl*
- **Route Planner:** *www.viamichelin.com*
- **Traffic Information:** *www.trafficnet.nl*

Women's Clubs

- **Federation of American Women's Clubs Overseas:** Has information about the more than 75 American Women's Clubs around the world.
  www.fawco.org
- **American Women's Club:** Sites have links for newcomers to the Netherlands, as well as information and events for those who have been here for awhile.
  - The Hague: *www.awcthehague.org*
  - Amsterdam: *www.awca.nl*

Help Us!

The American Women's Club of The Hague is striving to make this book as valuable as possible. If you have an update for the next printing or a suggestion for additional information, please let us know.

Please return this form with completed information to:

The American Women's Club of The Hague
Nieuwe Duinweg 25
2587 AB Den Haag
E-mail: *athomeinholland@gmail.com*
www.awcthehague.org

Updated Information:

Chapter:

Page number:

Update:

Suggested Additions:

Index

C

D

E

I

J

K

L

M

N

O

P

Q

R

ISBN: 978-90-5972-286-6

Production: Eburon Academic Publishers, Delft (www.eburon.nl)
Cover painting: John Proctor
Cover design: Studio Hermkens, Amsterdam
Graphic design: Textcetera, The Hague